HORSEBACK Across
THREE Ame

by Verne R. Albright

HELLGATE PRESS   ASHLAND, OREGON

HORSEBACK ACROSS THREE AMERICAS
©2020 Verne Albright

Published by Hellgate Press

(An imprint of L&R Publishing, LLC)

Hellgate Press
PO Box 3531
Ashland, OR 97520
email: sales@hellgatepress.com

Cover and Interior Design: L. Redding
Illustrations by William E. Jones

ISBN: 978-1-55571-998-2

Printed and bound in the United States of America
First edition 10 9 8 7 6 5 4 3 2 1

**Other Books Written by Verne R. Albright
and Available through Hellgate Press:**

Playing Chess with God
The Wrath of God

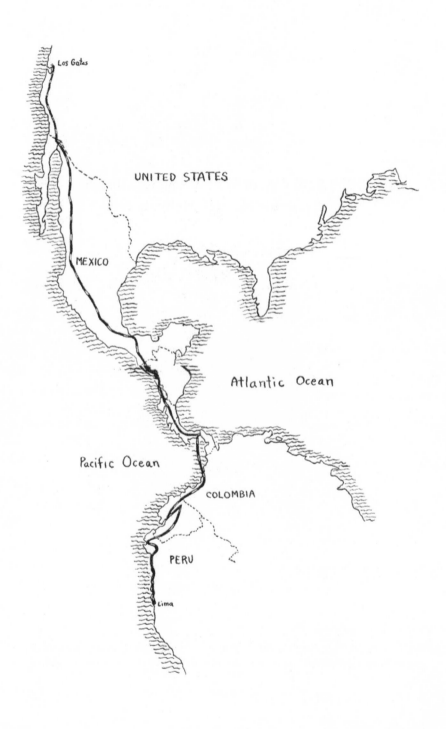

CONTENTS

PROLOGUE

Be Careful What You Wish For

Since my horses and I had left Peru and entered Ecuador, I'd been made uneasy by prominent posters in every village that urgently recommended inoculation against malaria. When I reached a large city I went straight to the Peace Corps office and spoke with an American nurse.

"I can't give Americans medical advice," she said. "I'm authorized to work with the local poor only."

"Can you recommend a doctor?"

"We're not supposed to do that," she replied in the same monotone, "and to tell the truth there aren't any I'd go to if I were sick."

"Thanks for your time." I turned to go.

"What brought you to Loja?" she asked.

"I'm on my way to the States on horseback."

"Oh my God! I hope you're being careful. You have no idea of the diseases they have here. Where and what are you eating?"

"Anywhere and anything I can."

"Rules be damned," she said, obviously concerned. "I'll give you a hepatitis shot and pamphlets describing precautions you should take against malaria, typhoid, tuberculosis, cholera, and bubonic plague."

In those days tuberculosis was a familiar threat, but I'd thought typhoid, malaria, cholera, and bubonic plague existed only in history books and horror stories. Suddenly however, they were among the threats I faced in Ecuador's Andes—along with bandits and avalanches.

I'd landed in this predicament because of boredom, which had emboldened me to tackle what I'd thought would be an exciting experience. All my life I'd longed for adventure, but I'd done so without realizing it was almost always a consequence of carefully laid plans going badly wrong—something much in conflict with my orderly German nature.

By the time I was nine, my family had moved ten times to new homes in seven states. Instead of making me long for continuity, all that uprooting and replanting made me restless for change whenever things stayed the same for very long.

We were never in one place long enough for me to get past being an outsider.

Every year I was the new kid in school and my classmates teased me mercilessly, mostly about my exceptional height. In response, I'd look forward to our next move in the hope that life would be better wherever we went next.

According to my mother, horses were the only thing that claimed and held my interest back then. As a young child I begged for horse books, and later I began pleading for a horse. When our family finally settled down in Reno, Nevada, my long-standing request was granted.

I was eleven when my father bought Trixie, a mustang mare

born wild and captured on a Nevada desert when old enough to ride. She was a bit small for me and sorrel, a color now called chestnut. Her energy and aloofness distinguished her from all other candidates my dad and I considered while horse shopping.

Trixie lived up to my expectations as nothing else ever had. I spent every second of my free time with her and joined a youth group sponsored by the Washoe County Horsemen's Association. My favorite of its many activities was an annual hundred-mile ride that took us into the wilds for three glorious days.

Newly arrived in Reno and socially clumsy, I didn't fit in with the other members and soon acquired a nickname, Tom Mix Up—inspired by a famous movie cowboy.

Trying to be a good sport I laughed when my fellow riders called me that. But clearly an insult, it stung.

By the time I was a freshman at Reno High School I'd sprouted to a whopping six-feet nine inches, outgrowing Trixie. I sold and bid her farewell with the same casual ease I'd left people and towns during my childhood. But it took years to find her equal.

My next horse—a Quarter Horse mare, Miss Rosetta—was phlegmatic and calm.

Her lack of energy made me long for Trixie's enthusiasm—a quality called *brio* in Peruvian Paso horses. My interest in this new mare, never strong, expired after I tried out for the Reno High School varsity basketball team and was unexpectedly chosen.

I sold Miss Rosetta and concentrated on this new challenge. Having grown like a weed, I was still coping with height to which I wasn't accustomed, and was too awkward to be any good. But as Coach Lloyd Trout told a newspaper reporter, "When a boy is built that close to the basket, he's liable to come in handy."

In my senior year I finally came into my own. Our team made it to the State Championship game — which we lost by three points — and I was named to Northern Nevada's All Star team. Following basketball season however, I was once again bored.

After a year at Portland State College in Oregon, my tolerance for dull routines was exhausted. Hungry for adventure I left school and never looked back.

Soon after Anne Mossman and I married that summer, I received a job offer from Roy Chamberlain, the man I'd worked for in Reno during high school. He'd been transferred to a new Skaggs Payless Drug Store, and he tempted Anne and me to Salt Lake City by saying he'd make me a department supervisor.

Two months before Christmas — following the store's grand opening — I was assigned to manage the toy department. Nothing I'd ever done had been as exciting. For two months I had to move fast and learn faster. Exhilarated and obsessed, I was in the store from before it opened to after it closed, seven days a week.

"You're doing a great job," Mr. Chamberlain told me one evening. "The owner's wife told him that our toy department is the best one in town."

As he'd expected, I was inspired to redouble my efforts. The predictable letdown came on December 26th.

With Anne's enthusiastic approval I decided working in a foreign country might be more to my liking, and I wrote John Cooke, an ex-girlfriend's father. A geologist who'd worked outside the States for years, he gave me a letter of recommendation and the names of foreign employers who might give me a job. I sent applications for months, but nothing came of it.

Finally I took the bit between my teeth and asked Mr.

Cooke, "If I were to just show up someplace, where would I have the best chance of finding work?"

"Peru," he replied. "I have a friend there who'll be happy to help you."

Anne and I spent half our savings on my one-way ticket to Peru. If I found a job, the rest of our money would fly her and our ten-month-old daughter, Vicki, to join me.

Otherwise, it would bring me back home.

On the flight to Peru, I met a lady who offered me a job teaching English, but I was hoping for something more interesting. Peru, I soon discovered, offered many appealing adventures but no interesting jobs for which I was qualified. Running out of money, I hired on as an English teacher at the Instituto Cultural and sent for Anne and Vicki.

By the time they arrived I was supplementing my income with private English lessons and saving for one or more adventures a travel agent had recommended.

* * *

Two months later Anne met Hillary Dunsterville and Lu-Bette Herrick, who'd checked into the boarding house where we were. They'd driven there from New York and were headed for South America's southernmost tip. Their Jeep station wagon Matilda, had developed mechanical problems shortly before reaching Lima, and the cost of repairs was a major setback.

The three women became friends and unbeknownst to me, discussed the possibility of having Anne, Vicki, and I join Lu-Bette and Hillary's adventure-in-progress. When Anne revealed that possibility to me, I was intrigued — but apprehensive.

"Having two strangers and a toddler move into Matilda," I told her, "will be hard for them."

"They know that," Anne assured me, "but our contribution toward expenses is as attractive to them as the prospect of adventure is to us."

Unable to contain my excitement any longer I asked, "Where are they going next and when do we leave?"

At the mechanic shop where Matilda was waiting to be repaired, I spent the next three afternoons building a collapsible wood and canvas tent on its roof rack. There Anne, Vicki, and I would sleep during what we hoped would be a memorable three-month trip to Santiago, Chile via the Andes of Peru, Bolivia, and Argentina.

Hillary and LuBette eventually found corporate sponsors, permitting them to reach their goal in Tierra del Fuego and then go north to Alaska. By then however, Anne and I had spent our savings, and we took a freighter from Santiago to the U.S. East Coast, then hitchhiked back to Oregon.

* * *

Several months after that I went to work for George Jones, who managed a finance company in San Francisco.

"I'm looking for ways to invest some money," he told me one afternoon over lunch. "Did you see anything in South America we could sell in the States?"

For weeks I offered suggestions we evaluated until George rejected them. Eventually I got the impression he enjoyed our hopeful conversations as an end in themselves. But he kept asking for ideas, and we amused ourselves for hours — George searching for a lucrative investment, me dreaming of another adventure.

Then one day during lunch, I made a suggestion that changed my life.

"I don't know why I didn't think of this sooner," I began.

"Peru has a unique horse breed that could be sold for good money in the States."

Sensing potential profit George gulped a half-chewed mouthful and asked, "What makes them special?"

By the time I'd described the breed's lateral four-beat gait, smoothness, beauty, and energy, he knew as much about Peruvian Pasos as I did. Impressed, he set up a petty cash fund so I could explore this idea. Gradually a concrete plan evolved. We'd import one of these horses and see how people reacted.

Soon I was on my way to Peru carrying a heavy burden of responsibility. The horse I bought would have to be impressive, but all I knew about Peruvian horses was that they lit me on fire. In Peru fortunately, a breeder named Fernando Graña took me under his wing.

A month later at the harbor in San Pedro, California — near Los Angeles — George got his first look at Malagueña, the sample I'd chosen. Soon he was almost as vocal about Peruvian horses as I. Our continuing efforts led to further importations, and within two years there were over a hundred Peruvian horses in the States.

To promote the breed, George and I founded the American Association of Owners and Breeders of Peruvian Paso Horses. He served as its first president, and I as the second. At twenty-three years of age, I'd finally found something that was never — not for an instant — boring.

My favorite among our promotions was importing Marinera, a mare I'd chosen to compete in cross-country endurance races. We sold her to Julie Suhr — an emerging endurance rider — and I became obsessed with their progress.

In 1966 Julie rode Marinera in California's grueling hundred-mile-in-one-day Tevis Cup Ride, and the gallant little mare represented her breed admirably.

Remembering those hundred-mile rides of my youth, I ached to get involved in endurance racing. But though slender I weighed two hundred pounds, and very few successful endurance riders were an ounce over one twenty.

I could however, ride Peruvian Pasos from South to North America. By then, Anne and I had gone our separate ways and the longer I considered that ride, the more it appealed. Here was a way to live life to the fullest. And after my journey I'd enter my best horse in the Tevis Cup with a rider who weighed far less than I—step one of a campaign to further promote Peruvian horses.

"You have a potentially fatal case of Paso promotion fever," George said when I pitched my brainchild.

When I mentioned my idea to others, their reactions made his seem optimistic. But such a ride was achievable. As a youngster I'd several times ridden a hundred miles in three days. All I'd have to do as an adult was string together fifty such trips. Right?

* * *

In the 1920s Aimé F. Tschiffely had made an epic, ten-thousand-mile, two-and-a-half-year ride from Buenos Aires to Washington, D.C. on two Argentine Criollo horses. His journey created the kind of publicity for Argentina's horses that I hoped to generate for Peru's.

"It's time to come to your senses, Albright," was George Jones's reaction.

I was undaunted. Those hundred-mile rides of my youth had taught me a great deal about long distance riding. The Jeep trip with Hillary and LuBette had familiarized me with traveling and crossing borders in Latin America. I was physically and emotionally capable of such a journey. Marinera had shown that the same would be true of well-chosen Peruvian horses.

All that remained was to do it. To give my best horse and its race-day rider time to work together before 1967's Tevis Cup, I'd have to be back in California in nine months—not enough time to ride five-thousand-plus miles. But what the heck, I didn't have enough money either.

George had declined to contribute to this venture and my life savings amounted to a little over two thousand dollars. Would that be enough? I couldn't prepare a budget. Not even the *Wall Street Journal* publishes the current cost of hay in Guatemala, grain in Panama, horseshoes in Costa Rica, dinner in Ecuador's highlands, and paperwork for horses to cross eleven borders.

All I knew was that I'd have to buy supplies, a plane ticket, horses, feed, hundreds of meals, and whatever else I needed along the way. My destination would be Joe and Pat Gavitt's ranchette near Los Gatos, California. They were avid Peruvian horse fans, and Pat had agreed to ride one of my horses in the Tevis Cup, a task for which she was well qualified.

After purchasing supplies, I wrote Tuco Roca Rey, secretary of Peru's national Paso horse breeders association, and informed him of my impending arrival. I hoped he and Peru's breeders would be enthusiastic about my plans because I would desperately need their advice and assistance.

1

PABLITO

"Goodbye," the Peruvian schoolgirl beside me said, pressing her forehead against the Boeing 707 jet's window so she could see the sun as long as possible. "I won't see you again or feel your warmth for a while."

Her words were prophetic. As our plane knifed down into the cloudbank that hangs over Lima in August, I saw the sun for the last time in many days.

After a turbulent descent, Peru's arid coast came in view. We passed above a farmer and oxen plowing a field, then oil derricks with flames burning off natural gas. Briefly we paralleled a highway with burros hurrying along its shoulder and boys straddling their rumps behind clay pots, probably full of water for homes that had no plumbing.

"What brought you to Peru?" the schoolgirl asked.

When I answered, her brown eyes lit up with amazement.

"Wish I were a boy," she said wistfully, "so I could have adventures like that."

After landing I cleared immigration and picked up my duffel bags in baggage claim. But first I had to battle porters for the right to carry them. Once I'd cleared customs, more porters aggressively offered their services. I'd soon learn it was best to ignore them rather than explain I didn't have money for tips.

Outside the terminal, the sidewalk was congested with people waiting for arriving passengers. My ears were assaulted by the sound of traffic and rhythmic cries from shoeshine boys, taxi drivers, agents for hotels, and tour guides.

Taxis there were the expensive tourist kind. Around the corner I found much-less-costly *colectivos*, cars that carried up to five passengers for a standard fee. People could get on or off anywhere on their predetermined routes. Before going out of style in the States, such vehicles cost five cents and were called jitneys — American slang for a nickel in those days.

When the driver discovered I spoke his language, he asked what brought me to Peru. Glad for the opportunity to practice my Spanish, I told him. His predictable response started with amazement, then moved on to disbelief and finally enthusiasm.

"If only I were young again," he declared, "I could have such adventures."

The other passengers nodded in agreement. Since I'd left Los Angeles no one had expressed the slightest doubt about my eventual success. Latinos consider it rude to rain on people's parades. But they underestimated the difficulties I faced and if I didn't succeed, they'd see me as having failed to reach an easy goal.

In Miraflores I left the colectivo and hailed a cab. Minutes after that I reached the Asociación Nacional de Criadores y Propietarios del Caballo Peruano de Paso (ANCPCPP), the national Peruvian Paso breeders association.

Before George Jones and I had imported Malagueña two

years earlier, I'd written the Asociación several times. When the secretary finally replied, he'd answered none of my questions and instead offered his assistance when I got to Lima. When I'd shown up on the Asociación's doorstep, he and other members had been supremely gracious and helpful.

The ANCPCPP clubhouse had an office, bar, dining room, kitchen, and courtyard with a fountain. The breeders present that night invited me to their dinner-in-progress, and afterward Tuco Roca Rey translated my last letter aloud for them. I'd known he wouldn't answer it — but as his notes in the margins confirmed, he'd already given considerable thought to my project.

"What can we call you?" Carlos Luna de la Fuente, one of the ANCPCPP's founders, asked, perplexed by his inability to pronounce my name.

"Let's give him a Spanish name," Carlos Gonzalez, the immediate past president, chimed in.

Playfully they suggested possibilities, their laughter very different from that of my classmates as they'd chosen my many hated childhood nicknames.

"From now on you're *Pablito*, little Pablo," Luna abruptly declared.

"Perfect," Gonzalez said, then told me, "Pablito is a famous, very short comedian."

I'd feared these busy, important men wouldn't have time to help me but laughing and patting my shoulder, they gathered around to ask questions and offer advice.

When Fernando Graña came in, he instantly replaced me as the center of attention. He was the most polished, elegant, intimidating man I had ever met. I'd been in awe of him since seeing a primetime U.S. television interview during which he described Peru's social problems in perfect English. Later he'd sold me Malagueña, the first horse George Jones and I imported.

As the evening progressed, a problem I'd had other times in Peru resurfaced. I don't partake of alcohol, which is an indispensable part of Peru's social life. Again and again someone offered to buy me a drink and was insistent after I declined.

"I don't have moral objections," I explained again and again. "I simply don't like the taste or effect."

But no matter how often I repeated those words, my abstinence seemed to offend or at least make them uncomfortable.

I cringed when Fernando Graña approached, presumably to try his luck.

"This has gone far enough," he declared. "Come with me please."

I followed him to the bar.

"Pour two fingers of Coca Cola in a glass," he instructed the attendant, "then add four fingers of soda water."

Studying the result he asked me, "Does the color look familiar?"

"Most definitely," I replied, grinning.

Handing me the glass he said, "As long as you're holding this scotch, no one will bother you."

Carlos Gonzalez noticed my duffel bags in a corner and asked, "What's in those?"

"Supplies for my ride," I told him.

"Would you mind displaying them on our conference table?" he asked, leading me into the office.

When my exhibit was to his satisfaction, González opened the door and herded everyone in. Nothing there would've attracted attention in the States, but in Peru almost everything did.

"You gringos may have a highly advanced country," exclaimed an elderly man who'd obviously never seen Levi's jeans, "but these pants made of canvas must be uncomfortable."

No one could resist removing my Bowie knife from its

sheath to admire the blade and double-edged tip. My water purification tablets brought predictable comments about gringos' fussy stomachs.

"Rain will pass right through these," one man predicted pouring a splash of scotch on one of my nylon horse blankets. To his considerable surprise it beaded up and rolled off.

For reasons I couldn't understand, everyone—though accustomed to exquisitely braided leather halters and lead lines—greatly admired my simple nylon ones.

As the room emptied, I was given two suggestions.

"Your horses will need grain," Carlos Luna, a professor at La Molina College of Agriculture, told me. "You'll need feedbags for that."

I made a mental note.

"And this cowboy hat isn't appropriate for riding our horses," Fernando Graña gently scolded. "You need a proper Peruvian sombrero."

I couldn't work up the nerve to disagree with him. A Peruvian sombrero however, was out of the question. They were stylish but expensive, and didn't stay put in wind or hold their shapes when wet.

I couldn't believe where I was or who I was with. The Asociación's members belonged to a social class I could never have approached without our mutual enthusiasm for their country's National Horse.

"Would you like Carlos González and me to help you find horses?" Fernando Graña asked around midnight after most members had left.

"Yes, please," I replied.

"We'll meet you here for breakfast at eight o'clock tomorrow morning."

Locking doors after we were alone, Tuco Roca Rey asked, "Where are you staying?"

"I don't know," I replied. "Can you recommend someplace inexpensive?"

"You'll be on the trail for nine months," he said, "and should start conditioning your body. If you want you can sleep on our meeting room floor, buy food at the market, cook it in our kitchen, and do your laundry in our bathroom."

I thanked Tuco for his tactful suggestion.

Alone after he left, I unrolled my sleeping bag and dedicated myself to conditioning my body on a tile floor that was probably more comfortable than most places I'd sleep in months to come.

* * *

"How many horses do you want and where do you plan to buy them?" Fernando Graña asked after breakfast the next morning.

"Two mares," I replied. "I thought I'd start looking at the Hacienda Casa Grande."

The world's largest plantation, located north of Lima, had the most horses and lowest prices of all Peru's breeders.

"Mares in your price range are little more than incubators," Don Fernando said. "Few get trained and those that do are seldom ridden and therefore not accustomed to hard work."

"Geldings," Carlos Gonzalez chimed in, "have a well-deserved reputation for endurance, which is the reason we refer to castrated males as *caballos de trabajo*, work horses — instead of *capónes*."

"Though Casa Grande's horses are strong and have excellent endurance," Fernando continued, "they grow up on a flat desert at sea level in soft sand, and aren't accustomed to cold, rain, altitude, horseshoes, steep climbs, or uneven terrain. I'd recommend horses from Cajamarca, which is in the Andes at seven thousand feet."

With his usual hyperbole Carlos González added, "Horses

raised there have gigantic lungs, huge hearts, legs of iron, and hooves of steel."

If they hadn't been who they were, I would've wondered what they had to gain by changing my plan.

"At Juan Miguel Rossel's farm," Graña continued, "there's a gelding named Huascarán you should consider. He's gray, seven years old, tall, sturdy, and absolutely beautiful. I'd be proud to own him, and that's the highest recommendation I have."

"I doubt I can afford such a horse," I said.

"At the moment Juan Miguel is at his Lima house. I'll find out how much he wants."

The quintessential man of action, Graña had the waiter bring a telephone to our table and called. After a quick conversation he hung up and told me, "He quoted an excellent package price for Huascarán and his half-brother Lucero, a black with extraordinary energy—subject to your approval of course."

I'd never bought a horse without seeing and riding it. But translated from Peruvian *soles* to U.S. dollars, the price was irresistible and included transportation from Cajamarca to Jorge Baca's farm near Chiclayo, an excellent place to start my ride.

"If you're in a hurry," Graña offered, "I'll call back and have Juan Miguel ship the horses. Plenty of people around Chiclayo would love to own those two geldings. If you don't like either or both, I'll arrange a trade."

I trusted him completely. He'd shown considerable integrity when I purchased Malagueña, an eye-catching gray mare I liked because her contrasting black mane, tail, and points were attention-getters.

"Before you make up your mind," he'd cautioned after

quoting a price, "I have a confession. I believe horses should be shown naturally so their qualities will be genetic and hopefully passed on to their offspring. I never would've done this for a show but for a recent parade, I had Malagueña's mane and tail dyed. When they grow out, there'll be a few gray hairs."

Bringing me back to the present Fernando asked, "Do you need more time to decide?"

"No," I replied. "I'll do as you recommend."

Fernando picked up the phone and closed the deal, then he, Carlos, and Tuco hurried to their cars leaving me alone and emotionally drained. I'd been in Peru less than sixteen hours and already had horses. I could hardly wait to see them.

2

THE BULLFIGHTER

That evening the *Asociación's* directors voted unanimously to endorse my ride and provide me with an official letter introducing me to Paso aficionados along my route. Then a member I'd never seen before offered to set up a ham radio network to follow my progress.

"I'll help take out your horses' export permits," Tuco Roca Rey offered after the meeting ended. "To gain time I'll have Juan Miguel send photographs, bills of sale, and veterinary certificates to me before he ships your horses to Jorge Baca's farm."

The following day Juan Miguel Rossel invited me to lunch at his house in Lima.

Tall and dignified, he greeted me warmly, then closed his library door to prevent interruptions and spent the afternoon showing me photos of Huascarán, Lucero, and their relatives. I was so impressed I bought a third horse — Inca, a bay.

All three were sons of Genio, a proven sire. According to photos taken from every angle they were muscular with straight clean legs, well-angled hocks and pasterns, broad chests, and deep bodies. All three also had well-sprung ribs, which promised the typical lung capacity of horses raised and worked at high altitude.

After Juan Miguel had gone through several albums I said, "You really love horses, don't you?"

He looked up and said something I've heard expressed in much the same words by several Peruvian breeders, "I don't raise horses in order to sell them. I sell horses so I can afford to raise them."

Before I left that evening Juan Miguel promised to ship my horses to Jorge Baca's farm soon. He also gave me photos to submit with my application for an export permit.

When I'd taken Malagueña to California I'd been required to get an export permit— though she was mine according to her registration certificate. Why? Because the process includes numerous fees and taxes.

Tuco orchestrated my effort to get that permit but left the leg work to me. On foot I went from the Ministry of this to the Ministry of that. The first day those long hikes were drudgery, endured to avoid paying for taxis. The next day however, I came to see that walking as part of my condition-ing program and tackled it with enthusiasm.

I didn't realize it then, but I was also being psychologically prepared for future battles with Peruvian bureaucrats. Gov-ernment officials everywhere put things off, but in Peru it was an art form. I was repeatedly frustrated by the difference between my definition of *mañana* (tomorrow) and theirs (at some convenient future time).

The day I took my application to the Ministry of Agriculture for a signature, a secretary cheerily promised it would be ready at noon *mañana*.

When I returned mañana at noon she told me, "Your papers

haven't been signed yet. You can pick them up tomorrow at 11:00 a.m."

I arrived a little ahead of time.

"The Minister isn't here yet," the secretary informed me curtly, as if being early was rude. "Come back in an hour."

An hour later a different secretary told me, "The man who signs export permits just left. You should have been here sooner."

"I was," I growled, "and the secretary you replaced told me to come back at this time."

"Sorry," she said. "They'll be ready at 2:30 tomorrow afternoon."

The next day I phoned an hour before my appointment.

"I'm sorry," one of the secretaries told me, sounding bored, "but you can't pick up your papers until 4:00 p.m."

I arrived at 4:00 and was told, "You have terrible luck. Unfortunately you'll have to return *mañana*."

I was sorely tempted to make today so unpleasant she wouldn't want to deal with me again *mañana*. But I'm not wired that way. The following day, however, I was.

Told by the embarrassed secretary to return yet again, I lost my temper. I was still angrily reciting a list of her many broken promises when—to my amazement—her boss walked out of his office and handed me my signed paper.

* * *

I still needed more signatures and had to collect them in order at ministries on opposite sides of Lima. No one would sign until I'd collected every signature preceding his. For days I squandered money on taxis, and once returned to the same office twice in one day for two signatures.

Every official collected a fee. I especially resented paying the Secretary of the Navy. After all I wasn't exporting seahorses.

An English novelist, L.P. Hartley, once wrote: 'The past is a foreign country, they do things differently there.' The Peru I'd seen so far was a foreign country living in the past, and things were done very differently. While most of the world's governments were promoting exports, Peru's had erected roadblocks that discouraged them, but brought money into its Treasury.

Making matters worse my height brought staring, laughing, jeering, and honking—unwanted attention that made me dread leaving the *Asociación's* protective confines. But my stay in Peru's beautiful, history-filled capital had compensations, the greatest of which was the time I spent with Tuco Roca Rey, a fascinating combination of old world elegance and impish humor.

One afternoon on a sidewalk downtown he stopped, staring at workers on a scaffold scraping paint from a building. Fingers to his lips he whistled, stopping them. After the powder and flakes stopped falling, we walked past. Without a word, Tuco's imposing presence had spared us and our clothes from what had threatened to be an unavoidable soiling.

The next time I saw his unexpected artistry as a funnyman, he made a mistake while dialing the rotary-style telephone in his home library. Thanks to Lima's antiquated phone system, breaking the connection meant waiting—probably quite a while—for a new dial tone. Briefly he glared at the offending finger, then punished it with a ferocious, pantomimed bite.

An accomplished amateur bullfighter he'd fought in the company of several famous Spanish toreros. He proudly showed me photographs of himself in a suit of lights dueling brave bulls in Lima's Plaza de Acho.

"He was talented enough to have been a professional," his wife told me as she served lunch, "but his family wouldn't allow it — not because of the danger but because they considered it beneath him."

After we ate, Tuco took me to a cockfight. One wave of his hand and the man in the ticket office returned my money and said, "Welcome. Today you'll be our guest."

We'd arrived an hour before the fights, but all the best seats were taken. Among the early arrivals were two ragamuffin boys who'd claimed front row seats they offered to give up for twenty Peruvian *soles*. After Tuco paid, they moved back to empty seats and were soon offering to leave those for ten *soles*.

"Guard my seat with your life," Tuco told me, then went to mingle with the roosters' owners, trainers, and handlers.

When two of my Peruvian horse enthusiast friends arrived, one called out, "Stay where you are or someone will take your seat. We'll come to you."

Our conversation was an enjoyable prelude to the fights. Adding to the magical atmosphere, two young men strummed guitars and serenaded pretty señoritas.

Later handlers carried two roosters into the ring and tied razor-sharp knives beside their natural spurs. Those deadly blades were the reason I hadn't enjoyed the cockfight I'd seen during my previous trip to Peru.

"I want to understand this sport so I can appreciate it," I told Tuco when he returned. "Do you mind if I ask questions during the fights?"

"I'm going to watch from the staging area," he said, turning to survey the seats behind us, "but I see someone who can answer your questions."

Tuco waved to Javier La Rosa, a promising young Peruvian Paso aficionado. I was still answering his questions about my ride when the first two roosters were turned loose face-to-face in the small, round arena's center. Angrily they circled, feathers fluffed.

Javier focused on them as if I wasn't there.

After the fight he asked, "You didn't enjoy that, did you?"

"All I saw was a flurry of feathers," I replied. "What should I watch for?"

"Put yourself in one of their places," he suggested, "and watch the other very closely. Consider ways to attack and defend yourself. If you concentrate hard, your eyes will slow the action."

The next feathered gladiators were a red and a white. Shortly after their battle began, Javier recoiled as though he'd been struck.

"Did you see that?" he asked. "I'm the white one, and the red just got me right there." He tapped a finger against his ribs.

By then the white was sitting — as if on a nest — its feathers bloody where Javier had indicated.

"How did you see that?" I asked. "Everything happened so fast."

Absorbed by the still unfolding drama, he didn't answer.

Declaring victory the red flapped its wings, crowing, strutting, and ignoring his fallen opponent — a big mistake. Abruptly the white leapt to its feet and inflicted a wound in his adversary's chest. Their legs simultaneously buckling, they sank to sitting positions. Neither had won. This was a fight to the death, and both were still alive.

The loser would be the first one whose beak touched the sandy arena floor. As their heads slowly drooped forward, bedlam broke out. Owners and handlers screamed encouragement. Spectators directed pleas to the rooster they'd bet on.

"Don't die."

"Stay alive."

As if synchronized, both heads slowly drooped forward. Then the white cock's bill stabbed into the sand closely followed by the red's.

"That was the most exciting fight I've ever seen," Javier said as wagered money changed hands.

That was the last cockfight I saw for years. Seeing such beautiful birds die had been difficult and no less so after a Peruvian sitting behind us defended the sport to his American companion by saying, "Yes it's sad to see them die but without cockfighting, they wouldn't have been born."

Fighting cocks were a special breed, created and maintained expressly for these contests.

* * *

After Tuco alerted Lima's media about my ride, the editor of the English-language *Peruvian Times* magazine asked me to send monthly articles from en route. Then two newsmen visited me at the Asociación and wrote small articles that were buried deep inside lesser newspapers. But the reporter who next came looking for me was from a major paper.

After a detailed interview Juan put a roll of film in his camera and said, "I want photos of you on a Paso horse. Let's see if we can find one."

We crossed the street to the Club Hipico but found only jumpers and dressage horses.

"You'd think we'd could find a Peruvian Paso a hundred meters from the national association," Juan complained.

When a man drove up in a Toyota, Juan perked up.

"Hugo Bustamante," he whispered reverently. "I wonder if his horses are here."

The unassuming young man who got out of the car didn't

strike me as a famous *torero* who fought bulls from horse-back.

"I need photos of this gringo riding a Peruvian Paso," Juan said, holding up his camera. "Can you loan us one of yours?"

Bustamante replied directly to me, "Would you like to ride Relicario?" Astonished I replied, "I'm not qualified to ride him."

"Don't worry." Bustamante grinned. "You'll just be a passenger. He knows what to do."

He entered a stall and brought out a beautiful gray stallion I'd seen in many photos.

After saddling Relicario, Bustamante instructed me to ride in a circle around him, and cautioned, "Don't touch the reins."

Holding up one finger on each hand to represent horns Bustamante, on foot, charged again and again. Each time, Relicario avoided him with cutting horse maneuverability that had me holding the saddle with both hands.

Finally satisfied with his photos, Juan glanced at his watch.

"I have to leave now to get my article submitted in time for tonight's edition," he said, then dashed to the street and flagged down a taxi.

I stayed while Bustamante unsaddled Relicario. Juan and I had invaded his privacy in one of the few places where he could escape his adoring fans and be himself. Eager to avoid overstaying my welcome I said goodbye and turned to go.

"Do you have time to talk?" Bustamante asked.

"*Claro*," I said.

He showed me his other two bullfight horses, then brought chairs so we could sit in front of their stalls. I wanted to know more about him, but his questions about my ride persisted until I was convinced he was truly interested and opened up.

"Who's Relicario's sire?" I asked after a while, hoping to change subjects.

"All three of my horses are Genio sons," he replied.

"That makes them half-brothers to my geldings," I exclaimed, inadvertently returning to the subject I'd tried to change.

Getting into his car at dusk, Bustamante said, "Tomorrow there's a police-sponsored charity event with bullfights and a Peruvian Paso exhibition. Would you like to come as my guest?"

"Absolutely."

"Meet me here at 6:30 a.m. We'll ride to the plaza in the truck with my horses."

That evening as I cooked supper in the Asociacion's kitchen, its fulltime employee Estanislao Ostos couldn't stop grinning. After he showed me the reason, neither could I. A feature article written by Juan and illustrated with his photos was on the front page of Lima's most prestigious newspaper.

* * *

"Have you seen this?" I asked, handing Hugo a copy of Juan's article at daybreak.

"Yes," he replied, locking his car door. "That reporter wrote too much about me and too little about you."

"I'll stand in your reflected glory any day," I teased. "Why do you suppose Juan's article didn't mention you're fighting a bull today?"

"This is a charity event with amateur fights," Hugo explained. "I'm participating in the Peruvian Paso exhibition only."

The army troop carrier scheduled to take Hugo's horses to the Plaza de Acho bullfight arena came an hour and a half late.

"Those look like leg-breakers to me," Hugo muttered, looking at knee-high benches permanently attached to the floor in the truck's cargo area. "I'd rather ride my horses to the plaza than put them in there. Will you please be my third rider?"

"With pleasure," I said.

Talking and laughing Hugo, his groom, and I rode along Avenida Arequipa's park-like median on lush grass shaded by leafy trees. When policemen at intersections recognized the famous *torero*, they immediately stopped traffic for us.

Downtown the median strip ended and we were funneled into narrow, congested, canyon-like streets between buildings that trapped and amplified the sound of automobile horns as well as the roar of worn-out mufflers.

Every time a policeman's shrill whistle cut through the racket, I looked to see if I'd done something wrong. But the officer's attention was always focused on clearing a path for one of Peru's best-known bullfighters.

Cars had the right-of-way in Lima. I never saw a driver chase a pedestrian on a sidewalk, but between the curbs people on foot had to be careful. The same was true of people on horses. A few drivers recognized Bustamante. The rest treated us with the same consideration they showed people who were walking.

I couldn't imagine a worse place to ride an unfamiliar horse, and mine was a young stallion still in training. Fortunately his priority was pleasing me and despite competition for his attention, he kept both ears pointed toward me. Even when I couldn't hear myself cluck to him, his quick responses got us out of tight spots.

At Lima's Plaza de Acho — South America's oldest bull-ring — an attendant opened the livestock gate and saluted as Hugo rode past.

"Wish I'd known you'd be here," Hugo told me after we stopped inside. "Having you ride in this exhibition would've been excellent publicity for your ride, but unfortunately I've already lined up another rider for the horse you're on."

"No problem," I assured him.

What he thought was bad luck was actually a blessing in disguise. I had a great deal to learn about getting a good performance from a Peruvian horse.

* * *

At three in the afternoon during bullfight season, the Plaza de Acho's expensive seats are shaded while the rest are exposed to the sun's heat. But under that day's overcast sky, rich and poor alike enjoyed a comfortable temperature.

Inside the packed stadium I didn't find a seat until after the scheduled starting time. Peru's bullfights start on time — never mind that nothing else does. When this one didn't, spectators vented their displeasure by whistling, stomping, and throwing rented seat cushions into the arena.

The crowd was in an uproar by the time the show began.

First was an exhibition of what the announcer introduced as: "Highly trained police dogs."

His description seemed exaggerated when the bloodhound couldn't track down the fugitive, who was hiding nearby and half-exposed. Then the German Shepherd attack dog wouldn't let go of the criminal and had to be carried from the arena with the poor man's padded arm clamped between his teeth.

The police motorcycle group's demonstration went well until the leader fell off his bike amid howls of laughter.

Having come for the bullfights, the crowd grew restless when the announcer told them how much they would enjoy the two remaining preliminary events — a police drill team on trotting horses, followed by a presentation of *caballos Peruanos de paso.*

As Hugo later told me, a rivalry had broken out while the trotters and pasos were warming up, and a police sergeant had insulted the pasos by calling them, "Silly little animals that shouldn't be anywhere near real horses."

"Let's settle this like gentlemen," Hugo proposed.

"What do you have in mind?" the sergeant asked.

"That each rider in both groups puts five hundred *soles* in a pot which will go to the team that gets the most applause."

"My men don't have that kind of money," the sergeant scoffed.

"If you're afraid to bet that much," Hugo tweaked him, "just say so. You don't have to make excuses. How about a hundred Peruvian *soles* each?"

The sergeant accepted and collected from everyone in both groups.

Now competing for what was a lot of money to them, members of the police drill team entered the arena intent on winning. After an impressive start, a trooper was thrown. On foot he couldn't catch his horse and when two of his mounted comrades tried to help, they added to the confusion.

Bursting into the arena, Hugo Bustamante guided Relicario with his legs during a spectacular capture of the elusive trotter.

"Congratulations Hugo," a spectator shouted. "So far no one else in this entire show has accomplished what he wanted to."

Prolonging a standing ovation, Hugo guided Relicario sideways around the circular arena, facing the audience all the way. Ever the showman he waved one hand and held his *sombrero* high with the other. By the time he'd finished, the discouraged mounted police had left.

Not interested in amateur bullfights, I rejoined Hugo and his groom and we rode back to the Club Hipico. The three horses arrived fresh and alert, a good omen I hoped, for my Genio sons.

* * *

More than two weeks into the nine months available for my journey I still hadn't seen—let alone ridden—my new horses, and I decided to go to Chiclayo. Shepherding my paperwork in Lima would take longer from there, but I'd gain more time than I lost if my horses were ready to go when their export permit was finally issued.

"I'll watch over your application," Tuco Roca Rey kindly offered, "and send your permits to Chiclayo as soon as they're ready."

On my last afternoon in Lima, Hugo and his wife took me to lunch at an excellent restaurant and then to his home. There we watched movies of him and Relicario fighting bulls in the Plaza de Acho.

"I didn't realize how dangerous your style of bullfighting is," I said after he turned off his projector.

Spanish *rejoneadores*—the best-known mounted bullfighters—are only briefly close to the bull and are protected for all but that instant by their horses' superior speed. During Hugo's *suerte nacional* however, Relicario pivoted on his forehand with the bull chasing his hindquarter. And for a long, heart-stopping moment Hugo was as little as a foot away from those deadly horns.

In the brief time we'd known each other, the torero and I had become friends. We were both adventurers but not the same kind. He craved brief periods of intense danger, whereas I preferred constant-but-milder stimulation. That night, after his wife went to bed, we continued our last conversation until daybreak, then said goodbye outside his car at the Asociación clubhouse.

I slept in a vacant office until 2:30 the next afternoon, then went downtown and bought a ticket on that night's cheapest bus to Chiclayo. Back at the *Asociación* I prepared my dinner. As I finished eating, Carlos Luna and Carlos González arrived. Often found together they were an unlikely pair— Luna intensely serious in contrast to the effervescent, playful González.

"We should drink a toast to Pablito's ride," González said.

The bartender winked at me and followed Fernando Graña's special recipe while mixing my counterfeit scotch.

Then Luna raised his glass and proposed Peru's traditional toast, "*Salud.*"

I responded with the English equivalent, "To your health."

"I like this one much better," full-of-fun González said, grinning. Raising his glass he said, "*Arriba.*" Lowering it to his belt he followed with, "*Abajo.*" Bringing it chest high, he ended with, "*Al centro y adentro.*" He drained his glass with a single gulp.

That clever toast is now common, but back then Luna and I had never heard it and we chuckled. It translates as: "above, below, to the middle, and inside." In Spanish it rhymes, adding to its charm.

After the two Carloses left I hailed a taxi. The driver opened his trunk and helped load my baggage. Augmented by acquisitions made in Lima—including a saddle—it had become more than one person could manage.

Sad to be leaving friends and familiar surroundings, I sat quietly during the drive to the bus station. Ahead were strangers who might or might not be friendly—not to mention an ambitious task that could end badly. I was excited to be on my way but sorry to be leaving.

An hour later, I would bid Lima goodbye with no regrets.

* * *

The taxi driver left me in front of the station where I'd purchased my ticket. The door was locked, the lights were off, and there were no buses. Thirsty and tempted to visit a nearby soda fountain I was afraid that if I stepped away, my baggage would disappear on the backs of street urchins amusing themselves by calling me giraffe and sundry less flattering names.

None too soon for my taste a clerk from another bus station chased them away.

"This company's bus broke down," he told me. "Mine has tonight's last available seat to Chiclayo."

His ticket was more expensive than the one I'd bought earlier, but he offered to accept mine as partial payment.

"You must hurry, *señor*," he warned, starting toward the depot from which he'd come.

"Don't let the bus leave without me," I called out.

I rushed back and forth with portions of my baggage, frantic that someone would steal something from one bus station while I was at the other.

"You're in seat 1-A, *señor*, next to a pretty nurse," the clerk said, handing over my ticket after I paid the balance due plus an excess baggage charge.

The driver shut the door and pulled out the instant I got in, presumably to protect the clerk who'd charged a premium price for what he'd claimed was the last ticket, when in fact, there was only one passenger in the first row. Too tired to care, I dropped into seat 1-A beside the pretty nurse, who was at least twice my age.

"What brings you to Peru?" she asked.

"I'm going to ride horses from Chiclayo to the United States," I replied.

Her response was predictable. "Wish I were a man so I could have such adventures."

3

THREE TO GET READY

F ollowing a pleasant conversation with the nurse, I closed my eyes well after midnight. Only then did I realized why the other passengers had chosen to sit farther back. All night oncoming headlight beams came through the windshield and pierced my eyelids. I slept fitfully and stopped trying five hours north of Lima when the sun came up.

The nurse was still asleep and I slid into the seat behind the driver.

When he heard what I was doing in his country, he dreamily said, "If I were single, I'd do something like that."

"Do you know Reque?" I asked after we'd talked long enough that I felt comfortable asking a favor.

"It's a village a little south of Chiclayo," he replied.

"Can you let me off there at Jorge Baca's farm, La Quinta?"

"I'm not familiar with La Quinta," he said. "The best I can do is leave you in Reque."

Later he stopped in a rural settlement and motioned for me to follow.

"Anyone here should be able to direct you to La Quinta," he said after pulling my belongings from the baggage compartment.

As he drove away I looked up and saw the sun for the first time since just before landing in Lima. It was a cheery and up-lifting sight, made even more so by surrounding fields of green, a welcome change from the gray of Lima's monotonous desert.

"Can you direct me to La Quinta?" I asked a nearby Indian woman.

"One kilometer," she mumbled, pointing.

If I'd known that earlier I could've gotten off the bus at the front gate and saved myself miles of walking. I shouldered as much of my gear as I could carry and made my first of three trips, harried by half-wild dogs.

After setting my last bag outside La Quinta's locked gate, I called to an elderly man standing on the driveway. He held up a hand—which I interpreted as a signal to wait—and walked away.

Pushing a cart with a platform between two wheels the old man returned, then unlocked the gate and said, "Señora Baca said to bring you to the house."

We loaded my baggage, which he insisted on pushing by himself—a considerable chore at his age. The lady on the porch of a two-story Spanish style house had a puzzled expression that didn't change after I told her who I was.

"You can leave your things here," she said. "No one will bother them. Have you had breakfast?"

"No but you don't have to—"

"Do you like rice and fried eggs?" she interrupted.

"That sounds wonderful."

"I sent a boy to bring my husband from the fields. He should be here soon."

I'd met Jorge Baca two years earlier at Lima's National Championship Peruvian Paso Horse Show. He'd been enjoying himself thoroughly and I'd had grave doubts about his reputation as a hard worker.

I was still eating when he came into the dining room.

"Pablito," he said boisterously—arms outstretched—then gave me an *abrazo*, one of those back-slapping hugs with which Peruvian men greet male friends. "What brings you here?"

"Didn't Tuco tell you I was coming?" I asked.

"Tuco Roca Rey? No."

"Did Juan Miguel Rossel send three geldings here recently?" I asked, panic tugging at my sleeve.

"Yes. I've been waiting for someone to tell me why."

Amazed when I told him about my ride, he said, "We'll talk more at dinner, but right now I have an emergency at my milking barn. Please make yourself at home. You and your horses can stay as long as you need."

"Where are my horses?" I asked.

"Over there." He pointed toward a stable and hurried back to whatever I'd interrupted.

* * *

Located near La Quinta's worker housing, the stable was shaded by leafy *algarrobo*, carob trees with yellow, string-bean-like seed pods. Bursting with anticipation I opened the first four in a row of stalls. They were empty.

"The horses from Cajamarca are that one," a boy told me, pointing.

"All in one stall?"

"*Si, Señor.*"

"Thank you. What's your name?"

"Pablo."

"Then we're *tocayos*," I said. "We have the same name. I'm Pablito."

He grinned, amused by the absurdity of my being a giant and having a diminutive nickname.

I opened the stall door he'd indicated. A gray, a bay, and a black huddled in a corner looked at me suspiciously.

"Why are they together?" I asked Pablo.

"They wouldn't stop calling to each other and we couldn't sleep."

"I need to put them in separate stalls, and when I do that, they'll be noisy again. Will that be a problem?"

"Not during the day," he replied, clearly pleased to have been consulted. "But they'll keep us awake after Don Baca turns off the generators."

Earlier Señora Baca had told me Reque had no public power. Gas-powered generators produced La Quinta's only electricity, and they were turned on for two hours at dawn and three more after dark. If my horses didn't settle down by bedtime, I'd have to put them back in one stall until tomorrow.

Eager to see Huascarán—named after the highest peak in the Peruvian Andes—I led the regal dappled gray from the stall. He was tall and handsome, as Fernando Graña had promised. Having been reserved for Juan Miguel Rossel's infrequent use, he was also overweight. But his muscles were rock hard and when I had him circle me in gait, he moved willingly and easily.

Lucero, the smallest, had a dull black coat and a protruding convex profile I hadn't noticed in his photos. Called a Roman nose in the States and a sheep's head in Peru, this unattractive feature was thought to indicate a horse strongly influenced by the blood of North Africa's Barb breed.

A leading breeder, Alfredo Elias, had taught me to evaluate horses from the ground up and the hindquarter forward, which focuses attention on the parts most important to performance. But I'd been unable to resist starting with Huascarán's beautiful sculpted head and Lucero's ugly Roman nose.

While evaluating Inca, I violated Don Alfredo's rule again. The pupil of his left eye was marred by a jagged white scar. Passing my hand back and forth in front of it brought no reaction. He was half-blind, a serious defect in a horse I planned to ride on dangerous mountain trails. It would also make him difficult to sell.

After putting my geldings in separate stalls I told Pablo, "I'll come back when I can."

"You're not going to ride?" he asked, looking disappointed.

"Tomorrow."

Today I had to figure out what to do about Inca. Initially surprised by his defect, I was now upset. Why hadn't I been told?

When I mentioned Inca's eye to Jorge Baca at lunch, he said, "I know. That was the first thing I noticed."

"May I please use your telephone to call Fernando Graña?" I asked. "I'll reimburse you for the cost."

"There are no phones in Reque," he replied. "You'll have to use one of the long distance booths in Chiclayo. I'll drive you there after work."

* * *

"I'm sure Juan Miguel doesn't know about that eye," Fernando Graña said after I'd explained the reason for my call. "No doubt he'll refund part of your money. I can arrange a trade with a breeder near you. But I once had an excellent one-eyed polo pony I wouldn't have sold for love or money. Why don't you ride Inca and see if you like him?"

As Jorge Baca drove me back to La Quinta I asked his opinion. "I agree with Don Fernando," he replied. "A friend of mine, Lucho Valverde, once took a trip in the Andes. He had a riding horse but needed another to carry supplies, so a friend loaned him a half-blind pack horse. He wound up riding the borrowed horse exclusively because it had more than compensated for its handicap by sharpening its other senses."

The next morning I tried to sneak up on Inca's blind side and he immediately sensed my presence. That afternoon I rode him on a rugged, busy trail where he was never surprised by — or walked too close to — anything.

Finding another horse of his quality would be difficult and I'd also have to apply for a new export permit. There were good reasons to keep him and I decided to do so, unless he disappointed me the next time I rode him.

* * *

Different physically, my geldings had comparable personalities, identical tastes in feed, and were spooked by the same things. The second day I rode them, none reacted to creaky groaning oxcarts or burros practically invisible beneath huge loads of alfalfa, firewood, or long sugarcane stalks noisily dragging the ground behind them.

All three calmly passed pumps noisily gushing water into irrigation ditches. But Lucero was terrified by one that was turned off. I had to coax for a long time before he finally sidled past. When Huascarán and I reached the same pump, all hell broke loose.

Later Inca too was suspicious and resisted passing, but briefly and far less forcefully. He had what O.M. Pat Smith — the mentor who'd taught me most of what I knew about horses — called a good mind.

* * *

That evening all three geldings surprised me again, this time by refusing to eat corn or barley. They were work horses and not accustomed to such luxuries, a serious problem because they'd need grain's vitamins, minerals, and other nutrients during our journey.

While Jorge Baca and I enjoyed a cool breeze on his porch that evening, I asked how he'd suggest getting my horses to eat grain.

"I'd put it in feedbags," he said, "and leave those on until they try it, no matter how long that takes."

In Lima Carlos Luna had suggested feedbags as a convenient way to feed grain, and they'd come in handy whether Jorge's plan worked or not. I cut and hand-sewed canvas until after midnight.

The next morning while my horses hungrily nickered for breakfast, I put corn in their new feedbags and tied those on their heads. When none had tried this offering by dinnertime, I gave up and fed them hay for the first time in twenty-four hours.

The next day I tried barley with the same result. In the States I'd fed rolled barley—which after being steamed and flattened—resembled oatmeal. But whole barley was the only kind available in Chiclayo. Its unappetizing, rock-hard kernels were difficult to chew, and the few my geldings sampled emerged whole in their manure—nutrition still locked inside.

That afternoon I soaked barley in water and crushed it with a mortar and pestle, to make it palatable, digestible, and easier to eat. By then however, Huascarán, Lucero, and Inca had decided they didn't like it. Period.

"Keep trying," Jorge Baca told me at lunch. "Some horses are slow to figure out that to eat from a feedbag, they have to lower their heads until its bottom is on the ground."

The following morning at Chiclayo's outdoor market I found a vendor selling whole oats. In the Peru of those days cereal grains were threshed by oxen, which trampled the stalks on the ground mixing the kernels with grit and other contaminates. These impurities could provoke colic, and my German heritage compelled me to pick them out.

While I was busy with this dreary, time-consuming chore, my young namesake Pablo asked, "Why don't you feed your horses algarrobo? They'll love it and all you have to do it pick it up off the ground."

Back then most Peruvians believed algarrobo's string bean-like seedpods were rich in protein because they gave quick energy. However, a leading breeder had told me he'd sent samples to a laboratory for analysis that revealed a high sugar content and little nutritional value.

But if my horses liked algarrobo, I could add sweet chunks to corn, barley, or oats, making them more palatable.

When I did this Lucero and Inca ate theirs with gusto and wanted more. And fussy Huascarán consumed most of his before removing his nose bag, something he'd learned to do no matter how tightly I tied it.

* * *

Sunday before dawn I was jarred awake by men stampeding past my bedroom window and voices full of urgency. Still buckling my belt I rushed outside and stumbled across uneven ground toward flickering lanterns near the milking barn corrals.

As my eyes adjusted to the darkness I saw four groaning Holstein-Friesian cows flat on their sides, grotesquely bloated. Jorge Baca was barking instructions to workers as they pried the stricken animals' mouths open and poured liquid down their throats. All around men were keeping other cows on their feet and moving.

I knew little about cows, but it's crucial to keep horses from lying down when they have colic and that seemed true of cows as well. When another dropped to the ground—her breathing labored—I vaulted the fence and seized both ears before she rolled onto her side. Another man grabbed her tail and someone else prodded her with a stick.

We got her back on her feet, but she refused to walk and went down again, eyes glazed, blood trickling from both nostrils. This time she wound up on her side.

"Make room," a man running toward us screamed, brandishing what looked like an oversize ice pick. With a swift stab he punctured the cow's stomach between two ribs and air hissed from the tube left behind to keep the wound open. With three more of those detachable sheaths, he performed the same operation on other cows that had gone down.

As suddenly as it had started, the crisis ended. One cow was dead and several had holes through which foul smelling air hissed, relieving the pressure in their stomachs.

I had no idea what had happened or why.

* * *

"My cows eat freshly cut alfalfa, which can ferment and cause bloat," Jorge Baca explained at breakfast. "To prevent that, we feed rice straw at the same time. This morning however, a new worker fed alfalfa only."

"Should I give my horses rice straw with their fresh alfalfa? I asked, concerned.

"No. It doesn't bloat horses. Cows have multiple stomachs where it stays long enough to ferment. The worst horses get is diarrhea, which yours haven't."

4

FOUR TO GET READY AGAIN

Two mornings later at breakfast, Jorge asked gently, "Have you heard the expression: 'In Peru, the medicine arrives after the patient is buried?'"

"Uh-oh," I said. "What's wrong now?"

"Tuco Roca Rey sent a telegram. The Ministry of Agriculture won't issue your export permit until they receive certificates proving your horses have been inoculated for glanders, sleeping sickness, and strangles."

"My geldings had those shots in Cajamarca," I protested. "I personally delivered the certificates to the Ministry in Lima."

"Those injections should've been administered by a government vet. But they weren't and now everything has to be done again—applications, inoculations, photographs, all of it."

"That's outrageous."

"Yes," he said, "but take my word, fighting our government is a waste of time."

For two frustrating weeks, I devoted my mornings to shepherding a second round of paperwork in faraway Lima. This frustrating delay would've been unbearable without the relief provided by my afternoon rides.

I'd begun to see differences in the half-brothers I'd first thought were almost identical.

All I had to do was point Huascarán and Inca down a trail and they followed it like powerful machines. But if I didn't pay constant attention, free-spirited Lucero—like a car with loose steering—constantly veered off the beaten path, merrily on his way to nowhere in particular. He was also more easily frightened than his half-brothers.

If not for the white blotch in Inca's eye, I wouldn't have known he was half-blind. I never saw any other evidence of that while working around or riding him. He had less energy than the others but used it efficiently. Never on parade like Huascarán he was surefooted, tireless, and definitely a keeper.

The first time I took my geldings on the trail together they quickly learned to travel single file—no matter which I rode. And finicky Huascarán was eating ever-increasing amounts of corn, barley, and oats—though I'd ceased flavoring them with algarrobo bits.

* * *

"Have you noticed that Huascarán is conceited?" Jorge Baca asked one afternoon at the stable.

His droll observation made me laugh, but he was right. My big gray didn't like being told what to do. When Inca or Lucero failed to follow orders, it was because they didn't understand. Huascarán however, would defy me. Evidently his size and power had convinced former handlers to give him his way if he persisted.

I'd been amused by his haughty expression after removing his feed bag by himself. But when the government veterinarian came to La Quinta I saw that look for what it really was — pure defiance. Unhappy with being poked and prodded during his examination, worming, and inoculations, Huascarán suddenly pulled back — jerking a hitching post out of the ground.

My countermove was to tie him to a substantial tree. His counter-countermove was to break his lead rope three more times before the vet finished. Rather than reward this behavior by freeing Huascarán in his corral, which was what he wanted, I tied him to the tree with my strongest lead rope and started cleaning stalls.

I was almost done when young Pablo rushed up to breathlessly announce, "Señor, Huascarán is loose and near the highway."

My big gray was in front of his stall when I caught him. Determined to prove my brain superior to his brawn, I spliced the lead rope and passed it behind his ears. This so-called "nerve line" would apply pressure next time he pulled, which he soon did.

Surprised by the unexpected punishment, he surged forward, angrily shaking his head.

I made sure no one was watching and growled, "Hope you've learned your lesson."

He backed up pulling the rope tight, then slung his head violently until he'd slipped out of his halter, freeing himself. By the time I caught him it was too dark to safely continue our test of wills.

"Tomorrow," I swore as I turned him loose in his stall, "I'll teach you humility."

Responding to my tone his look said, "You'll be glad you didn't say 'or die trying.'"

After working Inca and Lucero the next afternoon, I rode Huascarán twice as long. Far from worn out he broke two metal snaps and destroyed another leadline while I unsaddled and bathed him.

"Hope you've learned your lesson," his eyes said after his third escape.

Then I did what I should've done in the first place: snugged the noose of a lasso around his body at the withers, threaded the free end between his front legs and through his halter ring, and tied it to the tree. Walking away I chuckled with anticipation.

That familiar sly look in his eyes, Huascarán set out to break yet another rope. But as the lasso squeezed him more tightly his expression changed. By then I didn't care if he pulled until his eyes bugged out—but he was too intelligent to punish himself in a lost cause, and stopped.

After that he wouldn't pull no matter how much I provoked him—as long as I had the heart rope on him.

* * *

A day later I introduced my geldings to the art of carrying cargo.

Somewhat humbled after losing our last battle, Huascarán carried the packsaddle and duffel bags without incident. Inca was his usual trusting, cooperative self. Lucero didn't mind the saddle, but was suspicious of my duffel bags. He worked himself into a frenzy while I tied them down.

As I tried to lead him around the stable he jerked me off my feet, and dragged me until I let go. His mad dash threw one bag to the ground, broke the snap holding the other shut, then scattered its contents before he jumped a fence and charged into La Quinta's reservoir.

I·fished his leadline from the water with a stick, then coaxed him ashore and left him tied to a hitching rail while I retrieved my gear. The only casualty was my tin cup, which had been altered to a shape more suitable for begging than drinking.

Next I emptied both duffel bags and stuffed them with straw. Before Lucero would let me load them on the pack-saddle I had to put *tapa ojos*, eye covers, on him. Never having seen a blindfolded horse move, I was caught off guard when he charged forward after I untied him, almost trampling me before crashing into a tree headfirst. He was terrified — not defiant.

Concerned for his safety and convinced I'd never be able to trust him with the cargo I decided to make do with two packhorses.

*   *   *

The next time I went to Chiclayo my opinion of its residents soared to new heights. People were smiling and friendly. A shopkeeper I asked for directions closed his business long enough to guide me to a feed store. As I struggled to bring my hundred pound sack of oats aboard the bus to La Quinta, two passengers left their seats and helped me.

"Sorry, your money's no good here," the driver said when I tried to pay my fare.

Every seat was occupied, some by more people than they were designed for. I stood with passengers in the crowded aisle, doubled forward, the back of my head and neck pressed against the low ceiling. Seeing my discomfort, a boy gave me his seat. A conversation with his delightful parents shortened the trip to La Quinta, where two passengers unloaded my oats.

That night at dinner, Jorge Baca told me, "There was an article about your ride in the newspaper, but it was sold out by the time I got to the newsstand."

"I'd love to read it," I said. "What paper was it in?"

"*La Industria*. You can get a copy at their office tomorrow."

The following day when I went to get a copy, Chiclayo showed its other face.

I reached *La Industria* an hour after opening time. Its door was locked and the shades drawn. Everywhere I went while running other errands, people made fun of my height. When I was through I returned to find *La Industria* still closed.

The bus to Reque was an hour late and people—mostly women who'd arrived after I had—elbowed me aside and filled the seats and aisle. I had an appointment with a horse-shoer and couldn't wait for the next bus.

I took a taxi and the driver tried to charge double.

"I refuse to pay more than the regular fare," I told him.

"If I don't open my trunk," he countered, "you won't be able to reclaim your purchases."

They'd cost less than he wanted, so I sent him on his way. Then I waited hours for a blacksmith who didn't come.

I fed my geldings in the dark after sunset and found Huascarán's stall door shut but not latched. Someone had looked in and left it ajar. If he'd nudged or brushed against it, he'd have had a clear path to the highway—where drivers sped past with only parking lights on, risking death or injury to extend the lives of their batteries.

After a day during which everything had gone wrong I was thoroughly discouraged and homesick. Rather than risk having to be sociable on the way to my room I simmered on a boulder beside the highway, watching passing traffic.

Most of Peru's inter-city buses had previously belonged to Greyhound Lines in the States, and the names of former destinations were still displayed above the windshields. Seeing them pass — supposedly going to Green Bay, Houston, Chicago, or my hometown, Reno — I didn't feel as cut off from the world where I'd grown up, was comfortable and wished I still was.

The issue of *La Industria* with the article about my upcoming journey was sold out next time I went to Chiclayo, and I never did see it.

* * *

I was cleaning stalls when Jorge Baca drove up and got out of his car the next afternoon.

"If you're wondering why I look pleased," he said, "it's because I just arranged for the best farrier at Chiclayo's racetrack to shoe your horses tomorrow." Jorge handed me four horseshoes. "He has only aluminum shoes — too soft for anything besides racing — so I bought these iron ones from the mounted police."

"Thank you very much," I exclaimed, wishing I could think of a more original expression of gratitude.

"I have more good news," he said. "My brother's a senator and is going to ask the Minister of Agriculture to expedite your permit."

* * *

Because Peru's Paso horses are usually ridden barefoot, mine had never been shod. Even Lucero had reacted well the times I'd picked up their hooves and tapped the bottoms with a hammer. Nonetheless I was worried about their reactions to the real thing.

Fortunately the farrier, who arrived right on time, managed to nail on twelve shoes with only minimal resistance.

At lunch Jorge Baca had more good news.

"Your export permit is ready," he said, patting my shoulder. "Carlos Luna will bring it on Saturday. I've arranged for riders on horses from nearby haciendas to escort you to Chiclayo's most exclusive private club, where some leading citizens will toast you. Then you'll be on your way at last."

5

THE BISHOP'S BLESSING

Several times I'd regretted hatching the idea for my ride, but that last day at La Quinta more than made up for all of them. The magic in the air when I woke up lasted all day.

During breakfast Jorge Baca answered a knock on his door and returned with an elderly neighbor who'd come to wish me good luck. Painfully polite, the man apologized for interrupting our meal and insisted on waiting until we finished eating. When we rejoined him in the living room, he stood and ceremoniously handed me a sealed manila envelope.

"Gringo," he began, using an affectionate nickname as though we were longtime friends, "you must promise to not open this until you reach Los Gatos."

"You have my word," I told him.

"One of the three things inside," he continued, "is my prediction of your arrival date."

"When do think that will be?"

"You'll see when you open the envelope." He smiled warmly. "The second item is the image of a saint who'll assist with your journey. And the last is a gift I hope you'll like. Good luck."

"I'll keep this with my passport and other important papers," I told him as he left.

Jorge Baca told me what to expect during the next day's farewell ceremony, which was going to be more elaborate than I'd envisioned. A parade and an interview on national television seemed excessive. After all, I hadn't yet accomplished anything and might not.

"I expected a small private affair," I said.

"That would be inadequate," Jorge said, "especially since Carlos Luna is flying from Lima to see you off in the Asociación's name."

Later Jorge Baca's brother, who'd arranged the TV interview, called to advise that it had been canceled. I received that news with mixed feelings because it would've publicized the breed, one of my ride's main objectives.

Again someone knocked on the door. Jorge opened it to reveal a tiny, withered lady with the hooked nose, protruding chin, and sunken eyes of a storybook witch.

"I'm Miss Ward," she introduced herself, "a reporter for the *Peruvian Times*. I believe my editor told you I was coming?" Turning to me, she added, "I won't take much of your time and would like to start by taking photos of your horses if you don't mind."

Peruvian Times was a respected magazine distributed to Peru's large English speaking community. I'd read some of Miss Ward's past articles. She was a British expatriate and — in contrast to most women of that era — lived exactly as she pleased. To her credit however, she did so without the slightest trace of feminist abrasiveness.

She clearly needed to watch expenditures, and her appearance hadn't been enhanced by coming from Lima on the cheap, overnight bus.

I had much to do, but took her to my horses' stalls and opened Inca's. Listening to her evaluate him I realized she knew more about horses than I did, which made her approval reassuring.

"May I see him move?" she asked. "No need to ride him."

I ran him back and forth on halter so she could see his gait.

"It's good he has so little *termino*," she said, referring to the distinctive swimming motion of a Peruvian Paso's forelegs. "It makes this breed unique and beautiful, but in working horses it wastes energy."

When I finished grooming Lucero for Miss Ward's photo, she handed me her notes and said, "Here's what my article will say about him."

"Lucero," she'd written, "is a horse I had wanted to buy when I rode him at the annual horse show in Lima two years before. I liked his sheep's face, also known as a Roman nose, a conformation which is supposed to denote stamina."

"He was terrified when I tried to train him to carry cargo," I told her, "and has been off his feed since then."

"It might help if you put him in a corral with Huascarán and Inca."

Of course. I should've thought of that.

Once in with his lifelong companions, Lucero was instantly comforted by their presence and started eating.

"I suspect he might be too high-strung for the job ahead," I told Miss Ward.

"I wouldn't worry," she said softly. "He calmed down as soon as he felt secure."

When I brought Huascarán from his stall Miss Ward abandoned her English reserve long enough to exclaim, "Goodness. He has the shoulders of a bull."

Her high opinion of my big gray gelding was later evident in the article where she described him as, "...a magnificent steed and a perfect ride, easily gaited, very light mouthed, his powerful muscles giving a sense of great force."

She'd been away from England long enough to adopt Peru's relaxed lifestyle and would've been content to while away the day. But sensing I had a lot to do she graciously ended our interview, despite having come five hundred miles to conduct it.

I liked her a lot. She had the face of a witch but the soul of an angel.

* * *

The next day's long send-off from Chiclayo meant I'd probably reach Lambayeque — about seven miles to the north — after dark. Wanting to arrange accommodations for my horses in advance, I took a bus there and visited Augusto Carpena, a friend of Jorge Baca's.

"I'll be honored to stable your horses and have you stay in my home," he offered. "And since you won't likely find hay between here and Piura, I'll send some ahead to your nightly stops."

For an hour he helped me select those on a map.

Eager to express my gratitude, the best I could do was, "That's incredibly kind."

"In order to harvest," he smiled, "one must first plant."

"Where can I buy oats to send with your hay?"

"You won't find any at this hour."

"I'll bring some in the morning."

That night I slept at La Quinta for the last time, confident my horses were, as Miss Ward had said, "As fit as human hands could make them."

Determined to keep them that way, I took the early bus to Chiclayo and bought a hundred pounds of oats. I put these in five burlap bags and delivered them to Señor Carpena. Then I splurged on a taxi to take me back to La Quinta and set out for Chiclayo riding Huascarán, leading his half-brothers, and accompanied by Jorge Baca's trainer, who'd scarcely spoken to me before that day.

Riding a beautiful bay, he had a good laugh over my horses' awkward movements caused by the unfamiliar weight of their new shoes. By the time we were halfway to Chiclayo, they had adjusted and were moving comfortably.

That morning's short ride provided a discouraging preview of the difficulties I'd have with my duffel bags. Repeatedly I had to reposition them on the packsaddle. The trainer was no more experienced with cargo than I. He could only offer encouragement, which I would gladly have traded for some old-fashioned, how-to instructions.

A group of Paso horses and riders, *chalánes*, were waiting on Chiclayo's outskirts, and a police motorcycle escort led us into town. Our first spectators, vendors pushing fruit and vegetable carts, studied us silently. Farther along our audience was more appreciative.

In other countries our horses would've been the center of attention. Their stylish four-beat gaits easily kept pace with the police motorcycles, and they carried themselves as if leading a conquering army, while giving the chalánes and me unbelievably smooth rides.

But Peruvians are accustomed to their National Horse and all attention was on me. Groups of children tagged along shouting, "Pablito. Gringo."

People called out encouragement.

"Que le vaya bien."

"Buen viaje."

"Buena suerte."

I appreciated the enthusiastic applause, but was also embarrassed since I hadn't yet accomplished anything.

A group of young ladies showed particular enthusiasm. Flirting, I tipped my hat and said, "Thank you very much."

"Why do you thank us?" one returned, eyes sparking wickedly. "We're clapping for the horses, not you."

Everyone within hearing distance laughed and all eyes turned to me. Peruvians enjoy word games, and these waited to see if I was any good at them. I wasn't but something similar had happened to my Peruvian friend Alfredo Elias.

"I know," I told the girls, taking his words for my own, "but my horses can't talk and I'm speaking for them."

Again the crowd laughed, then waited for the girls' retort. Fortunately for me, they didn't have one.

Our little parade entered the Central Plaza, packed with people whose applause swelled to a crescendo when I stopped Huascarán. Displaying impressive horsemanship the chalánes flowed into the plaza in pairs, then stopped side-by-side in a long, perfectly straight line.

Behind me, Inca stood unperturbed and Lucero was predictably agitated.

I dismounted in front of an exclusive private club, where a man took charge of my horses as Jorge Baca introduced me to Chiclayo's Mayor and Bishop, a bank president, and two plantation owners. Then I leaned toward Carlos Luna—there to represent the national Paso breeders Asociación—for a back-slapping *abrazo* before we went inside.

After cocktails and hors d'oeuvres Luna, who'd attended a university in Germany and been on the podium during one of Adolf Hitler's speeches, stepped to the microphone and presented me a parchment scroll from the Asociación.

"This," he announced, "is for the American Association of Owners and Breeders of Peruvian Paso Horses."

Written in the formal language of Cervantes, it expressed gratitude for North America's growing interest in Peru's National Horse.

During the mayor's speech, he handed me an envelope and said, "When you reach your destination please deliver this to the mayor of Los Gatos."

Filled with the melancholy that comes over me when I leave familiar places, I scarcely heard the other speeches. Then the room went silent and everyone looked at me.

I hadn't prepared a speech but in my flawed Spanish said, "I've never been in a place as friendly as Chiclayo and won't forget the people here, especially Jorge Baca. He's one of the busiest men I've ever met but always found time to help with my problems. My profound gratitude also to the *Asociación Nacional de Criadores y Propietarios del Caballo Peruano de Paso*, which couldn't have been more supportive. And finally, thank you Carlos Luna for coming all the way from Lima to see me off."

I tried to remember who else I should mention. Augusto Carpena occurred to me but too late. Someone had called for a toast and uniformed waiters were passing out glasses of scotch and water. I would've preferred Fernando Graña's alcohol-free recipe, but this time mine was the real thing.

Glasses were raised and someone said, "*Salud, pesetas, amor, y tiempo para gozarlos,*" which seemed rather incongruous since it meant: "Health, money, love, and time to enjoy them."

I swallowed a sip of scotch that burned my throat and brought tears from my eyes, then set my glass back on the waiter's tray. Next the Bishop blessed my enterprise in Latin while making the sign of the cross in the air.

Back outside, reporters clamored for a final comment.

"Please," I requested, "ask your readers in places where we spend a night to provide stalls or a corral for my horses."

My private parade continued to the city limits, where I stopped and faced the chalánes. One by one they rode forward, shook my hand, and wished me good luck. More than the Mayor, Bishop, bankers, and reporters, they understood the magnitude of my task.

Then the police turned their motorcycles around and led my mounted escorts back across the city toward the trucks that brought them.

I rode in the opposite direction, into the desert.

6

THE ROYAL ROAD

As I rode along the highway shoulder a northbound vehicle came alongside and slowed—windows rolled down and occupants wishing me well.

"How will you find your way," a woman asked.

My simple answer no doubt disappointed her, "I'll follow the Pan-American Highway—not always this closely, but I'll keep it in sight."

The Panamericana was probably the western hemisphere's best-known road.

Centuries earlier Spain had built the portion called El Camino Real, the Royal Road, to connect its colonies in North, Central, and South America. Three years before my ride, all nineteen thousand miles had finally been completed, making it possible to drive from northern Alaska to southern Argentina—except for the impassible jungle in Panama's Darien Gap.

When I'd read about that famous road, the word highway had misled me. In Peru it was vastly inferior to California's back roads and rarely had a centerline. Drifted sand, cavernous potholes, and unsupervised livestock slowed traffic. Luxuries like signs, guard rails, banked curves, rest stops, emergency telephones, and lighted intersections were nonexistent.

Traffic included countless out-of-date vehicles, and people often had to make complicated on-the-spot repairs. The soft, sand shoulders — where vehicles easily got stuck — encouraged doing this work in traffic lanes, where drivers warned others to slow down with stacks of rocks. These were sometimes whitewashed and often left behind to become greater hazards at night.

To make a bad situation worse, Peruvians' extraordinary courtesy evaporated when they slid behind a steering wheel. California drivers wouldn't have dreamed of slowing to my horses' speed, obstructing the only northbound lane while carrying on leisurely conversations — something that happened frequently that evening.

At dusk in Lambayeque, I reached the Carpena farm and began what would become a nightly routine: cooling and brushing my horses, shoveling the leavings of previous occupants from their stalls, feeding and watering, giving rubdowns, and cleaning the next morning's grain.

When finished, I left my geldings under the night watchman's protection and walked to the house, where Señor Carpena and his wife graciously dismissed my apologies for delaying dinner.

"In our culture," the Señora softly explained, "we always eat late."

She served a meal made all the more splendid by potatoes instead of the rice or yucca Peruvians appreciate more than I do.

After dinner Augusto Carpena gave me a fat envelope of

newspaper clippings. My send-off in Chiclayo had been front page news throughout northern Peru, and proving Peruvians can be extraordinarily efficient, many were illustrated with photos taken mere hours before publication.

"I've arranged," Augusto then told me, "for you to spend tomorrow night at the Hacienda La Viña, which is famous for its fighting bulls. They'll have feed for your horses, so I didn't send any there."

The perfect end to a memorable day was a restful sleep.

* * *

At the crack of dawn I quietly closed the Carpenas' front door, surprised by the desert's early morning chill and by a young boy sitting on a Paso mare near the barn.

"I read about your ride in the newspaper, Señor," he said respectfully, "and got up early so I wouldn't miss you. I can show you how to miss the worst traffic while crossing town."

"Thank you," I said, touched by his hero worship. "That will be a big help."

When my horses were ready, we rode to the house. Apparently having heard our approach, Señora Carpena stepped outside.

"Jimmy," she greeted my young friend, pronouncing his name *Yimmy*. "Would you like to join us for breakfast?"

"I didn't want to disturb your sleep and was planning to just eat some fruit," I told her.

"Nonsense," Augusto said, joining us. "It will be a cold day in hell when I don't eat breakfast at least this early."

Sensing I was eager to be underway, Jimmy ate as quickly as I did.

Then I told my hosts, "I don't know anyone anywhere who would've shown a stranger the hospitality you showed me. Thank you very much."

"*De nada*," Augusto replied.

Americans typically respond to expressions of gratitude with, "You're welcome."

Peruvians say, "It was nothing."

"It wasn't nothing," I told Augusto. "It was very special and greatly appreciated."

I followed Jimmy to where the Panamericana headed north from Lambayeque. Before we parted company he gave me a small photo with a high-school-yearbook-type inscription and his signature on the back.

As I tucked it in my wallet he handed me one of the previous night's newspaper clippings about my ride and asked, "Will you autograph this please?"

Touched I dedicated my journey to him in one of the margins, then signed and said, "*Gracias*, Jimmy. You saved me a lot of time, and don't tell me it was nothing."

"If I were grown up I'd go with you," he said.

"If you were grown up I'd welcome your company."

I turned Lucero toward the desert, amazed once again by the complete lack of any transition between Peru's desert cities and the barren landscape around them.

* * *

As I rode toward Jayanca, most people in passing cars waved enthusiastically or slowed to ask how they might be of service. Like it or not, I was a celebrity.

A man on a Vespa motor scooter pulled up beside me, then matched his speed to mine and in Italian-accented English asked, "Where are you going?"

I told him.

"I myself am making a similar trip," he exclaimed. "I estimate it will take four or five weeks to reach California."

"It will take me much longer than that," I said.

"Wish I had time for an adventure like yours." He smiled and sped out of sight. I never saw nor heard of him again.

Near Jayanca a man rode out of the brush.

"I'm Felipe," he introduced himself. "May I guide you to La Viña?"

"How did you know who I am and where I'm going?" I asked.

"I was with Augusto Carpena in Lambayeque yesterday. He asked me to do whatever I can to help you."

Before we'd ridden far, a couple slowed their car and the woman called out, "Felipe, would you and your friend care to join us for lunch?"

"I will if you will," Felipe told me.

At their home she served a scrumptious vegetable omelet.

"You sure know how to eat in this country," I complimented her. "I've never had such delicious food."

"The world is starting to discover Peruvian cuisine," she said proudly. "Our restaurants in other countries are doing extremely well."

Unlike Americans, who also consider it impolite, Peruvians seldom eat and run.

By the time Felipe and I continued on, the sun was low in a pinkish-orange late afternoon sky.

His horse moved crisply and stylishly, head and neck beautifully collected. I was riding Lucero who by comparison, looked embarrassingly humble. When I started explaining why I rode in such a relaxed way, Huascarán, behind me and carrying the cargo, passed a telephone pole on the opposite side from Inca, who was behind him and tied to the packsaddle.

The pole snagged the rope between them and in the resulting confusion the two became hopelessly entangled. It took me a while to sort out the resulting mess.

"Now you'll never believe I know anything about horses," I told Felipe, shaking my head.

With classic Peruvian sensitivity he assured me, "Don't worry, Pablito. I know you ride that way to conserve your horses' energy. If I were making a trip like yours, I'd do the same."

7

THE PHANTOM OF LA VIÑA

Felipe and I reached La Viña after sunset. A typical Peruvian hacienda, it seemed ancient and deserted. There were no electric wires or phone lines. No lights were on, no dogs barked, and no machines chugged. The only marks on the dirt driveway were our horses' hoof prints.

"You should see this place during bullfight season," Felipe said, eyes scanning the facilities from which countless *toros bravos* had been shipped to Lima's Plaza de Acho bullring.

The architecture was typical of Peruvian haciendas—adobe walls, pillars supporting overhanging red tile roofs, and no asphalt. We stopped in front of a house Felipe said was at least a hundred fifty years old. When his knocking went unanswered, we set out to search nearby corrals, shops, and storage rooms.

"*Aló,*" he periodically shouted from between cupped hands.

He may as well have been calling people into Tombstone's main street during a gunfight. The only living things we saw were the mothers of fighting bulls, calmly munching hay.

Where was whoever had fed them?

As I followed Felipe in pitch darkness, a stooped old man materialized from the shadows, carrying a sputtering lantern.

"Why are you trespassing?" he demanded, sinister in the faint light. Felipe stammered an explanation.

"I didn't expect company," the old man said curtly, "and don't have any available facilities or feed. Our bulls have been eating only once a day during the drought."

That was bad news. Augusto Carpena hadn't sent feed there.

"This *Norteamericano* is riding to the United States," Felipe said, "and—"

Turning toward me, the old man raised his lantern and squinted behind his thick-lensed eyeglass.

"You're the one in the newspapers," he declared. "*Bienvenido.*"

I didn't feel welcome as much as I felt like the perfect fit for some diabolical plan.

Uneasily I watched Felipe ride away, leaving me with a man who—though half my size and several times my age—seemed threatening. Beckoning for me to follow, he shuffled off, feet sliding instead of stepping. Out of courtesy I dismounted and walked with him, leading my geldings. They hung back, suspicious of the sputtering lantern.

Powerful snorts came from a corral with adobe walls and I saw the silhouette of a fighting bull through an opening. Ignoring one of the world's deadliest animals, the old man reached through an opening and casually appropriated an armload of hay from a feed trough. He dropped it into a beat-up wheelbarrow and brought more.

"Put your horses in there," he instructed, pointing to a corral full of milk cows.

"If possible I'd rather put them where they can be alone," I said.

"I didn't know you were coming or I would've prepared a place," the old man said. "But it's too late now. After you care for your horses, come to the house."

While cleaning Huascarán — brush in one hand, flashlight in the other — I discovered a swelling inflicted by the pack-saddle's cinch. Damn. No matter how often I'd adjusted the cargo that day, it had ridden badly. I rubbed the swollen area with liniment, and after brushing Inca and Lucero, put the hay in a feed trough and turned my horses loose.

Having eaten recently, the cows were down on their bellies chewing cud. My geldings made a beeline for a corner and began scrounging scraps of straw from the ground. Sighing, I moved their hay and watched them dig in as if starving. Apparently when feeding them, as when buying real estate, location was everything.

Carrying my gear to the house required three trips, one for each duffel bag and another with my saddles and horse gear. I knocked on three exterior doors before one opened.

"Welcome," the old man greeted. "Put your gear against that wall."

He led me to a spacious, primitive kitchen where he'd laid out a wash basin, pitcher of water, bar of soap, and towel.

"We don't have running water," he explained, then poured some on my hands before I washed and again while I rinsed.

Next he led me past a servant frying beans and rice on a wood-burning stove.

"You can leave," he told the man. "I'll serve our guest's dinner."

The huge dining table in a cavernous room lit by a single candle was a perfect setting for an Edgar Allan Poe tale featuring a tall North American lured to a terrible fate by the Phantom of La Viña. I couldn't help wondering if he'd dismissed the cook so he could add special flavoring from a bottle with a skull and crossbones label.

My meal, however, wasn't big enough to contain a fatal dose of poison. Unaware he made me uncomfortable, the old man refilled my tea cup after every sip, slid the salt closer though it was within easy reach, and apologized for his inadequate hospitality. His extravagant kindness was a clear attempt to compensate for not having enough food on hand.

Later the Phantom showed me to a cubicle with no door. A socket and bare light bulb hung from its ceiling, but La Viña's generator wasn't running. The tiny cot prompted more apologies.

"This is more than satisfactory," I said. "I wasn't expecting anything elaborate."

Wealthy hacienda owners lived rustic lives when they left their mansions in Lima. Going to their farms was the equivalent of roughing it.

After the old man left with his lantern, I felt my way around in pitch-darkness while unrolling my sleeping bag on the cot and then filled the howling vacancy in my stomach with fruit and candy bars from my saddlebags.

* * *

At first light I padded the packsaddle's cinch ring so it wouldn't do to Inca what it had done to Huascarán. Eager to be underway I ate dry toast and steaming boiled milk served by the old man. In the light of day he looked like what he was—kind, harmless, and doing his best to be the perfect host under trying circumstances.

He seemed delighted by my enthusiastic thank-you.

I rode Huascarán bareback to avoid having a cinch further aggravate his swelling. Carrying the cargo, Inca was next in line followed by Lucero, tied to the packsaddle with my riding saddle on his back.

That afternoon a tumbleweed tangled itself in Inca's tail. Startled he surged forward as Lucero shied in the opposite direction, breaking the packsaddle's wooden tree. Using the straps and snaps on my duffel bags, I attached them to each other and draped them across Inca's back — one on each side. He accepted this indignity with his customary calm.

In a small hamlet I heard snarling and whirled, expecting to see German Shepherds or Dobermans snapping at my horses' heels. The growls came from a rooftop. In Lima dogs were routinely kept on flat-roofed houses that were attached to their neighbors and had no yards. This, however, was the only time I'd seen dogs up there in a rural area.

The ruckus brought two men dashing outside.

"We saw your picture in the newspaper," one said as they followed me. "It's a privilege to meet you."

"We'll make note of the date and time you were here," the other declared gravely. "Someday that will be of historical value."

Their enthusiasm wasn't as flattering when I realized both were roaring drunk.

8

ALMOST BEYOND OLMOS

With only the weight of my fastened-together duffel bags holding them in place, I was reduced to a maddeningly slow pace and didn't reach Motupe until almost 10:00 p.m.

Obsessed with the need to find accommodations for my horses, I avoided eye contact to make it obvious I was in no mood for small talk. Nonetheless a man stepped in front of Huascarán, stopping me.

"You must be the famous Pablito," he said pleasantly.

"I don't know about famous," I replied, "but I am Pablito."

Evidently detecting my sense of urgency, he got to the point. "I'm Pedro Arraya. My wife and I would be honored to have you as a guest in our home and can offer a corral for your horses."

"You're the answer to my prayers," I said, relaxing. "I was afraid I might not find a place for my horses this late."

Walking beside me and talking nonstop, Pedro guided me to his modest home.

Soon his four children were brushing Inca while I did the same with the less trustworthy Huascarán and Lucero. When I turned all three loose in the corral, Señora Arraya offered to cook me a late dinner.

"Thank you very much," I said, "but first I have to feed my horses."

"With the drought," Pedro replied, "you won't find anything for them to eat."

"Fortunately," I told him, "a friend sent hay and oats to the gas station."

The gas station, I discovered after walking there, was a nightly gathering place for the town's men.

When I asked about the feed Señor Carpena had sent, the attendant looked me up and down and said, "No hay was delivered today."

"What about yesterday?" I asked.

"Nor the day before."

"Is there another gas station?"

He busied himself with other tasks—not interested in my problem. His atypical abruptness showed me how people in Motupe must have felt when I ignored them after my arrival—a discourtesy I resolved not to repeat.

"There is another gas station, Señor," a man volunteered. "I'm Lucho and I'll take you."

It was a long walk and a waste of time. My hay wasn't there either.

"Where can I buy hay and grain?" I asked Lucho.

"There isn't any. You might as well be seeking..." he frowned, then blurted out, "the Seven Cities of Cibola."

"Where's the nearest farm?"

"There are none worth mentioning," Lucho said. "It won't kill your horses to go a night without eating."

Meant to be reassuring, his words had the opposite effect. I combed the area for hay, then accepted the unavoidable truth. My horses would go hungry unless I took a bus south to Lambayeque and bought feed there.

Back at the first gas station—which also served as Motupe's bus stop—the driver of a northbound bus was unloading his departing passengers' luggage. He dropped a familiar-looking burlap bag on the ground, followed by a hay bale. Better late than never, my horses' dinner had arrived.

This brought good-natured razzing from Lucho.

"If you'd taken my advice," he pointed out, "you'd be where you are now—but with a full stomach."

When I returned to their house Pedro and his wife were asleep. Their eldest son was waiting, eager to help. By lantern light we cleaned oats on the kitchen table, and gave them to my horses with generous amounts of hay. Then he brought cooking oil for inside Huascarán's crusty ear, salt to replace what my geldings had sweat out, and a pine-tar-soaked rag to plug the leaking water trough.

In my bedroom after midnight I opened the window overlooking the corral, then fell asleep to the soothing sound of my horses chewing.

* * *

At dawn I sent my duffel bags and broken packsaddle by bus to my next stop—the Guardia Civil outpost in Olmos. Returning to the Arraya's house I bought cocoa butter and applied it generously to my painfully cracked lips.

As this flavored my breakfast, Señora Arraya answered a knock on the door.

"I'm a reporter," the man there said. "I came to interview Pablito and take photos."

She looked at me with raised eyebrows. I was eager to get started, but nodded. After all, a newspaper article had inspired her husband to offer their hospitality, and I would need many more such invitations.

"I'll appreciate it," I began my interview, "if you'll emphasize the Arraya's kindness in your article."

After the reporter left, I saddled up with half the town looking on. As I mounted Inca, Señora Arraya surprised me with a sack of sandwiches and fruit. A lonely childhood had led me to have a negative opinion of my fellow man. I wanted to say her family's kindness had done much to erase that. But those flowery words stuck in my throat.

So I thanked her, waved goodbye, and turned Inca toward Olmos.

* * *

The morning was cool and my horses were fresh and energetic. Without urging they left Motupe at a brisk pace, a welcome contrast to our arrival the previous evening. A mile into the desert two men on a bicycle caught up, one peddling, the other sitting on the handlebars.

"I'm a newspaper photographer," the passenger shouted, jumping off. "Look your best please."

He took photos as we passed, then reseated himself on the handlebars for the ride back to Motupe.

Next a delivery truck pulled over, and the driver brought me an armload of soda pop and a bottle opener. I thanked him and put his welcome gifts in my saddlebags.

Later a bus slowed and another photographer hopped out. The vehicle kept pace with him as he snapped pictures.

Waving he shouted, "See you later," and scrambled aboard.

Peru's newspapers had fulltime reporters and photographers,

but also bought articles and pictures from freelancers. This inspired the latter to extraordinary efforts. Like the country's other small entrepreneurs, they contrasted sharply with the American stereotype of our supposedly lazy Latin neighbors.

I couldn't wait to see what would happen next, but the day's remaining surprises were unpleasant. The Desierto de Sechura's brutal temperature continued climbing. Each day since Chiclayo had been hotter and drier. Once flowing in rivers, water now had to be cranked up from wells. Few people ventured outside during the heat of the day.

I rode for hours without seeing a vehicle or another human being. I'd grown up in a Nevada desert but its heat hadn't affected me the way Peru's did. I couldn't dismiss it from my mind. To make matters worse, Lucero started short-stepping. I palpated his foreleg and inspected his hoof, but found nothing wrong.

Later Inca became listless, and I rode Huascarán instead. Soon my little bay's ears were drooping and almost parallel to the ground. Sick — not merely overheated — he locked his legs, forcing Huascarán to tow him several steps before agreeing to resume his lethargic walk.

Next time I looked back Lucero was having difficulty lifting his right forehoof as he strode forward. Soon we were going so slow an observer would've had to line us up with a stationary object to be sure we were moving. Without food, water, or shelter we had to keep going — until we reached Olmos.

Every time we crested high ground I searched for a town ahead, only to see another long stretch of empty desert. By then I'd finished my soda pop and the water left in my canteens was too hot to drink.

Trapped in what seemed like an unending nightmare, I could only flog myself to the next viewpoint, then the one after that. Even after my first glimpse of Olmos, we didn't reach it for two hours. We arrived looking like what we were, a pathetic caravan broken down four days into a seven-month journey.

Olmos was as hot and parched as we were. It could've been an outpost deep inside Arabia. Its buildings were made of unplastered adobe bricks. Burros, goats, pigs, and chickens were loose in the streets. Ignoring the debilitating heat dark-eyed, grinning children rushed outside to get a close look at us. Their parents called the girls back inside.

The boys gathered around when I stopped at a kiosk. There I delighted them by guzzling a family-size bottle of Coca Cola, pausing briefly to breathe, then downing another.

"Where's the Guardia Civil post?" I asked.

"Over there," several replied in unison, pointing north.

They returned to their homes and I continued on, asking directions every time children came outside. As far as I could tell from their vague answers, I was headed in the right direction.

* * *

At the Olmos headquarters of Peru's national paramilitary police, a Guardia Civil sergeant stood on the porch.

"Good afternoon," he greeted. "We've been receiving things for you."

"Hope that didn't cause any inconvenience," I said.

"Not at all," he assured me. "Your baggage arrived this morning and the horse feed came last night, along with a note from Señor Carpena telling us to expect you. Your bed is ready, and one of my men will take you to your horses' accommodation."

What he'd called an accommodation turned out to be the prisoners' exercise yard, attached to the jail and surrounded by high walls. To my relief both cells were empty.

With my luck, if the *guardia* had a prisoner, he'd have made a daring escape on Huascarán.

When I turned my horses loose, Inca stood in a trance, covered with flies, tail hanging motionless instead of trying to chase them away. Lucero was dragging his hoof. I soaked his sore foreleg in water for an hour and applied liniment.

At sunset a cool breeze came up. Huascarán and Lucero started eating the hay I'd given them earlier, but Inca ignored his. I cleaned their rations of grain and offered those with the same results. Next I gave all three rubdowns.

By the time I was free to look after myself, I didn't have the energy and collapsed on my bed in the *guardia's* bunkhouse without dinner—thoroughly discouraged. For weeks I'd neglected myself in favor of horses that were falling apart after four days and a mere hundred miles.

At least I had enough hay for a while. The bale sent to Olmos would last at least four days. After that I could bring back some of the hay and oats Augusto Carpena had shipped to our next two destinations.

* * *

At sunrise Inca still had no appetite or interest in his surroundings, but he was cool to the touch—which meant he didn't have a fever. By then Lucero had covered the exercise yard with drag marks while hobbling on three legs.

Adding to my worries, the guardia sergeant was much less friendly when I asked if my horses and I could stay longer.

"Only if you provide your own water," he replied sternly. "Last night your black horse spilled three buckets of ours while you were soaking his leg."

"I'll replace what I used and supply my own from now on," I promised. "Where can I buy some?"

"At the wells outside town. But if you use as much as you did last night, you're in for a big expense and a lot of work."

Pointing at the Andes Mountains he added, "You can blame those. They're the reason Peru has deserts in the tropics."

Beyond those peaks, torrential rains watered the world's largest rain forest and fed the Amazon River—which was deep enough to accommodate ocean-going freighters and up to fifty miles across. But the Andes, sometimes two or three ranges wide, blocked clouds so effectively that rain had never fallen on much of Peru's coast.

When it did however, wild grass grew as high as a mule's belly. Plans for diverting east-flowing Andean rivers to the fertile Olmos Valley had been proposed but never financed. As it had been for centuries, Olmos's most precious natural resource was still pulled up in buckets from hand-dug wells.

The wells had unpredictable hours. That morning I walked from town but found them unattended and covered with padlocked metal covers. When one finally opened I bought water and hired a deliveryman to transport it to the *guardia* post on his "tricycle," a three-wheel work vehicle built on a bicycle frame with a platform between two front wheels.

The rectangular containers were twice as tall as wide, had no lids, and were prone to tipping over. When this happened, it was at my expense. And water wasn't cheap. No wonder the sergeant had resented my casual waste of it.

To reduce the amount my horses used, I started holding their buckets while they drank, then soaked Lucero's leg with what was left, and sponged the remainder on Inca to cool his rising temperature. The *guardia* officers watched my efforts with ill-disguised amusement.

"If this gringo's pampering is good for horses," I heard one ask another, "why are his having problems?"

That of course, was a question for a priest.

9

FROM FRYING PAN TO FIRE

While doctoring Lucero's injured leg one afternoon, I found his fetlock hot to the touch and went looking for ice. But Olmos's residents preferred beverages at room temperature, and the available food didn't require cooling. An ancient refrigerator in one restaurant however, had a freezer compartment.

Twice that day I bought all the ice it had produced and put it in a plastic bag, then molded it around Lucero's fetlock and wrapped it with an elastic bandage.

Inca hadn't improved, and I suspected he'd picked up an infection.

"Is there a veterinarian in town?" I asked the guardia sergeant.

"No," he replied. "People here treat their own animals."

"Where do people go when they're sick?"

"Diego Campos does what he can to help them, but he doesn't have a license."

I visited Campos.

"If your horse has an infection," he told me, "I can inject him with antibiotic."

Proudly he opened the velvet-lined wooden case containing his hypodermic syringe. More impressive than its modern, disposable, plastic counterparts — it was metal and glass.

His policy however, was BYOM — bring your own medicine. Olmos's dirt-floored, scantily stocked pharmacy had neither electricity nor refrigeration, and I didn't expect to find penicillin there. But the druggist carried a powdered German brand in hermetically sealed glass ampules and had enough for three days of shots.

In the guardia's exercise yard I handed Campos the ampules, which looked like test tubes with narrow necks and bullet-shaped heads. He scored the neck of one with a tiny saw blade and flicked its head off with a forefinger. Using the syringe he squirted distilled water in with the powder to dissolve it. Then he pulled the mixture into his syringe and injected it in Inca's neck.

Next morning my little bay was chasing flies with his tail and had regained his appetite. Soon after that he began exploring the exercise yard to which he'd previously been oblivious.

With Inca's appetite restored, my hay would soon run out so I went ahead to my next scheduled stop in Ñaupe and picked up most of the hay and grain Señor Carpena had sent there. When that was almost gone, I traveled to a settlement known as Kilómetro 65 to appropriate some of the feed waiting there. This seemingly simple task expanded to fill an entire day.

The morning bus left Olmos earlier than scheduled, and I missed it. With the next one long overdue, I hiked out to the highway and caught a ride with a farmer in a pickup truck. A few miles down the road his left front tire blew out.

"Fixing this will take time," he said, gathering rudimentary tools from behind his seat. "You may as well thumb another ride."

When I finally succeeded he was still forcing his patched tire back onto its rim.

At the Guardia Civil outpost in Kilómetro 65 I picked up my oats and all but one night's supply of Señor Carpena's hay. Then I stood beside the highway with my thumb extended until a huge ore truck stopped.

"There's plenty of room in back," the driver called out.

I climbed into the trailer and joined a dozen or so of Peru's indigenous mountain dwellers, *Serranos* — still referred to as Indians in the days before political correctness. They worked in an Andean mine and two spoke Spanish, but the stiffly sprung trailer's metallic clattering drowned out our attempts at conversation. With nothing better to do, I began cleaning my oats.

Bouncing around I couldn't pick out the grains of sand — so I strained them through holes in my straw cowboy hat's crown. These were big enough to let sand out and small enough to keep kernels in.

I was halfway done when I noticed my fellow passengers' curious stares.

"Why," one finally asked, "are you pouring oats in your hat and then...doing what?"

Not satisfied with my answer he said, "You told us those are for horses — not *Cristianos*."

Serranos frequently refer to people as Christians, a custom tracing back to Spanish missionaries who'd converted their ancestors.

"Why go to all that trouble for horses?" he persisted.

"Because I'm crazy," I teased.

Not sure I was joking, he and his companions couldn't help smiling — something I'd never seen Serranos do. It was nice to see their human side.

By the time the truck dropped me off at the intersection where my trip had started, the sky was dark. I carried the heavy hay and oats to the guardia post, fed my horses, jogged to a padlocked well, and then located one still serving customers and hired a deliveryman.

It was almost midnight when my geldings drank their fill and I soaked Lucero's leg. To avoid waking the temperamental sergeant I went to bed quietly, without eating.

* * *

After unappetizing meals in all Olmos's eating establishments except The Hungry Pig, I decided to do my own cooking. At the outdoor market however, the only food available was what restaurants served. Not to mention that I didn't like to cook and wasn't good at it.

At first I wished I'd gone to The Hungry Pig sooner. Typical, it had no glass in the windows but was cleaner than most and had fewer flies.

Requesting a menu would've been pointless. The town's restaurants served the same meal — usually goat, beans, rice, and yucca. In the tradition of Madison Avenue this was the Daily Special. The goat was heavy on bone, gristle, veins, and cartilage. The yucca was dry, fibrous, and tasteless. I'd never cared for rice and didn't like the local beans.

But the alternative was expensive canned food and cooking for myself.

After I ordered, the waiter brought an agricultural sprayer from the back room.

Moving fast he pumped its tank full of air and sprayed

poisonous mist without regard for where it—or the dead flies—wound up. When several oilcloth table covers were damp and littered with little black corpses, a boy wiped them with a dirty cloth.

I'd lost my appetite by the time my meal was served, revealing that the day's cut of goat wasn't loin, brisket, rib, or flank. It was lower jaw, and gums were pretty much the only meat. Most of the teeth were where they'd always been, but there were several indentations in the jawbone. My dinner looked like the photos dentists use to motivate people into getting check-ups.

I couldn't look at my meal—let alone eat it. Goat's jaw was probably no worse than hot dogs, but at least they didn't have teeth sticking out.

* * *

The morning of my fifth day in Olmos, Huascarán and Inca were full of energy, having been cooped up too long.

"They need exercise," the sergeant belabored the obvious.

"I know," I said, "but I can't exercise them until I get them out of the exercise yard."

His smile revealed that he—like most Peruvians—appreciated word games.

The day I'd arrived with my horses, he'd let me lead them through the post's front door, past a desk, down the hallway in front of then-empty jail cells, and out the back door. But now he had a prisoner.

"Taking horses through the office in front of our guest won't promote respect," the sergeant told me. "I'll show you another way."

The other way was a narrow concrete walkway between adobe walls, with an open gutter down its center. I led Huascarán in, his right hooves on one side of the channel and his left on the other. Before I could shut the gate, poor unlucky Lucero—distressed to see his stablemate leaving—charged in.

In the narrow passageway Lucero slipped and fell, groaning as his injured foreleg hit the gutter's concrete edge. Intent on helping him get up, I dropped Huascarán's lead rope to ground tie him. Overexcited my gray whirled like a big cat, then slid past his fallen stablemate. Lucero scrambled to his feet and wouldn't let me touch his shin.

Back in the exercise yard I examined the abrasion on Lucero's leg. It looked and felt superficial, but he flinched in anticipation of my slightest touch. When I turned him loose, he hobbled away—his reinjured foreleg bearing as little weight as possible.

Having witnessed this fiasco, the unsympathetic sergeant declared, "Lucero may not be the right horse to demonstrate the Peruvian Paso's toughness."

* * *

That afternoon I rode Huascarán and then Inca several brisk miles. They were clearly ready to continue our journey, but Lucero wasn't. I might have to go on without him. To help me decide I led him on a slow evening walk through town. As he warmed up Lucero limped less and by the time we returned to the exercise yard, he was moving better.

I decided to wait before giving up on him.

Having seen horses strain a sound leg while trying to spare an injured one, I soaked all four of Lucero's in saltwater, thirty minutes each, three times a day.

During our walk the next afternoon Lucero continued to favor his foreleg. When distracted however, he moved almost normally. This led me to suspect he sometimes limped—not because his leg hurt, but because he was afraid it would.

Moving at Lucero's slow pace that day, I saw Olmos in a new light. Far behind the times, it was also a friendly, happy town where people were seldom rushed or stressed. Though I was still working and would be for hours, people in the central plaza were enjoying a refreshing breeze and listening to music from a loudspeaker.

Watching them I came to a long overdue conclusion: if I didn't slow down, I'd burn out.

* * *

I limited my next day's work to eight hours at a reasonable pace. Soon the tension left my body and I actually felt my sour expression fade. This change of mood must have been apparent because soon after a stranger approached me for a friendly chat, a shopkeeper asked how Lucero was doing.

Then children who'd always watched from a distance followed me into a shop and gathered around my table at lunch. They'd have been unwelcome before I relaxed but their company was delightful that day.

One brought me a newspaper to read.

"Why would I read when I can talk to you?" I asked.

Smiling he told me, "There's a trail outside town where dogs won't bark when you walk your horse today."

"Good," I said. "They make him nervous."

That afternoon, accompanied by even more children, I walked Lucero on that trail. When a snake boldly came toward us, unconcerned by our numbers, I stopped, suspicious of its brazen confidence. The boys threw rocks until it slithered away.

"Those are poisonous and can kill," one boy said.

"Thank you for protecting me," I responded.

He giggled at the thought of protecting someone who towered over him.

I hadn't been around children for a while and was re-minded of Vicki, my daughter, and her younger brother Scott—born two years before my divorce.

* * *

In the plaza after dinner, a man my age approached and introduced himself as Tomás.

"It's about time you finally relaxed," he said, shaking his scolding finger. "Would you like to attend a birthday party tonight?"

Later in front of a humble adobe home, Tomás, I, and other guests announced our presence by setting off homemade fire-works—one for each year of the life we'd come to celebrate. Then the birthday girl opened the door and invited us inside.

Her mother's hors d'oeuvres were simple, inexpensive, and exquisite.

"These shish kebobs are delicious," I told her. "What are they?"

"Goat," was her surprising reply.

"Yours is a lot better than what the restaurants serve."

"That's because they don't take time to marinate the meat."

When the music started I helped clear the floor for dancing and sat on the couch.

"If you see someone you like, ask her to dance," Tomás suggested.

"I don't know these dances," I replied.

"My sister will teach you." He waved for her to join us.

I'd never enjoyed dancing—or a party—as much as that night.

The next day a group of girls who'd been at the fiesta smiled as Tomás and I passed.

"Why didn't you smile back?" Tomás asked.

"Because they were smiling at you," I replied.

"You're confident in most situations," he said, "but lack confidence with the opposite sex. Idiot. They were smiling at you — not me."

"That's hard to believe."

"It's true," he insisted.

"If so, those smiles weren't because of my charm. They were because I'm a tall, blue-eyed, sandy-haired oddity in a town where everyone else is short with brown eyes and black hair."

"You're not exactly a hopeless romantic, are you?" he asked, frowning.

Actually I was. But I didn't want to set myself up for disappointment.

* * *

After two days of conversations and socializing, my sense of duty reared its ugly head. I decided to resume my journey to Piura where I could find a veterinarian for Lucero. As I prepared at top speed in the Guardia Civil barracks, the sergeant happened by.

"You should take precautions," he warned. "You can start in the early morning, but whatever you do, don't travel after dark. That's when bandits are most active."

I'd been told otherwise, but he was a policeman and should know better than anyone else.

"People call the desert ahead the *Despoblado*, the unpopulated place," he continued ominously. "If you have an accident or are assaulted by bandits, there won't be anyone to help you."

Continuing to work while he droned on was rude, but the price of days of relaxation was a long list of last-minute chores.

"You're not listening," he said gruffly.

I gave my full attention until he started repeating advice he'd previously given.

Changing the subject, I asked if there were really deadly snakes outside Olmos.

"Yes," he replied. "Every time you stop your horses, look around. They often cool themselves by lying in livestock's shadows. Do you know what to do if bitten?"

Having heard his thoughts on that subject I reminded him, "I have a snake bite kit."

"Yes, but do you know how to use it? First—"

"I need to get my packsaddle repaired," I interrupted, then hurried out the door.

At teatime I took Lucero for a walk. He didn't take a lame step for the second straight day, validating my decision to leave in the morning. If asked to carry his own weight only, he should be fine.

On our way back to the exercise yard we passed two men. They were locking up the pigs they released every morning to eat table scraps townspeople threw in the street. This mutually beneficial arrangement was the reason Olmos had no skinny pigs and no garbage in its streets, unlike most of rural Peru.

10

A RISKY GAMBLE

I had intended to be in bed early but first Tomás and his sister, then two groups of my other new friends came to see my horses. I wasn't done with my preparations until midnight. Exhausted I slept three hours before strapping on my Bowie knife, a rather melodramatic gesture since I'd never used a knife for anything other than cutting or spreading.

Riding Huascarán while leading Inca and Lucero, I rode through Olmos's deserted streets and into the *Despoblado*, hoping to get to Ñaupe before nightfall, when bandidos began looking for victims.

After a few miles Lucero developed a shuffle that spared his foreleg but reduced our speed. My wildly optimistic goal had been to reach Ñaupe before the desert was unbearable, but it got that way before we were halfway there. Just breathing hurt, and shimmering heat haze distorted every view.

A promising afternoon breeze soon felt as though it came from a blast furnace.

The oppressive heat did more than cause discomfort. It sapped my will, killed my appetite, depressed my spirit, and produced the boredom I'd hoped to escape during this ride. I'd slept only three hours the night before, and the soothing swish of hooves in sand lulled me into shallow naps.

Repeatedly I was brought back to reality—by a thorn tree's clawing branches...then buzzing insects...next as Huascarán slowed to avoid a lizard wriggling across his path...later as he detoured around a carcass and evil-smelling buzzards that refused to give ground. I was reminded of the cartoon where one vulture tells another, "Patience, my ass. I'm gonna kill something."

Whenever I took a sip from my canteen, I gave each horse a taste. There was no point conserving water that would soon be too hot to drink. I'd rejected the sergeant's suggestion that I carry a container with enough water to maintain a drinkable temperature. That much liquid would shift constantly—even on a smooth Peruvian—making it an intolerable burden.

I'd always found water somewhere but the *Despoblado* had no wells, farms, or people—and few passing trucks. I flagged one down and asked if the driver had water cool enough for my horses.

"Yes," he replied, pointing to a fifty-gallon drum, "but it's for sale."

My geldings were glad to get it.

"How much will you charge to take my black horse to Piura?" I asked as the driver climbed back into his vehicle.

"I'm not going that far," he replied.

"To Ñaupe then?" I persisted.

He answered my question with one of his own, "Without an embankment, how will we load him?"

* * *

82

Fourteen hours after leaving Olmos we reached Ñaupe's Guardia Civil checkpoint. Days earlier when I'd picked up three quarters of the feed sent there by Señor Carpena, the officer in charge had invited me to stay the night.

His equally hospitable replacement said, "We have a spare bunk and your horses can stay in our courtyard."

Like the exercise yard in Olmos, this was attached to the building and accessible only from inside. A guardsman and I rearranged furniture, and one-by-one I led my horses through.

They drank gallons of water but ignored their hay.

I ate a serving of corn fritters at a kiosk and hurried back to see if my geldings were eating yet. They were, but Lucero was walking on three legs and hopping on the other. Adding insult to injury, Huascarán had diarrhea and Inca had a cough—in the desert of all places. I doctored them as best I could and collapsed on my bunk.

There'd been little daytime traffic because intense heat is hard on motors and tires. At sundown however, trucks started rolling and all were required to present documents at Ñaupe's guardia post. The constant coming and going produced a cacophony of engines, mufflers, brakes, grinding gears, and people trying to be heard.

Fearing I'd be awake all night, I made myself as comfortable as possible on a small bed.

* * *

When I woke up the next morning I hadn't moved.

"You must have been exhausted," the guardsman on duty said. "You slept in the same position all night."

Fearing the worst, I looked in on my horses. Huascarán and Inca were no better, and Lucero was worse. I'd asked too much of them. Yes, I had demanded even more from myself, but I saw purpose in the suffering and hard work while they saw only suffering and hard work.

Lucero clearly wouldn't get better without a long rest. I'd have to leave him behind in Ñaupe and come back for him from Piura with a truck.

I'd been knocked down once too often and was certain that putting forth another thousand efforts would only bring a thousand and one new obstacles.

"I need to see your horses' documents and your passport," the officer at the desk said as I trudged past.

Looking for those in my important papers pouch, I came across the sealed envelope from Jorge Baca's neighbor. He'd said it contained the image of a saint who would help me during my journey.

I laughed bitterly. That saint was doing a damn poor job.

* * *

Halfway through breakfast at one of Ñaupe's restaurants I felt hope springing eternal. I couldn't imagine why, but there it was. Somehow I'd get Lucero a free ride to Piura. But who would grant me such a huge favor when I didn't know anyone within two hundred miles?

There was one possibility, admittedly a long shot. In Lima Carlos González had written the name and phone number of Piura's premier Peruvian Paso breeder on a slip of paper. However I'd been told his hacienda was far from my planned route and hadn't kept it.

I was still trying to recall that breeder's name when a pickup truck pulled off the highway and parked.

"You must be the famous Pablito," the driver said as he sat down at the next table. "I'm Ricardo Espinoza. I read about you in the newspaper."

We stood and shook hands, then—thinking our conversation was over—I started toward the cashier.

"Last I heard," Señor Espinoza said, "you were delayed in Olmos."

"And now I'm delayed in Ñaupe."

"Do you have a moment?" He gestured to the other chair at his table.

"I have all the time in the world." I sat down.

"What's wrong, and how can I help?"

"Are you a veterinarian or do you have a horse trailer?" I asked.

"No. I'm an engineer and know nothing about horses."

"Is there a well-known breeder of Peruvian Pasos near Piura?"

Piura was a large city, and my question was a long shot.

"You mean José Antonio Onrubia?" he asked.

"Yes, that's him. I remember now."

Another of my problems was solved when Señor Espinoza offered to drive me to Onrubia's hacienda. While he finished breakfast I checked on my horses and asked the guardia sergeant to please keep an eye on them until I got back.

Espinoza was in his truck when I went outside. Watching the desert flash past from inside his pickup was disheartening. Every five minutes we traveled farther than I could ride in an hour. My time on that soft padded seat would translate into two twelve-hour days on horseback—if all went well, which it never did.

* * *

In Piura, Ricardo, as he'd asked me to call him, took me to his house so I could shave, shower, and change clothes. After a simple lunch that seemed splendid after Olmos, I was eager to press on. In those days however, siestas were the norm. At midday businesses shut down for three hours while people went home for lunch and a nap—not a good time to ask favors.

When we set out for Señor Onrubia's hacienda, San Jacinto, I didn't realize I was headed for an audience with a very important person. If I'd known he was Peru's richest man I wouldn't have had the nerve to ask for his assistance. He didn't know me and no doubt received requests for help from people with problems more important than mine.

After Ricardo introduced us and left, Señor Onrubia, remarkably down-to-earth despite his position and power, patiently listened to my tale of woe as if he had nothing else to do.

When I finished he matter-of-factly said, "You're welcome to stay in my guest room. Tomorrow I'll have my overseer drive you to Ñaupe in the ranch truck and bring Lucero here. Then we'll look after him while you ride Inca and Huascarán the rest of the way here."

"I appreciate your kind offer," I told him, "but my horses have no feed. I have to take them some tonight."

"When a man is more concerned about his horses' comfort than his own," he observed with approval, "it's the unmistakable sign of a true horseman. As soon as my stable manager returns I'll have him drive you to Piura and find you a ride to Ñaupe. May I show you my horses in the meantime?"

He didn't have to ask twice. I'd heard his horses were among Peru's best. And I was especially taken with his famous stallion, Piloto, a sire that would play a starring role in one of my future adventures.

That evening Señor Onrubia's manager took me, a bale of hay, and twelve pounds of oats to Piura's southern outskirts. After driving back and forth among truck stops, we finally found four cattle trucks traveling together and headed in the right direction. One of the drivers had read about my ride.

"I'll be happy to take you," he said, "but I hope you're not in a hurry."

Ricardo had brought me from Ñaupe to Piura in two hours. It was soon apparent the slow-moving convoy would take much longer to make the trip in reverse — not that we traveled in reverse gear. It only seemed that way.

Not far down the road the convoy pulled over while a driver repaired a motor so old that parts were no longer available. While I waited and watched, my driver took a pinch of coca leaves from his belt pouch and chewed them.

"These keep me alert," he explained.

Coca is a mild stimulant, comparable to strong coffee. Back then, however, I only knew that it was the source of cocaine. I was exhausted, but my concern about traveling a hazardous highway at night with a drug-impaired driver kept me vigilant.

For hours the dim headlights revealed roadside crosses, marking sites of fatal accidents. Most, according to my over-active imagination, had surely been caused by truckers who chewed coca instead of taking NoDoz.

In the wee hours, my hungry horses greeted me enthusias-tically. I fed them and slept soundly, but not nearly long enough.

* * *

Up early I was eager to be on my way to Kilómetro 65, so named because it was sixty-five kilometers from Piura. After wolfing down a quick breakfast, I emptied my duffel bags. Then I filled one with rainy-weather gear and other unneeded items I could send to San Jacinto with Lucero. After that I packed the other with supplies I'd need during my ride to Piura.

It seemed I'd waited forever when Onrubia's pickup truck, its bed enclosed by a metal stock rack, stopped near Ñaupe's Guardia Civil post. I'd never seen the driver before. He was hours late, but I could still get to Kilómetro 65 by dark. Or so I thought before he strolled into the restaurant and sat at the counter. Wanting him to eat, not talk, I waited outside.

To my dismay he struck up a conversation with the man beside him, and it was past noon when he finally backed his truck up to an embankment so I could load Lucero. In those days there were no horse trailers in Peru. Even rich men transported horses in trucks of one sort or another.

Lucero went aboard easily, which was fortunate because the driver was afraid of him and wouldn't have been much help if I'd needed it.

Once aboard, Lucero slipped and fell, obliging me to doctor his cut leg.

Afterward the driver, suddenly in a hurry, asked, "Can I leave now?"

His vehicle's slippery metal floor combined with his fear of horses convinced me to change plans.

"I'm ready," I said. "Let's go."

"Are you coming, too?" he asked.

"Just as a precaution."

"Don't worry about Lucero. I'll look after him."

"He's difficult to handle. I'd better go along."

"*Macanudo.*" He gestured to the passenger seat. "You'll be good company."

"I'd better ride in back with my horse."

That was a good decision. Twice on curves I kept Lucero on his feet. But I had difficulty staying on mine as I leaned against the metal rack and dozed during long, monotonous straightaways.

* * *

At San Jacinto Señor Onrubia's jovial trainer, Eusebio Rodriguez Baca, helped me settle Lucero in a corral, then invited me to his house.

"Please sit down," he said in his living room. "Would you like a *gaseosa*?"

Gaseosa turned out to be Peruvian slang for a carbonated soft drink. Rodriguez brought me a bottle of Inca Kola, a refreshing Peruvian beverage with a taste similar to cream soda. Thirsty I drained it, pausing only to swat a persistent slow-moving stable fly whose untimely death didn't discourage the rest of his swarm.

On her own, Rodriguez's youngest daughter picked up a towel and swung it at my winged tormentors. I wouldn't have been more embarrassed if she'd peeled a grape for me.

"Please. You don't have to do that," I told her.

"She wants you to be comfortable," Rodriguez said. "May I bring you another Inca Kola?

I was still thirsty, but declined. On a trainer's salary, gaseosas were expensive.

Eager to return to Ñaupe I said goodbye and offered Rodriguez's daughter a coin.

She looked at him for permission to accept.

"That's not necessary," he assured me.

"Maybe not," I said, "but she earned it."

"Very well." He nodded at his daughter.

"*Gracias*," she said, smiling shyly as she took the coin.

* * *

I don't remember the trip back to Ñaupe and for good reason. I dozed off soon after the truck carrying me left Piura and didn't wake up until it stopped at the Guardia Civil station. Half asleep I fed and watered Inca and Huascarán, ate my last candy bar, and slept until the *madrugada*, the hour before dawn.

Yesterday's rest had been good for my horses. Inca was no longer coughing and Huascarán's stools were normal. Since a good appetite is a sign of a healthy horse, I was pleased when both ate every every stalk and leaf of their larger-than-usual breakfast.

That morning for the first time, my journey was everything I'd imagined—including dangerous. Huascarán vigorously carried me across a rugged range of hills enveloped in cool, low-lying mist. Cutting that road in such steep terrain had been expensive, which explained why it was narrow and had almost no shoulder.

Trucks coming from opposite directions slowed to a crawl and slid past one another, left-side tires on the pavement and right-side tires off. Twice this pinned my horses and me against sheer rock walls. Those drivers couldn't easily see us in the mist and glaring headlights, adding to the excitement.

When we were back on flat ground that day's ride became enchanting and finally exhilarating. Since leaving Chiclayo we'd seldom gone faster than a walk, but all afternoon Huascarán carried me in a brisk paso llano gait, asking for more rein so he could go even faster.

On the outskirts of Kilómetro 65 we passed a highway repair station. The watchman waved me over and gave my horses water.

"How long will you stay and where?" he asked.

"All night," I replied, "at the Guardia Civil checkpoint."

"There's no corral there," he said. "I'll make you one."

While I unsaddled he arranged portable road barricades in a square. When my geldings were cool, I put them in this enclosure and walked up the highway to claim what was left of Señor Carpena's hay—along with revenge on a sergeant I'd met the previous day.

"The newspapers didn't mention any plans to transport your famous horses this way," he'd needled with mean-spirited delight when Onrubia's truck stopped for inspection. "Why don't you sell them and buy one of ours? We never have such difficulties."

I tried to downplay my problems but the sergeant knew every detail, thanks to his counterparts in Olmos and Ñaupe.

"Paso horses are rich people's pampered playthings," he sneered, returning Lucero's health certificate.

Now the shoe was on the other foot. Huascarán and Inca had covered thirty-two difficult miles in excellent time.

"You're here already?" the surprised sergeant asked, eyes wide. "You must have ridden all night."

"No," I said. "I left Ñaupe at 3:30 this morning, and you can verify that with the officers there. How long does that ride usually take you?"

Thanks to his boasting the previous day, I knew the answer was embarrassing.

And he knew I knew.

I'd planned to overnight at Kilómetro 65 and continue on to Piura the following day, but that meant riding fifty miles in one day. It would be better I decided, to continue on to Kilómetro 50 when the afternoon was cooler. That would shorten tomorrow's ride and spare me a tense night with a certain sergeant.

When the afternoon cooled I sent the next morning's hay and oats, along with my duffel bag, to Kilómetro 50 on a passing truck. Ready to get underway, I walked to my makeshift corral, where a man in a guardia uniform was studying Huascarán. When closer, I recognized the sergeant.

"Something's wrong with your gray horse," he said.

11

BANDIDOS?

Huascarán's temperature and breathing were normal, but he was lethargic and hadn't eaten or moved his bowels. Suspecting constipation had followed his diarrhea and hoping light exercise would do him good, I set out for Kilómetro 50, leading him and riding Inca. Huascarán's next manure was closer to normal, which seemed to confirm my diagnosis.

But his stools became progressively looser until he was passing murky green liquid. And though it was more a feeling than an observation, Inca seemed exhausted. Rather than make him carry my weight I dismounted and walked.

For a while I stayed far from the highway — not wanting my horses seen in their conditions. But sinking into loose sand forced them to waste energy, so I angled toward the highway shoulder and its firmer footing.

"No, nothing's wrong. I'm just stretching my legs," I answered a motorist's inevitable question with forced cheerfulness.

Just before dark a bus passed, every passenger holding his or her hands near the windows so I could see — if not hear — their applause. They'd never know how much that picked up my spirits, but it didn't help Huascarán. He reached Kilómetro 50 with his head low, and dull eyes.

Before walking into the faint glow of open fires I washed the manure from my big gray's buttocks with a rubber curry comb and water from my canteen. The green stain however, was still visible when I led him into the light.

Kilómetro 50 was a hamlet astride the highway thirty miles south of Piura. Two small restaurants — made of sticks planted upright, side-by-side — catered to truckers.

Numerous small-time entrepreneurs prepared meals outdoors over open fires or offered cigarettes and candy from cardboard trays. And a withered Indian lady sold fresh milk extracted from her burro's udder.

People there had little, but willingly extended hospitality. My horses slept in a cramped storage yard and I dozed fitfully on my sleeping bag in a restaurant's back room.

When I got up to check on Huascarán at midnight, he hadn't eaten and looked terrible. I pinched up a pucker of skin on his neck. It flattened slowly, indicating dehydration, which often accompanies diarrhea. I topped off his water bucket.

Inca had no obvious problems. But seeing his lifeless eyes and frequent yawns, I decided I'd lead both my horses the rest of the way to San Jacinto.

* * *

Halfway to Piura a man rode a spotted mule out of the roadside brush, studying me with disconcerting thoroughness. As we passed I saw a pistol on his hip and considered sliding my Bowie knife to where he could see it. But if he was a bandido that could get me shot.

"*Buenos dias*," I greeted, hoping I looked poor and even bigger than I was.

"Where are you going?" he asked.

"North," was my intentionally vague reply.

I was preparing to flag down the approaching car when my pistol-packing visitor turned his mule into the roadside brush. Tempted to stop the oncoming driver anyhow, I had a disconcerting thought. If the man on the mule was a bandit, why hadn't he simply escorted me off the highway at gunpoint? There we'd have been out of sight and he could've taken everything I had.

Had he noticed that the oncoming car was new and expensive? Was he trying to scare me so I'd stop it and provide a more prosperous victim?

After the car passed, the rider came back on the road behind me. I swung aboard Inca without touching the stirrups. When I sped up, Huascarán—tied to my saddle—locked his legs, yanking Inca to a stop. Looking back I saw my big gray's stubborn look. When I insisted, he started forward but wouldn't go faster than a walk.

With another car coming, my pursuer rode back into the brush. He might have simply been staying a prudent distance from traffic, but why the pistol? A hunter would've had a rifle. Was he using me as bait? No one in his right mind would stop for him, but for me they might.

When I tried to speed up Huascarán stopped again, this time pulling my saddle back. Quickly I dismounted, repositioned it, tightened the cinch, and untied my big gray's lead-line from it.

Another rider came out of the brush, several hundred yards behind me. He had a rifle in his saddle scabbard.

That was all the confirmation I needed. Those two were trying to spook me into stopping a passing car so they could rob its occupants. They didn't know I had traveler's checks worth several times what they'd likely get from anyone in a car. They could probably cash those on the black market.

With Huascarán's lead rope in one hand instead of tied to my saddle, I swung aboard Inca and thumped both heels against his sides. He leapt forward. Huascarán stayed put, nearly pulling me from the saddle. I grabbed the rope with both hands. I'd never let him win any of our battles, and this time he gave in quickly.

We went as fast as Huascarán would permit until well beyond the roadside brush.

There I could see far enough to be sure the mule riders were no longer following us.

*   *   *

Such is human nature. Twenty minutes earlier I'd been glancing over my shoulder and fleeing for my life. Now I was trudging along, bored and looking, not for bandits, but for Piura. Surely it was just beyond the horizon. But when I reached high ground I saw only desert.

After another hour we passed towering sand dunes that resembled giant ocean waves rolling toward us from both sides. Beyond that we reached a welcome landmark, a river flowing under the highway bridge at Piura's southern entrance.

I led Inca and Huascarán down to the water and let them drink their fill. Next I unsaddled and led them out to where the slow moving, tepid current was deeper. It was time to get ready for the crowds we'd attract.

After washing the diarrhea from Huascarán's rear legs and tail, I scrubbed the green stain several shades lighter with a bar of lye soap. Using a feedbag as a bucket, I bathed and rinsed the rest of him. Overheated, he submitted to that indignity without his usual disgusted look.

By the time I started Inca's bath, a crowd had gathered on the bridge above and was watching a man with a camera hurry down the path to the river. He introduced himself as Armando and was evidently more reporter than photographer. He took only one photo and asked numerous questions while I saddled and mounted Inca.

Then he followed me up to the bridge, took a photo of me riding across it, and flagged down a taxi. Exhausted and hot I decided not to cross Piura until the afternoon cooled off.

I was still resting in the shade under the bridge when Armando brought me the late afternoon edition of northern Peru's most important newspaper. On its front page his two pictures were captioned: "Pablito Reaches Piura" and "Pablito's Horses Bathe in the Rio Piura." The article he'd written read as if this would just be another stop on my journey, an impression I'd given on purpose.

But I knew better. Huascarán and Lucero had serious problems. At best, I'd be at San Jacinto a long time. At worst, my ride was over.

* * *

Riding Inca and leading Huascarán I crossed Piura, avoiding commercial areas. But even in quiet residential neighborhoods people stopped what they were doing, their attention drawn to the fresh fecal matter on Huascarán's hind legs.

Disgusted a boy exclaimed, "What a pig."

After that I deflected attention from my big gray by squeezing my legs so Inca would strut, making himself the center of attention.

A surprising number of people knew who I was and thanks to the rumor mill, some had already heard that Lucero was at San Jacinto. Their encouragement and sympathy lifted my spirits as I rode past Parque Pizarro's impressive statue of Piura's founder, the conquistador Francisco Pizarro, on horseback.

When I was certain we were alone, my sense of humor briefly surfaced.

"Inca," I whispered quietly, "there may never be a Parque Pablito with statues of us, but don't worry. It's not your fault."

After crossing Piura I started down the rutted dirt road to San Jacinto, weak from hunger. By the time I'd left Lucero at San Jacinto, the banks had been closed and I'd gone back to Ñaupe with the equivalent of twenty U.S. cents in soles. Because traveler's checks couldn't be cashed outside large cities, that was all I'd had for meals.

In Kilómetro 50 it had bought four bananas and a cup of tea — not much fuel for a thirty-mile walk.

With no audience to impress, I dismounted to spare Inca the effort of carrying me.

Refreshed by his rest at Rio Piura and the cooler temperature, he pranced and misbehaved. I'd led him thirty miles that day and nine the afternoon before because I'd thought he was exhausted. Evidently he'd simply been conserving energy. Exhausted I put my foot in the stirrup and lifted myself into the saddle. If Inca had the energy to frisk and frolic, he could darn well carry me.

When we reached San Jacinto Señor Onrubia's trainer, Rodriguez, had bad news.

"Lucero's leg is worse," he told me solemnly, "and he's stopped eating."

"He does that," I explained, "when he misses Huascarán and Inca."

Delighted when I put them in his corral, Lucero joined Inca at the feed trough. Oblivious to them both, Huascarán stood lifelessly where I'd removed his halter.

* * *

In the morning Señor Onrubia's vet, Doctor García, studied Lucero's movements as I walked him back and forth near his corral.

"I can't find anything wrong," he told me after palpating my little black's fetlock, ligaments, and tendons. "It might do him good to stand shoulder deep in cold water, an hour twice a day."

Huascarán's examination lasted much longer.

"This could be any of several things," García said when finished. "I'll know more after I run some blood tests. How often do you water him?"

"Every hour," I replied.

"How much does he drink?

"It's hard to tell," I said. "Much of the water he sucks in comes back out his nostrils."

"That's not as unusual as you might think," Garcia said. "Is there an empty stall we can use?"

Rodriguez took us to one. García hung a bottle of plasma from its ceiling, then attached a plastic tube and a needle he inserted into a prominent vein on Huascarán's neck. When the plasma was gone he replaced the empty bottle with a full one of electrolytes.

After that one drained he said, "I'll drop by tomorrow to see how they're doing."

Soon after García's departure, Señor Onrubia, on his way to work, joined me at Huascarán's stall.

"What was García's diagnosis?" he asked.

"He doesn't know what's wrong with Lucero's leg," I replied, "and is doing blood tests on Huascarán."

"The results won't come back for at least a week." Señor

Onrubia patted my shoulder sympathetically. "It won't do any good to sit around worrying, and as luck would have it the Week of Piura starts tomorrow. It's like an American state fair. You're welcome to come with me if you want."

"I'd love to."

"You'll enjoy it," he assured me, "and by the way, we know each other well enough for you to stop calling me Señor Onrubia. I prefer José Antonio."

"I'd be uncomfortable calling you that," I said. "Would you settle for Don José Antonio? It's less formal and won't sound disrespectful."

"That would be uncomfortable for me," he replied. "Please, call me José Antonio."

* * *

Early next morning I showered, fed my horses, filled their water buckets, and stood Lucero shoulder deep in San Jacinto's pond. Then I enjoyed José Antonio's company during the first day of the Week of Piura's Peruvian Paso horse show. There was never a dull moment as we admired horses, ate delicious food, and talked with interesting people.

More often than not I forgot my problems.

Though the hour was late when we returned to San Jacinto, I soaked Lucero's leg again before going to bed.

At the showground the next day, I ate as never before.

A confirmed seafood hater, I tried *ceviche* at José Antonio's insistence and loved it. It's prepared by immersing fresh, raw, diced fish—usually sea bass or sole—in the juice of *limónes*, which are more acidic than lemons and cook the meat perfectly. The flavor is further enhanced by onion, corn on the cob, and sweet potato.

Other irresistible delicacies included beef heart shish kebobs — called *anticuchos* — several varieties of avocado, and two interesting kinds of banana. One tasted like an apple, and the other had a yellow peel but was pink inside and extremely tasty.

My favorite main dish was *lomo saltado*, a stir-fried mixture of sliced beef tenderloin, French fries, rice, plum tomatoes, garlic, yellow aji peppers, red bell peppers, red onions, vinegar, and soy sauce.

I became aware of the huge impression my eating was making when one of José Antonio's fellow exhibitors introduced me to his wife.

Seeing my height she exclaimed, "You must be the gringo who eats three double *ceviches* and drinks five Cokes before lunch."

Further evidence of my spreading reputation came that afternoon when a restaurant owner set a triple serving of lomo saltado in front of me and challenged, "This will be free if you can eat it all."

"He doesn't think I can do it," I whispered to José Antonio, absent mindedly lapsing into my native language.

"I'm sure you can," he replied in perfect, unaccented English.

I was surprised he spoke English, but shouldn't have been. Almost every book on the shelves in my bedroom at San Jacinto was in that language.

P.S. After finishing my lomo saltado I ordered dessert, *mazamorra morada* — an exquisite plum pudding.

* * *

Watching the weeklong Peruvian Paso Show was educational as well as entertaining. I knew little about the breeds' fine points, but felt that Huascarán, at his best, might have done well.

When I asked if José Antonio agreed, he said, "Would you like to enter Inca in the gelding class?"

"Is he good enough?"

"Let's find out."

The next morning he filled out the necessary paperwork and paid Inca's entry fee.

That afternoon his manager transported my little bay to the showground, where José Antonio hired an excellent rider to show him.

I'd never seen Inca looking as impressive as he did in the arena that day. While his class was still in progress several spectators congratulated me.

"He might win," one speculated.

Before the results were announced I imagined myself arriving in California aboard Northern Peru's 1966 Champion Gelding. But Inca placed sixth. The winner was a splendid gelding of José Antonio's.

After congratulating José Antonio, Juan Miguel Rossel, Inca's former owner, shook my hand. When he withdrew his, he left behind two folded thousand *sol* notes — the equivalent of eighty dollars, a considerable sum in those days.

"I'm honor bound to refund half of Inca's price," he told me in his generation's elegant language. "I never would have sold him to you if I'd known about his eye."

* * *

Having won many important prizes that week, José Antonio was buoyant as we drove home.

"What was your most satisfying award?" I asked.

"That's easy," he replied. "Champion of Champions Gelding."

His answer increased my already considerable admiration for this remarkably decent man. Without knowing Inca's quality, he'd made it possible for my little bay to compete against one of his favorite horses — and had even paid a top rider to show him.

12

THE WORST
FORM OF UNLUCKY

Doctor García was already at San Jacinto's stable when I went there at dawn on the show's final day.

"There's no point in continuing to soak Lucero's leg," he told me, yawning. "It's getting worse — not better. And until Huascarán starts eating, I'll have to feed him intravenously."

During the past week — gently at first, then more insistently — he'd cautioned that neither would be ready to go on for months, if ever. These latest deteriorations in their conditions were proof.

My ride had failed catastrophically.

Every night after the show, I'd fallen asleep telling myself I'd nurse my geldings back to health and in Ecuador we'd climb into the Andes. There we'd be in moderate temperatures and green valleys similar to those in Cajamarca, where they'd been born and built reputations for endurance.

That, however, had been wishful thinking. Even if Lucero's

leg healed, it would be prone to reinjury. And Huascarán's condition—probably provoked by changes in feed, climate, water, bacteria, and altitude—would likely recur if he was subjected to the same stresses again.

Only Inca had survived and even he had suffered more than a desert-bred horse would have. For reasons that seemed excellent at the time, I'd bought the wrong horses. Now I'd have to sell them for whatever I could get and go home.

During his famous ride, my idol, Amie Tschiffely, had ridden Mancha and Gato—two immortals of the equine race—from Buenos Aires, Argentina, to Washington, D.C. Like me and my horses, he and his had suffered immeasurably in the desert called *Matacaballo*, Horsekiller, in those days.

In his book he'd summarized his crossing of that hellish place in a single pungent line: "Dante's Inferno is a creation of stupendous imagination, but the Peruvian deserts are real, very real."

Mancha, Gato, and Tschiffely, however, had overcome its challenges and completed their journey.

* * *

During the show that day, Anibal Vásquez, a breeder from Paiján, took me aside and made an offer too good to be true.

I asked him to please repeat himself.

"You heard correctly," he said. "I have a hundred mares to choose from and will trade three for your geldings, straight across."

"I don't know how to thank you," I said, incredulous.

"You don't have to," he replied, gruffly. "We'll make arrangements before I leave."

As Anibal walked away, Dr. Horst Seifert continued our interrupted conversation.

"Anibal is my neighbor, and I know his bloodlines," he told me. "You couldn't do better."

Remembering that Fernando Graña had said geldings were superior for hard work, I asked, "Will mares be up to the challenge?"

"If you choose well," Seifert replied. "And desert-born horses will handle conditions in the Andes better than mountain-born horses handle conditions in hot places. That's important because most of your ride will be in deserts and the tropics."

Seifert's opinion was important. At the Hacienda Casa Grande, he oversaw forty thousand head of livestock. He knew horses and had helped Bayer AG, the giant German pharmaceutical company, develop equine products sold worldwide.

That night the show ended with a traditional Peruvian *pachamanca* barbecue. Exhibitors and their families sat outside at long tables where citronella torches kept insects at bay and canaries in black wrought-iron cages provided background music.

All day a suckling pig had roasted underground in a clay pot—with delicious results. I'd never eaten such juicy, tender, flavorful pork. The lima beans, sweet potatoes, yucca, corn, and tamales were mouthwatering. Dozens of people were in line waiting for seconds when the food ran out.

While we ate dessert several exhibitors stood to thank the show's organizers.

During his brief remarks, Anibal Vásquez reaffirmed his offer to trade mares for my geldings.

"I'll be driving to my ranch tomorrow," he said, looking straight at me. "You can come along if you'd like."

* * *

On his way to work at the crack of dawn José Antonio dropped me off at Piura's Plaza de Armas an hour before Anibal was due. I could've come two hours later on the bus. But public transportation was often far behind schedule, and I didn't want Anibal to get there before I did. Better I should wait than he.

Hungry and thirsty by the time he was two hours overdue, I decided against leaving the plaza to buy a beverage and snack. Anibal had struck me as a man who wouldn't appreciate being delayed and I wanted to walk up to his car the instant he arrived.

Hot, bored, and drowsy, I stretched out on a bench — just to rest my eyes I told myself — and dozed off, then felt a nightstick tapping my boot soles.

"No sleeping here," a policeman told me sternly.

An elderly gentleman with whom I'd talked earlier sat down beside me and asked, "Your friend still hasn't picked you up?"

"Not yet," I replied.

"I fear he isn't coming."

"Oh, he'll be here."

"Don't be too sure," he cautioned. "You've had awful luck. You may be *salado*."

Grimacing I said, "Anything would be better than that."

Literally translated, *salado* means salty. But another definition appears in the opening lines of Ernest Hemingway's masterpiece, *The Old Man and the Sea*:

> *He was an old man who fished alone in a skiff in the Gulf Stream and he had gone eighty-four days now without taking a fish. In the first forty days a boy had been*

with him. But after forty days without a fish the boy's parents had told him that the old man was now definitely and finally salado, which is the worst form of unlucky.

At 4:00 that afternoon Juan Luis Ruesta—a Paso breeder I'd met at the show— stopped his car near the bench where I sat and rolled his window down.

"Still waiting for Anibal?" he asked.

"Yes," I replied.

"He's at the fairground," Juan Luis said. "I'll take you there."

"I'd better stay here. I don't want to miss him."

"Take my word, you won't."

* * *

When we reached the fairground, Anibal wasn't as happy to see me as I was to see him.

"Something has come up," he said, his normally booming voice reduced to confidential tones. "I'm not going directly to my ranch. Can you meet me in Paiján in more or less two weeks?"

Back in his car Juan Luis sliced a finger across his throat and put my worst fears into words, "Anibal has changed his mind about trading horses with you. I sensed his second thoughts before going to get you."

Anibal's offer—made after several of Peru's high-alcohol beers—had brought cries of bravo when repeated during his post *pachamanca* speech. But afterward he'd changed his mind about trading three mares for a sick gelding, a lame gelding, and one that was half-blind. Though perfectly reasonable, his decision devastated me.

I was silent as Juan Luis drove me back to San Jacinto.

"You have problems, no?" he asked as we stopped at José Antonio's house,

"My photograph," I replied, "belongs in the dictionary next to the word *salado*."

"Maybe I can help."

I'd had several offers of assistance during the Week of Piura. Nothing had come of them.

"I'm not like the others," Juan Luis said softly, with his uniquely Peruvian ability to read my thoughts. "Have breakfast with me tomorrow and I'll explain what I have in mind."

13

HONEST JUAN'S
SLIGHTLY USED HORSES

"Beautiful, isn't she?" Juan Luis asked the next morning when he caught me admiring a young woman as I finished my ham and eggs. "She was mine once."

Not much older than I, he should've been footloose and fancy-free. Instead his nose was to the grindstone as he prepared to run his aging father's hacienda. One day no doubt, he'd enjoy that job immensely—but for now, still young, he dreamed of adventure and identified with mine.

"Will it help," he asked as we walked to his office, "if I sell your horses for enough to buy replacements?"

"No offense," I replied, "but who'll pay that much for horses that can't reproduce and are in sorry condition?"

"I have some candidates in mind," he said. "Your horses are related to Hugo Bustamante's Relicario and have had a great deal of publicity. That'll help."

That night I lay awake, adjusting my original plan. If Juan

Luis did the impossible and sold my geldings, I'd buy three of Casa Grande's mares, which were exceptionally well cared-for, could reproduce, and would bring better prices than geldings when sold in the States.

* * *

The next day with Juan Luis's help, I embarked on what could most accurately be called a horse sellathon. But it's misleading to say I had his help because that infers he had mine, and I was a mere observer. Fortunately several of Piura's farmers needed geldings, I had the only ones available, and Juan Luis was a virtuoso salesman.

Even after calling attention to Inca's blind eye, he demanded three times what I'd paid before Juan Miguel Rossel refunded half. The first interested party, an infamous tightwad, was offended by the price.

"I don't think he'll pay anywhere near what you're asking," I told Juan Luis after our potential buyer left his office in a huff.

"Neither does he," Juan Luis said. "I'll have to change his mind, which won't be easy. He's unbelievably cheap."

"Me, too," I teased, "but I prefer to be called thrifty."

"Yes, but this gentleman is..." He tapped his elbow.

"What does that mean?"

"It means that to get him to open his tight fist and turn money loose, you have to hit him there with a hammer. Fortunately I have one."

That afternoon Juan Luis offered Inca to a second buyer and let the two compete until the tightwad bought him for more than our original asking price.

Huascarán was eating again and looking better when a

young farmer signaled his interest by agreeing to Juan Luis's first price. His grandfather however, held the purse strings and refused to pay that much.

"It'll be hard to find another buyer for a horse in Huascarán's condition," I pleaded when Juan Luis refused to lower the price.

"Pablito," he said with an exasperated sigh, "have you heard the story of the scientist who conducted an in-depth study of pessimism and optimism?"

"No," I said cautiously.

"Well, he locked a rich boy in a room with every toy ever invented and a poor boy in a room full of manure. A week later he opened the first door and found the rich boy sitting on the floor, bored. But behind the other door the poor boy was digging in the manure like a dog looking for a bone.

"Asked why, he replied, 'With all this manure, there has to be a pony in here somewhere.' I want you to be as optimistic as the poor boy was. These buyers can afford my prices, and you need all you can get to finish your ride."

After that I silently watched my newfound friend do everything possible to get me as much as he could for Huascarán. Our deadlock with the grandson was finally broken thanks to an ingenious solution proposed by...who else?

When all was said and done, the grandson paid me a considerable sum on the sly before taking me to his grandfather's house where I accepted the old man's offer and collected from him.

Next Juan Luis offered to buy Lucero for a handsome price.

"Lucero is still lame and has an uncertain future," I told him. "Your offer is far too high. I won't accept more than half that amount."

After a strenuous objection he reluctantly agreed.

All told, my three geldings—two in poor condition—had brought in a great deal more than I'd originally paid.

Thanks to Juan Luis's genius as a salesman I had enough to buy mares. But I had to do that quickly. My available time was on the wing.

* * *

That night I caught a ride on a southbound cattle truck and, at its destination in Lambayeque, continued on to Chocope in a truck hauling bananas. There I took the early morning bus to Casa Grande.

When that legendary hacienda's founder—a German immigrant named Juan Guildemeister—first turned his attention to the Chicama Valley in the late 1800s, it had been home to a few large plantations and thousands of small farms. Over the next fifty years, he combined them all into a single entity a quarter the size of Switzerland.

Reputedly the largest privately owned plantation on earth, Casa Grande stretched from the Pacific Ocean, across the Andes, and into the Amazon Basin's vast jungle. The millions of tons of cane it harvested annually were transported on its railway, processed in its mill, sold through its world-wide organization, and shipped from its private seaport.

In round numbers its corrals and pastures held twenty-five thousand sheep, twelve thousand cattle, and five hundred horses. Many of the latter would be suitable for my purpose. But would any be in my price range?

I knocked on Dr. Seifert's door earlier than I would have if the lights hadn't been on.

"Verne," he greeted. "I'm just sitting down to breakfast. Will you join me?"

As we ate I explained why I was there.

"Buying horses on the coast is a good move," he said. "Casa Grande raises livestock down here and in the *sierra*. Animals that grow up here are bigger and healthier because the feed is higher in nutrition."

Before lunch and again after, his assistant guided me through fields of mares and I wrote down numbers branded on the thighs of those I wanted to try under saddle. With over two hundred to choose from, the list I took to Seifert's office was sizable.

He compared it with Casa Grande's private stud book and crossed off the numbers of those not for sale, pregnant or with nursing foals, too young or too old, or priced beyond my means. When he finished, every number but one had a line through it.

"Hamaca," Seifert said with approval. "I was going to recommend her. I'll have her saddled so you can ride her. But we only catch her when it's time for shots, worming, or tuning up her training. We'll have to rope her."

* * *

Only four, Hamaca was wily beyond her years. Sensing she was the ropers' target, she eluded them by hiding behind her pasture mates. We drove her and a few others into a smaller field, then waited for her to come clear as they circled us.

When a loop finally settled around her neck, Hamaca stopped in her tracks. She'd been roped before and knew struggle would be futile. Seen up close she was solid black without a single white hair, pretty, and well-built with straight well-muscled legs and well set-up pasterns.

"She's a bit short for you, but very strong," Seifert told me.

Her name meant hammock, appropriate because riding her was smooth with a gentle side-to-side sway. For hours she carried me on narrow dirt roads between monotonous walls of towering sugarcane. With a horse to evaluate and a decision to make, time and miles passed quickly.

At dusk I stopped Hamaca in front of Seifert's office.

"I'll take her," I told him. "One down. Two to go."

"To make sure you didn't overlook any candidates," he offered, "I'll go through the herd with you tomorrow."

At his home that evening we ate a delicious dinner with other administrators and their wives—all born and raised in Germany. For my benefit the conversation—whether or not I was participating—was in English, which they all spoke fluently and effortlessly.

"You're from Germany but speak perfect Spanish and English," I said, impressed.

"Germans speak several languages. I've never understood why Yanks limit themselves to one," a man named Heinz responded, strengthening my earlier impression that he didn't care for Americans. "Of course that's only one reason your countrymen are unpopular in most of the world. Have you seen the anti-American graffiti in Lima?"

I had. In those days it was everywhere and most said the equivalent of *"Cuba Sí! Yanquis No!"* or *"Fuera Yanquis!* Yankee Go Home!"

"I've never been treated badly by a Peruvian or heard one criticize Americans," I told Heinz.

"Of course not," he said sharply. "They're too polite for that and—"

Smiling but forceful, Mrs. Seifert interrupted, "Let's change the subject before poor Verne gets the idea we Germans have superiority complexes."

After that, the evening continued as delightfully as it had begun.

* * *

Early the next morning as I ate breakfast in Casa Grande's guest room, Dr. Seifert knocked on the door.

When I opened it he said, "Something unexpected came up. We won't be able to inspect the mares until ten o'clock. I've arranged for someone to show you our refinery in the meantime."

Unwelcome at first, this delay turned out to be fascinating.

My tour of the huge refinery began at a spur track where sugarcane arrived from the fields in gondola cars. Two hours later it ended where hundred-pound bags of processed sugar were being loaded on a long line of flatcars. Empty when I got there, they were now full.

After Dr. Seifert and I went through Casa Grande's mares without finding another that was suitable and in my price range, he drove me to nearby farms with the same result. Thoroughly discouraged, I swallowed my pride and telephoned Anibal Vásquez in Paiján. He was out of town for a week.

If, God forbid, I couldn't find two more mares in the Chiclayo area, I'd have to come back.

* * *

"A driver brought us a bull from Piura and offered to take Hamaca back with him free," Dr. Seifert told me during dinner at his house that night.

"Do you think he'll mind if I go along?" I asked.

"I thought you were going to Chiclayo," he said.

"Not until Hamaca is safely at San Jacinto."

"Don't worry. You can trust Raul."

"I prefer to go with her," I said.

It had always been difficult to trust others with my horses, and my memories of keeping Lucero on his feet in José Antonio's pickup were still vivid.

First thing in the morning I brought Hamaca to Casa Grande's loading ramp, where a boy was putting bags of Dr. Seifert's special equine feed supplement into Raul's truck.

"I thought Hamaca should have familiar feed her first few days at San Jacinto," Seifert explained.

Raul had already cleaned the dirty straw bedding from his vehicle's cargo area and replaced it with pulverized sugarcane waste. His truck seemed in excellent condition and had just delivered a bull that probably outweighed Hamaca three-to-one.

"I'll ride in back with my horse," I told Raul after loading her.

In the town of Chocope four miles into our journey, the floorboard beneath Hamaca's right hind leg snapped. She dropped to her stomach in a fog of cane particles, three legs sprawled at impossible angles.

Dangling beneath the truck, her other leg was inches from a rotating tire. If they came in contact, skin and flesh would be peeled to the bone. Unbelievably she ceased thrashing as soon as I knelt and stroked her neck.

Banging my fist on the cab I screamed, "*Alto*! Stop! Now."

The menacing tire ceased turning, but Hamaca's leg was still threatened by the broken floorboard's jagged edges. Raul broke them off with a crowbar. Next we locked arms behind Hamaca's rump and lifted until her leg was back inside. I tied her far from the hole in the floor, then looked for injuries and found none.

My adrenaline level declining, I felt a stabbing pain in one eye. Trapped beneath its lid, an irritating speck of bagasse dragged across my cornea every time I blinked. Raul lifted my eyelid and tried to remove the particle with his finger.

Giving up, he said, "Don't worry. God has provided for you."

Looking where he'd pointed I saw we were stopped near Chocope's hospital.

"Stay with Hamaca," I said. "I'll be back soon. I hope."

Hand over my eye I rushed to the emergency room. When no one answered my call, I hurried down a hallway and around a corner.

"This area is restricted," a nurse scolded, then saw the tears dripping from my jaw.

She left and returned with a doctor who tried several times before snagging the jagged speck with a tissue.

"There's no damage," he said after careful examination. "I'll give you some ointment for the discomfort."

Eye throbbing, I rejoined Raul.

"How's Hamaca?" I asked.

"Okay as far as I can tell," he replied. "She won't let me touch her."

With flattering trust she watched me inspect her leg again. Satisfied she was unhurt I borrowed Raul's flashlight, crawled beneath his truck, and inspected the floorboards before we continued on.

* * *

It was dawn by the time Raul backed up to San Jacinto's livestock ramp. He stood beside his truck's broken floorboard, making sure Hamaca didn't step in the hole while I unloaded her. Then, at least as tired as I was, he drove away.

Hurrying through the dark toward my bedroom's outside entrance, I almost bumped into José Antonio.

"Find any mares at Casa Grande?" he asked.

"One," I replied. "I'll look for more tomorrow in Chiclayo."

"You look exhausted. Go to bed. We'll talk later."

"After you see my new mare." I gestured for him to go first.

Hamaca was in Inca's former corral eating the hay I'd given her.

"You chose well," José Antonio enthused.

After he left for work, Rodriguez and I leaned against Hamaca's corral. He clearly liked her.

When I finally went to bed, sleep held me in its grip until dinnertime. I ate with the family, then checked on Hamaca who seemed glad to see me. I was petting her when Rodriguez returned from hunting birds. About to lean his shotgun against the corral, he saw a fox creeping toward the chicken coop. Stealthily he aimed and fired.

A geyser of dust erupted and the predator escaped as a startled Hamaca bounded to her corral's far corner.

Frowning Rodriguez said, "Hope that wasn't a bad omen."

He was superstitious—like most Peruvian trainers—and believed in divine warnings. Feeling optimistic about my ride again, I didn't want to hear any discouraging words and changed the subject.

* * *

The next day I crossed the Despoblado in yet another truck. Again the desert's long, monotonous gray stretches briefly gave way to towns and green farms where rivers flowed down from the Andes. But with summer giving way to autumn, the heat was less oppressive and I said goodbye to each oasis with less regret and looked forward to the next with less urgency.

The change of season was also a reminder that according to my original schedule, I should be at least six hundred miles north of Piura.

In Reque I visited Jorge Baca at La Quinta. He was surprised to see me and had no mares for sale. Helpful as ever he took the day off and drove me to Hacienda Cayaltí, another of Peru's immense sugar plantations. Its owners, the Aspillaga family, had created a bloodline that once dominated Peru's national Paso Tournament.

Pedro Briones — one of the trainers who'd escorted me through Chiclayo during my send-off — greeted us and confirmed my worst fears. Cayaltí's once-extensive herds were gone. Juan Rafael Cabezas, a new breeder in Costa Rica, had been there weeks earlier and bought eighty-some of their last remaining horses.

I looked at those still for sale and found them more suitable for the show ring than the trail.

"You should visit the small farms around Cayaltí," Briones suggested. "Their horses descend from our best lines."

That afternoon I encountered something new, Peruvians eager to sell horses. They treated me with lavish courtesy and insisted on calling me mister, a level of respect that made me uncomfortable. When I wasn't interested in buying their horses, prices came down until they were incredible bargains, if such can be said of something one doesn't want to buy.

Finding two more horses would be difficult. Management of Peru's haciendas was passing from old-fashioned gentlemen — willing to spend on horses — to modern capitalists — looking to cut costs.

Long after the same had happened in the States, stalls were being converted to storage rooms. Trainers and stable boys were finding other jobs. Cash crops were being planted where herds once grazed, and the price of good, trained horses was skyrocketing.

14

TWO FOR THE ROAD

"**W**here next?" Jorge Baca asked during our late lunch. "Pucalá?"

"Yes," I replied, "but you're busy and have already given me too much of your time. I'll take the bus."

"No," he insisted. "I'll drive you."

"Please, let me do the right thing."

Reluctantly he relented and left me at a bus stop.

Visiting Pucalá was a desperate last resort. Yet another of Peru's giant sugar plantations, it was that era's leading breeder of prize-winning Peruvian Pasos.

Anticipating a foreign market, Guillermo Cepeda, married to one of the owners and in charge of the horses, was increasing their supply.

I feared Pucalá's prices would be beyond my means and their horses too stylish for my purpose. But with few options, I felt compelled to look at them.

Named after a famous Peruvian singer, Ima Sumac was at least the tenth mare Pedro Torres, the head trainer, showed me.

She was four, black with a white star, and her pedigree was a who's who of champions. Even though she'd never been ridden, she was the best possibility I'd seen since Hamaca. Her price however, was double what I'd budgeted for two mares.

I opened the haggling by turning my back and asking, "What else do you have?"

When we ate lunch at his home, Torres said, "I still think Ima Sumac is right for you."

He'd detected the interest I'd tried to hide and was clearly being pressured to make sales. Because Ima hadn't been trained under saddle, I suspected he didn't consider her good enough to show, even though he was asking a show horse price.

"She's barely four," I told him, "too young for hard work."

"But," he countered, "she comes from a family of strong, sound horses."

Good. He was under a lot of pressure.

"I'd be a fool," I grumped, "to buy a young, untrained horse."

That afternoon we looked at more mares, none of which was what I wanted.

By the time we ate dinner with Torres's wife Ima's price was lower but remained beyond my reach. By then however, I'd decided to make my ride on only Hamaca and Ima. Provided of course, that I could buy Ima for no more than I had intended to spend on two horses.

"Well, Pablito," his wife said as she served supper, "did you find a horse?"

"Yes," I replied. "If Pedro can get me a price I can afford I'll be able to continue my ride, and the publicity will tell the world about Pucalá's wonderful horses."

"How much can you afford?" she asked.

I told her.

Eventually Pedro lowered his price again, but not quite enough.

"Does that include delivery to Piura?" I asked.

Sighing he replied, "If you insist."

* * *

The man assigned to transport Ima Sumac to San Jacinto knocked on the door of Pucalá's guest room soon after I returned from breakfast.

"I'm your driver, Samuel," he said cheerily, "and I'm ready when you are."

Ima Sumac was already inside the stock rack on the back of a pickup truck in the driveway. I rode in back with her—hoping that precaution would prove unnecessary.

If Samuel heard my pleas to slow down, he ignored them and soon sped into a situation he could escape only by slamming on his brakes. I did my best to keep Ima on her feet, but she went down on her knees.

Looking contrite Samuel hurried back to check on her. Angrily I pointed to her swollen knee.

"I won't drive that fast again," he promised.

He kept his word and by the time we reached San Jacinto, the puffiness in Ima's knee had gone down and her leg was bearing its full share of weight.

With Rodriguez looking on, I put her in the corral adjoining Hamaca's. They took to one another like the long-lost sisters they appeared to be. The most notable differences were the star on Ima's forehead and Hamaca's missing forelock—cut off as was customary those days with mares in Peru.

That evening I showed Juan Luis Ruesta what he'd made possible.

"I like Hamaca very much," he said, "but Ima doesn't look very strong."

"In my opinion," I told him, "that's because Pucalá's trimmer left her toes too long and cut her heels too short."

"It'll take months," Juan Luis cautioned, "for those heels to grow out."

"A good farrier can correct her stance overnight by trimming her toes and making her shoes thicker at the heel."

"I hope you're right." His expression said he doubted it. "We don't shoe our horses, and I have no experience with that."

* * *

Next morning I applied for Hamaca and Ima's export permits, intending to condition them while the paperwork was processed. Now familiar with the ins and outs of dealing with Peru's Ministries, I hoped to avoid what I called The Peruvian Factor, which had been so frustrating when I took out my geldings' permits.

Murphy's Law tells us anything that can go wrong will. My corollary, The Peruvian Factor, makes him seem optimistic. According to his law, Peru's long-predicted, catastrophic earthquake will drop the coast west of the fault into the Pacific Ocean. But according to my Peruvian Factor, everything east of that fault — Brazil included — will disappear into the Atlantic.

When a government veterinarian came to San Jacinto to begin the application process, he arrived right on time and examined Hamaca and Ima with outstanding professionalism.

"I won't be able to administer the required injections until tomorrow morning," he then said.

In the grand scheme of things, a one-day delay was hardly a big deal. Two days later I phoned his office.

"Our supplier has equine encephalitis vaccine," a secretary told me, "but had to order the glanders and strangles shots from Chiclayo."

At worst this was a mild example of Murphy's Law...so far. Hoping to keep it that way I visited the supplier.

"I can't find those vaccines anywhere," he told me.

At José Antonio's office, I broke my rule against asking for his help.

"I'll have my Chiclayo office send them by bus," he offered.

Piura's notoriously unreliable telephone service was down so he used his company's citizen's band radio.

When the vaccines didn't arrive as promised, he radioed Chiclayo and got the response I feared, "*Mañana.*" That *mañana* and two more passed before they came. Several days after that, the vet still hadn't come to inject them. This rather minor delay however, was far from bad enough to qualify as The Peruvian Factor.

Getting photos was proving equally difficult. The photographer didn't keep our first appointment. When I cornered him in his office bright and early the next morning, he promised to be at San Jacinto by noon. At 4:00 p.m. he promised to meet me at 9:00 the following morning.

At noon the next day he took the pictures.

"I'll have them developed by 11:00 tomorrow morning," he promised.

When I went to pick them up, his secretary said they hadn't turned out and would have to be taken again. This was closer to The Peruvian Factor, but not yet there.

I would've utilized these delays for training and conditioning my mares, but first they needed shoes. Minutes after keeping our first appointment, the farrier wiped the smile from my face.

"I'm here to measure your horse's hooves," he said, "and will finish the job after I make the shoes."

"You don't have ready-made shoes?" I asked.

"No." He was clearly insulted. "I do quality work, which requires custom-made shoes."

He measured my mares' hooves with only his eyes and without picking up their feet.

Pointing to Ima I asked, "Can you please make the heels of her shoes thicker so her pasterns will be at a better angle?"

"I would have done that," he huffed, "even if you hadn't asked."

I didn't speak with him again for a week, though not for lack of trying.

With those and other frustrations coming one after another, I still hadn't started conditioning Hamaca and Ima. It was time to acknowledge the horrible truth. I was dealing with the same dreaded Peruvian Factor that had delayed me for weeks in Chiclayo.

* * *

After José Antonio loaned me a car one morning, I found my tormentors one-by-one, then took each wherever he had to go to do whatever he had to do to finish his job. From Tuesday to Thursday I begged, badgered, and bullied until my mares were vaccinated, photographed, wormed, examined, certified, and shod.

Before calling it a day I drove downtown to Puira's telephone company and stood in a line of people waiting for booths from which they could place long distance calls. When my turn came I called the Asociación in Lima and brought Tuco Roca Rey up-to-date.

"Send your application and documentation on tonight's bus," he said. "Tomorrow I'll deliver them to the Ministry of Agriculture and do everything I can to get your permit issued quickly."

15

YET ANOTHER CHANGE OF PLANS

Hamaca had seldom been ridden and Ima Sumac never. To condition them quickly and with minimal stress, I started leading them across the sand dunes near San Jacinto—one tied to the other's tail. Climbing in deep sand was strenuous exercise. But since each carried only her own weight it didn't put undue strain on muscles or sinew

Daily I increased the distance. Soon Hamaca and Ima were covering more ground than would've been prudent if they'd been carrying me. In the evenings after the temperature cooled, I taught both to carry my duffel bags and began training Ima under saddle.

So far my mares had been more sensible, better able to handle heat, and more adaptable at mealtime than their predecessors. They easily transitioned from fresh sugarcane to cured alfalfa, and after I fed them the last of Dr. Seifert's special supplement they ate barley, oats, or corn with equal enthusiasm.

* * *

After making my three feedbags, I'd marked one with an H and another with an I — the first letters in the names of both their original and new owners. The resemblances were uncanny.

Ima was another Inca, friendly and calm. Dust made her sneeze as it had him and she had his baby face, but with two perfectly good eyes. Built along similar lines, she had a similar gait and the same fast, efficient walk. And like him she'd stick her head over the fence after finishing whatever was in her feedbag, so I could remove it.

Hamaca was a scaled-down Huascarán. Smaller she had the same deep, ample body and way of moving without wasted motion. She too was inclined to pull back when tied and showed bug-eyed frustration when I put the heart rope on her. Not to mention that both had quickly learned to take off their feedbags.

Hamaca however, had a virtue Huascarán lacked. She was eager to please.

* * *

Struggling up a sand dune while conditioning Hamaca and Ima one morning, I had an epiphany. Instead of conditioning my mares in circles that began and ended at San Jacinto, I could lead them to Peru's border with Ecuador. That way we'd be a hundred miles closer to our destination when my export permits were ready.

At lunch I asked José Antonio's opinion.

"Good idea," he said. "I'll have Tuco Roca Rey send your

permits to the border station at La Tina, and my stable manager can ship feed to your overnight stops."

That afternoon while Rodriguez and I gave Hamaca and Ima another lesson in carrying my packsaddle, its wooden tree broke. Again.

"Who can fix this today?" I asked Rodriguez.

"The nearest saddlemaker is in Catacaos," he replied.

Catacaos was a village where master craftsmen produced everything from the world's finest palm fiber sombreros to exquisite gold and silver jewelry. I hadn't been able to find the time to visit its shops.

"How long does it take to get there?" I asked.

"Quite a while on paved roads," Rodriguez replied, "but there's a direct cross-country route that's faster. I'll draw you a map."

Home for the afternoon, José Antonio loaned me his car.

Rodriguez's shortcut began as a dirt road and after a few miles was little more than a cattle trail. Twice José Antonio's car nearly bogged down in sand. Then the trail disappeared into a small river and reappeared on the opposite bank.

The only way to evaluate its muddy depth was to wade in. My foot on the bumper, I was untying a bootlace when a barefoot Indian on a small horse and leading pack mules rode into the water from the opposite bank.

"As you saw, Señor, it's safe to cross," the old man said, sweeping his hand back toward the river as he passed.

"I'd better make sure," I said, untying my other boot. "This is a borrowed car."

"It will be my pleasure to guide you."

He dismounted and rolled up his pant legs, then waded in and motioned for me to follow.

Full of dread I drove behind him, ready to reverse course on a moment's notice.

But the old mule skinner kept me in shallow water and on firm ground all the way across, then declined a tip.

"We were put here to serve," he said cheerfully and continued on his way.

* * *

The streets of Catacaos were unpaved and its humble adobe structures had no plumbing. Electricity was provided by gas powered generators and the only advertisements were for Coca Cola, Inca Kola, pain killers, and laundry soap. There was nothing to indicate that craftsmen with worldwide reputations lived and worked there.

"Why don't you have a sign?" I asked when I finally found the saddle maker's shop.

"What for?" he answered with a question of his own. "Everyone knows where I am."

"What about people from outside this area?"

"None come here. They buy my merchandise in stores."

Simple and polite he reeked of old fashioned virtues. It didn't seem right that middlemen benefited from his talents—undoubtedly more than he did.

While he repaired my pack saddle, I visited other shops. All had entry areas where glass cases displayed examples of the artisans' finished products. Closed doors hid rooms where they lived and worked.

As I admired one's display of silver jewelry, he offered, "I can duplicate anything there in twenty-four-carat gold. Or if you prefer *filigrana*..."

He pointed to a case of exquisite four inch fighting cocks, llamas, and *marinera* dancers, made by rolling and twisting silver wire.

Two hours later—with my newly repaired saddle in José

Antonio's trunk—I turned onto the main street ahead of a loudspeaker-equipped Land Rover I'd seen campaigning for a mayoral candidate in Piura. Soon the voice coming from its loudspeakers switched from Spanish to accented English and said, "Vote for Pablito. Only he can end this terrible poverty."

When I looked back, the driver and a man with a microphone laughed and waved. I didn't know them, but they knew me and plugged my undeclared candidacy all the way across town.

Wonder if I got any votes?

16

BORDERLINE

That afternoon Juan Luis Ruesta brought friends to San Jacinto's stable and gave me a gratifying compliment.

"You were right," he said. "With her new shoes, Ima Sumac's angles are outstanding. But are you sure she's in good enough condition for your ride?"

"For a while it won't be my ride," I began a play on words I thought he'd enjoy. "It'll be my walk. I'm going to lead her and Hamaca until they're fit enough to carry me."

Rather than get a halter when one of Juan Luis's friends asked to see Ima's gait, I fastened my belt around her neck. Unaccustomed to being controlled that way she didn't gait well.

Juan Luis slapped her rump to bring out more energy. Startled, she bolted. With only my belt to control her, I was forced to let go. She scampered into her corral and stood, eyeing Juan Luis suspiciously and snorting.

During her mad dash I'd turned my ankle. Already it was swollen and throbbing.

"Better stay off that a few days," Juan Luis said.

"No more delays," I declared. "I'm leaving in the morning as planned. Period."

When Juan Luis said goodbye I couldn't find the words to adequately thank him for saving my enterprise from certain failure. By that age however, hiding my feelings was an ingrained habit I couldn't break even when I tried. I could only hope my enthusiasm made up for my lack of eloquence.

After dinner that evening I had a similar experience when saying goodbye to José Antonio. I felt great affection for this soft-spoken man who'd done so much for me. His example had shown me what it meant to be a true gentleman, and he'd taught me a great deal about Peruvian horses as well as life in general. But I couldn't bring myself to tell him that.

* * *

The Onrubia family was still sleeping when I set out for Sullana.

Since Chiclayo, I'd been told the desert ahead was nothing but sand, but there'd always been at least some vegetation and a few creatures. That day, however, there were indeed stretches of only sand, the highway, and those inescapable roadside crosses— sometimes in clusters—that marked places where people had died in car crashes.

Though summer had become fall, the day was extremely hot. Whenever I stopped I had to lift one foot and then the other to keep the sand's stored heat from penetrating my boot soles. Most of the time I was able to ignore my sprained ankle, but even the slightest misstep sent lightning bolts of pain through it.

As recommended by Juan Luis Ruesta's father, I went as far at the picturesque cavalry fort on Sullana's outskirts.

When I showed the guard at the gate Señor Ruesta's letter of introduction, he called the *comandante's* aide-de-camp and gave it to him.

When the aide finally returned he said, "You and your horses can stay the night."

Inside the fort's tall, thick perimeter wall were barracks, officer housing, a dining hall, offices, exercise fields, and a barn—all connected by paths lined with whitewashed stones.

"Our veterinarian," the aide informed me, "will have to check your horses before you put them in with ours."

After a thorough examination the vet reported, "They're in excellent condition, but the one called Hamaca is in foal."

What? Two pregnancy tests at Casa Grande had been negative, and she'd come in heat at San Jacinto.

"Could you please check again?" I asked.

"That won't be necessary. I'm absolutely certain she's pregnant."

If correct his news was painfully ironic. I'd been unable to buy several excellent Casa Grande mares because they were pregnant and couldn't safely make the journey—let alone compete in the Tevis Cup Ride.

The aide showed me to a pair of empty stalls in an otherwise full barn.

In the U.S. Cavalry, tanks had long since replaced horses. I was glad that wasn't the case in Peru when the blacksmith checked my mares' shoes, found one of Hamaca's loose, and re-nailed it.

After dinner I took aspirin and wrapped my ankle, then went to bed with my foot elevated. Feverish I fell asleep slowly, but slept soundly and in the morning was well enough to set out for Hacienda Chilaco.

* * *

Climbing into the foothills from Sullana's stark desert, we went through an area where dry bushes lined both sides of the road. Hamaca took advantage of every opportunity to scratch herself by pressing against them as we passed.

She had an itch that never seemed to go away. No matter how long I curried her, she kept her upper lip extended with pleasure until I finished. When I rubbed behind her ears she looked ecstatic. And no matter how I tried to prevent her from rolling after baths, she did. Dust was her talcum powder and she wasn't comfortable without it.

Ankle throbbing and my fever now accompanied by other signs of dysentery, I reached Chilaco. Events there were reminiscent of my arrival at another seemingly deserted hacienda. Feeling what baseball player Yogi Berra famously described as "*déjà vu* all over again," I knocked on the door to no avail and later found an aging caretaker among the corrals.

Like the Phantom of La Viña he wasn't expecting me, but the similarity ended there.

"The feed you sent is in the tack room." He pointed to it and added, "Put your mares in that corral and make yourself at home."

When I knocked on the house door no one opened it. Worried that something had happened to the old gentleman I went inside.

"Anyone here?" I called. No answer.

I went from one empty, unfurnished room to the next— searching and calling to no avail.

Hmm. The caretaker hadn't said to meet him at the house. He'd told me to make myself at home. Evidently he'd chosen to escape the burden of being a host, which was fine because I was exhausted and didn't feel like being a guest.

Out-of-date and in bad shape, the once elegant mansion had no electricity or running water. Chunks of plaster were missing from walls. Its one saving grace was the main bathroom's ornate porcelain bathtub. I filled a pail again and again at my mares' water tank and emptied it there.

Lying up to my neck in that cold water was delicious. I soaked until the skin on my fingers and toes shriveled and my teeth chattered. Finally my fever broke.

After making sure all was well with Hamaca and Ima, I didn't feel like eating.

Exhausted I unrolled my sleeping bag in front of the fireplace by moonlight. Rather than crawl inside I stretched out on top, prolonging the marvelous sensation of coolness.

* * *

Well-rested but still not hungry in the morning, I left a thank-you note on the kitchen table and started for Las Lomas. All day Hamaca, Ima, and I climbed into the Andes. Gradually the shrubs, trees, wildflowers, and flocks of parrots — all of which had called my attention at first — became commonplace.

In Las Lomas I asked a man where I might keep my horses and he invited me to put Hamaca and Ima in his corral. When I fed them, his eyes narrowed.

"Where did you get such excellent hay and *concentrado*?" he asked, calling grain by a name I hadn't heard before.

"I sent them here by bus," I replied.

Instantly he became exceedingly formal, clearly under the impression I was wealthy. Who else would spend that much money on horses? And since rich men don't need favors, he demanded a healthy fee for keeping my mares in his corral.

My stay in the Guardia Civil checkpoint however, was free.

There weren't many trucks on the road that night, and few document checks interrupted my much-needed sleep. But I was repeatedly awakened by a mosquito. Finally I climbed from my upper bunk with a rolled-up newspaper, determined to silence my annoying tormentor.

"What's wrong?" the guardsman in the lower bunk wanted to know.

"There's a mosquito," I replied.

"Male or female?"

"How do you tell the difference?" I asked.

"The females make no sound when flying."

"Well this one needs a muffler, so it's definitely a male and will soon be dead."

Which he was, but two more—his brothers no doubt—came to avenge him.

* * *

In the morning—famished after not eating for thirty-six hours—I astonished my fellow patrons at a restaurant by eating three breakfasts before setting out for Suyo.

Telephone poles along the road that day looked like reflections in a fun house mirror. Like the region's stunted trees—from which they were made—they were inches in diameter, crooked, and not much taller than I. The single wire they supported was Suyo's only connection with the outside world.

In the bushes around them, patches of vivid color appeared to be flowers—but were small birds.

From a distance Suyo looked picturesque, but up close it was a collection of shacks under impressive roofs made with Spanish, half-barrel style, red tiles. Each of these had been handmade and shaped over its maker's thigh. Wider at one end, they overlapped perfectly.

I spent that night at a cavalry outpost where Hamaca and Ima shared the only available stall, to their mutual delight. They didn't like being separated.

While the post blacksmith replaced their worn iron shoes free of charge, gregarious troopers gathered around.

"If your horses get an open wound while in Suyo," a corporal warned, "clean it thoroughly several times a day. If it gets infected the pain will be so terrible that they'll seek relief by biting off chunks of their rotting flesh."

Not to be outdone a sergeant added, "You should have put *sabila* in your stall."

"Sabila? What's that?" I asked.

"A succulent that repels vampire bats." He pointed to a fleshy, spiny aloe leaf hanging in a stall.

Vampire bats was one horror story too many. I suspected they were trying to see how gullible I was.

After I'd finished caring for my mares the sergeant showed me a gelding that had been bitten on the neck by one of those filthy vermin — leaving a hideous, festering wound.

During his famous ride, Aimé Tschiffely too had been in vampire country and had written the following:

> I was puzzled how a horse or mule could let so big an animal bite him, when a mosquito or a fly will make him defend himself. At a later period I had the chance to observe how these bats attack, and I feel inclined to believe in the theory of some mountain people.
>
> Bats have a peculiar way of flying around the horse in circles until he becomes drowsy and half dazed. These bloodsuckers usually exist in deep quebradas, as the rugged valleys are called, and owing to the hot and damp atmosphere the horses perspire even during the

nights. Gradually the bats circle closer and closer around the now sleepy horse, and presently they hover near the spot where they intend to bite, all the time fanning air against the victim. Once the horse gets used to the pleasant sensation of feeling cool the vampire gently settles down and bites through the hide with his sharp little teeth, keeping up the fanning with his wings.

At noon the next day I reached my ride's first milestone, La Tina—the town where Peru ends and Ecuador begins. Hamaca and Ima had traveled a hundred miles to the first of ten borders we'd cross. But they weren't yet fit enough to carry me long distances, and I'd have to continue leading them a while longer.

Nonetheless it was time to take satisfaction in my ride's first small success.

17

THE SMUGGLER
IN THE MIRROR

I n La Tina I rented a corral for Hamaca and Ima at a small farm, then walked to the town's Guardia Civil post. My export permits had arrived, thank goodness.

José Antonio had known I wouldn't find anything for my horses to eat during my initial days in Ecuador. True to his word, he'd sent extra hay and oats.

"A word of warning," a Peruvian sergeant said as I loaded my feed into a borrowed wheelbarrow. "If you attempt to cross the border with that, the Ecuadorians will confiscate it."

Wondering how to avoid that—I checked into a hotel.

I'd always found showers conducive to problem solving and was soon turning the hotel's hot water on and off to conserve it as I formulated a plan. By the time I was clean I'd decided to smuggle my feed into Macará, the town on Ecuador's side of the border.

If the Ecuadorians caught me, I'd show the visa in my passport and tell them I had the right to enter their country and hadn't known the river was the border. Normally that would've worked. The locals didn't get visas every time they crossed the river to shop or visit friends. They simply waded across, and officials on both sides turned a blind eye.

But recently Peru and Ecuador had nearly gone to war over disputed territory.

Both militaries were on full alert.

* * *

By mid-afternoon I was knee-deep in a secluded stretch of river, following the man I'd hired to transport my feed to Macará on his mule.

In town my first stop was the army post, where the comandante's gracious welcome gave the impression my arrival was a welcome break in an otherwise dull day. Fortunately for me, no one asked to see my still-unstamped passport.

In the comandante's office I told him about my ride and asked if he'd please help me send hay and oats to my initial overnight stops.

"Of course," he replied. "But that's not your only problem. Empalme — the first place with enough flat ground for you and horses to spend the night — is forty miles away. And you have to get there on a narrow road that climbs thousands of feet and is little more than a ledge cut into steep mountainsides."

"There must be a closer place we can spend a night," I said.

"No." He shook his head. "If you're still on that road after dark, you and your horses will be difficult to see. What color are they?"

"Black."

"Oh my. You'd better get started as soon as the border station opens in the morning. I'll tell my men there not to delay you."

He spread a map on his desk and helped select my first six destinations, then wrote a letter on official stationery instructing Ecuador's military and police to help me whenever possible.

Outside I put equal portions of hay and oats in a half-dozen burlap bags and attached notes with my estimated arrival dates.

Later at the bus station I paid to have those bags shipped — one a day so they wouldn't arrive long before I did.

* * *

Macará, Ecuador, was like La Tina, Peru, with one notable difference. South of the border, structures were adobe. But north of that imaginary line they were wood.

Downtown Macará resembled a nineteenth century town in America's Wild West. Its restaurants were larger and more modern than La Tina's, so I ate dinner there before returning to Peru.

I was paying the bill when the town was suddenly infested by a plague of biblical proportions. In less than two minutes, locusts on the restaurant's screens were so thick I couldn't see past them.

"Right on time," the cashier said cheerfully. "The lights attract them."

Throwing open a screen door clogged with grasshopper-like insects holding on for dear life, I hurried outside. All around men were spraying walls, streets, and sidewalks while others swept dead locusts into piles. No one objected when dogs ate from those.

Evidently the insecticide wasn't harmful to them. Most dogs I'd seen in Peru were walking skeletons, but Macará's were plump. Even locusts are good for something.

It was dark when the excitement ended. I hired two boys to guide me back across the river and found my way to Hamaca and Ima's corral in La Tina. Somehow cows had gotten in with them — helped by their owners I suspected. They had finished off the hay and oats I'd thought would last until morning.

I shooed these invaders out and wired the gate shut, then woke a shopkeeper and bought rolled cooking oats, by far the most expensive grain I'd yet fed to Hamaca and Ima. Then with a borrowed lantern and machete, I cut elephant grass along the riverbank.

Before going to bed I punched a new hole in my belt so I could tighten it enough to keep my pants up. I'd lost considerable weight leading my mares some two hundred fifty miles during their training and our walk to Ecuador.

* * *

A half hour before the International Bridge opened I was first in line, anxious to quickly clear immigration and customs. I didn't want to be on that treacherous mountain road after dark.

The border's Peruvian side opened an agonizing twenty minutes late. The day before I'd talked with the sergeant there at considerable length. He knew I was in a hurry and cleared my horses and duffel bags expeditiously.

Stamping my passport he said, "Good luck, Pablito."

On the Ecuadorian side — thanks to the comandante who'd been so helpful the day before — the officials waved me through without asking to see my mares' health certificates or inspecting my duffel bags.

Energized by having crossed into Ecuador so quickly, I hurried through Macará and started into the Andes. Soon the steady climb had me wondering if I could maintain the necessary pace.

Coming around a curve I saw a group of Ecuador's mountain Indians, Serranos, coming single file — carrying machetes and observing me with suspicion. As we passed, the first man greeted me with a nod and, "*Buen dia*," which I repeated to him.

One by one the others said, "*Buen dia*," and I responded in kind.

From time to time this ritual was repeated with other similar groups. Andean courtesy it seemed, demanded that everyone I pass greet me with *Buen dia*, and that I parrot those words in return. That was fine with me. If people with machetes wanted to be sociable, why disappoint them?

Gradually the appearance of grim-faced Serranos ceased to be alarming and I tired of those monotonous exchanges. But then a group passed without returning my *Buen dia*. I felt a chill between my shoulder blades as soon as they were behind me.

Following a staccato exchange in a language I didn't understand, I looked across my shoulder as the last man disappeared around a bend. Why had they ignored me? Did they speak only their native tongue, or did they dislike white people?

Thanks to newspaper articles, Peruvians had known I was promoting their National Horse, and I'd been popular there. But to the Ecuadorians I'd seen so far, I was an oddball leading two perfectly healthy horses he should be riding.

My new surroundings, it appeared, might not be as hospitable as those I'd left.

18

THE ANDES

T hat afternoon we passed through a forest. Spread across steep hillsides, it must have been beautiful once. But now parasitic thistles were growing on its branches and sucking the life from their hosts. Already they'd killed hundreds of trees, and nothing was being done to stop their spread.

A peasant added to my dismay by pulling a double barreled shotgun to his shoulder and dropping two brightly colored parrots from a flock. Initially surprised, I was soon furious. What was wrong with that fool? Those gorgeous birds' habitat was being destroyed, and he was making that even more disastrous by shooting them.

My disapproval — I soon realized — was hypocritical and based on our very different circumstances. It wasn't his fault I saw parrots as pets. He needed food, and compared to him I was eating well. And to be honest, my conscience hadn't stopped me from hunting equally beautiful pheasants and wood ducks when I was a boy.

Beyond the forest Hamaca, Ima, and I climbed into barren mountains where I saw few people and no sign of where they lived. If I didn't reach Empalme by dark I was pretty sure following one of the steep footpaths from the highway would take me to Serranos' huts.

However, I doubted I'd be welcome and sped up. Under the darkening sky I saw fireflies blinking among roadside shrubs.

"Empalme," the comandante in Macará had told me, "is nothing more than a few ramshackle kiosks that sell meals, mostly to truckers."

Drained by my eleven-hour climb, I came around a curve and saw a place where the mountainside had been blasted away to make room for a checkpoint.

"Is there someplace my horses can spend the night?" I asked, handing the comandante's letter of recommendation to an officer standing behind a metal arm lowered to stop traffic.

"Put them in our holding pen." He pointed to a corral on the slope below. "They'll have company if we confiscate any livestock tonight."

Before taking Hamaca and Ima down that treacherous slope, I set out to find them a drink. Even in the desert I'd never had such difficulty getting water. The kiosk owners had to bring theirs miles and refused to give me any. Even after I offered to pay they wouldn't sell much. I had to patronize them all, then buy more at the checkpoint.

After watering my mares I hired a boy to hold Ima, then started down narrow switchbacks—following my flashlight beam toward the corral. Hamaca was no happier to leave than Ima was to be left. Frantically they called to each other.

Whirling toward Ima, Hamaca slipped off the path dislodging rocks that loudly bounced into the canyon. I held her leadline with all my might until she stopped sliding. Groaning I pulled as she struggled up toward me. Then she was back on the path— trembling and puffing, but okay.

As soon as her breathing was back to normal we continued toward the corral. This time Hamaca was careful where she put her feet, despite Ima's continuing calls.

Built on the hillside the corral was equally steep. The only place a horse could stand and eat was a shelf of rocks and dirt collected against the lower fence. I sat, slid a few feet, stopped, stood up, brought her forward, then repeated that procedure over and over. When we were on the narrow level area I turned Hamaca loose.

The gate at the corral's uphill side didn't have a latch. Before bringing Ima, I fastened it shut with my belt. On my next three trips — all uneventful thank goodness — I brought Ima, the feed sent from Macará, and a pail of water.

After one look at those filthy kiosks, I decided to eat several bananas and skip dinner. Then I spent an uncomfortable night on a small bench inside the checkpoint.

* * *

At sunrise I fed and watered Hamaca and Ima in their hillside corral. Then hungry enough to eat one of those gigantic Texas steakhouse meals that are free if you can finish them, I took another look at the kiosks. Even though my standards had been lowered in Peru, I was appalled by the lack of sanitation.

By then I had two simple guidelines. First: whenever possible eat food that comes in cans, bottles, peels, or shells. Second: insist all other meals be cooked — preferably boiled — long enough to kill even the heartiest bacteria and viruses.

I ordered a dozen eggs — fried until rubbery, four large rolls — baked until almost black, and beans — fresh from a brick oven. Not particularly tasty, that breakfast was as welcome as any I'd ever eaten.

When I went to get Hamaca and Ima, my belt was gone—stolen no doubt—and the gate was ajar. But my mares were where I'd left them. Hamaca—insecure on the steep slope—had all four feet on the dirt shelf inside the lower fence. Beside her, Ima sat like a dog—hindquarters straight uphill, rear legs tucked beneath her body, back horizontal, front feet on the level area.

Like the comedienne she was, she looked pleased with herself.

* * *

That day's journey took us to the village of Las Playas, where our arrival attracted part-Indian boys.

"The hay and concentrado delivered to our schoolhouse yesterday must be yours," one said.

"I'll pay you to bring it," I offered. "What's your name?"

"Juan."

Motivated by this opportunity to earn money, he speedily brought my feed, then asked, "What else can I do to earn money? If you want, you can pay me by the hour."

"You're hired," I told him. "Stand my mares in the creek for a while."

"Why?" Juan teased, grinning mischievously. "That won't make them grow big enough for you."

Later we removed two hazards in my rented corral, with me laughing almost nonstop as Juan further demonstrated his quick, delightful intelligence and wit.

He and his companions were the first in Las Playas to attend public school. Around a bonfire that night I saw the results. Inescapably harsh lives had made their parents pessimistic. But thanks to teachers, this new generation believed persistence brought success, people reaped what they sowed, and education resulted in good jobs and happiness. As a result they welcomed rather than endured life.

They'd also learned compassion toward animals. Their parents were indifferent to non-human life. They raised livestock to eat, but their only partners from the animal kingdom were mules. And as a consequence of poor care, those often let them down.

None of the older generation seemed to know the word horse. I was insulted the first time someone called Hamaca and Ima *mulas*, and he was astonished to see the time, energy, and money I invested in their care.

Earlier that day I'd seen a man on a small, skinny mule with a rear fetlock so hideously twisted I could see the bottom of its hoof from the side as it passed. Despite this it hobbled past at remarkable speed on three hooves and the side of its deformed pastern. All the while the rider demanded more by smacking its ribs with the flat of his machete blade.

He was cordial and considerate with me, but clearly didn't know animals have feelings.

19

MY FRIEND THE
WITCH DOCTOR

An hour after I fed my mares that evening Hamaca still hadn't touched her hay or grain. This worried me all the more when I noticed her carriage and demeanor were similar to Huascarán's before and during his epic diarrhea. I was examining her—trying to figure out what was wrong—when a man outside the corral started toward town.

"I'll bring the doctor," he called over his shoulder.

He soon returned with a dignified half blood who exuded confidence and clearly had both Indian and European ancestors. Regal in a suit and fedora hat, he wouldn't have looked out of place in a Humphrey Bogart movie.

I took hold of Hamaca's halter so he could examine her. He removed his coat and unsheathed the machete hanging from his belt.

"What are you going to do with that?" I asked.

"Cure your mare," he replied with calm self-assurance. "Hold her firmly please."

He touched the side of his blade to Hamaca's underside behind the foreleg and slid it to her flank, then tapped twice. I lost count of the number of times he did that. Then he rested the blade near her withers, slid it across the top of her rib cage, and tapped her loin twice. This too, he repeated over and over.

After walking to her other side, he did the same there. When he finished Hamaca lowered her head, sighed, and re-laxed. The cold steel massage had clearly been soothing.

Abruptly the half-blood started chanting and slashing his machete through the air above a now startled Hamaca. Ready to stop him if this got out of hand, I realized he was a witch doctor drawing mystic signs in the air so his god — or gods — would bless his efforts with success.

I breathed easier after his gyrations stopped and the ma-chete was back in its sheath. When he left without asking for payment, I relaxed completely.

At 2:00 a.m. I got out of my sleeping bag beside Hamaca and Ima's corral and checked on them for the third time. Clearly better, Hamaca was devouring hay. I couldn't help wondering if Huascarán too might have benefited from some witch-doctoring.

* * *

At sunup Hamaca showed no trace of distress. With only twelve miles to go that day and both mares full of vitality we pressed on. I however, must have looked as exhausted as I felt. Twice, passing truckers offered to take me, Hamaca, and Ima all the way to Quito at no charge.

Free rides for two horses wouldn't often be available, and

to reach California before the Tevis Cup we'd have to travel thousands of miles in vehicles. But I preferred to do that in Mexico's monotonous deserts. With its Serranos, witch doctors, and towering mountains Ecuador was an experience to be savored.

As Hamaca, Ima, and I entered Catacocha—the first modern Ecuadorian city we'd seen, people stopped to stare. We must have been quite a sight—two plump, sassy black mares led by an emaciated gringo giant who kept his pants up by tying his front belt loops together with a handkerchief.

In a plaza Serrano Indians stood in a long line with pails and other large containers. Their common goal was a concrete structure with protruding pipes discharging water for the poor. This seemed like a good place to give Hamaca and Ima a drink, so I joined them. The lady in front of me—evidently surprised I was white—waved for me to go ahead.

"No, thank you," I said. "I'll wait my turn."

These people's forefathers had ruled Ecuador before their Spanish conquerors arrived. Now they were outsiders. Until then I'd thought Ecuador's Indians ignored me because they disliked whites, but what happened next suggested otherwise.

"Are your mulas for sale?" the lady in front of me asked.

"No," I replied. "I'm taking them to my country."

"They don't have mulas there?" a man asked.

My answer brought questions from all sides, as if speaking with me was a rare opportunity. Talking for almost an hour as people left the waterspouts carrying full containers, we slowly moved toward our goal. No one seemed to mind spending so much time on a chore I'd always accomplished by simply turning a faucet handle.

* * *

Built on hillsides and densely populated, Catacocha had no visible stables nor corrals. Forced to settle for whatever lodging I could find, I arranged to sleep in a repair shop's spare room and turned Hamaca and Ima loose in its storage yard. Businesslike and distant, the owner demanded more than I'd offered before outlining his rules and collecting in advance.

The window in my second floor room overlooked my mares' enclosure. Seen from above they looked like black mice in a maze as they explored rows of parked cars, trucks, and buses waiting to be repaired.

In downtown Catacocha my faith in the essential goodness of Latin Americans declined a little every time a cashier presented me an inflated bill. Shamelessly all persisted in trying to collect even though they should've been embarrassed I'd caught them trying to cheat me.

But those who saw me as an opportunity were greatly outnumbered by others who saw a man on unfamiliar ground and in need of help.

A group of Good Samaritans intervened when I was about to give money to a beggar with an empty sleeve, then shamed him into revealing his supposedly missing arm—strapped behind him, under his jacket.

As I left a bank after cashing a traveler's check, a teenager pointed out a short innocent-looking orange thread on the shoulder of my shirt.

"It was put there as you left the bank," he explained, "by that pickpocket's partner, to mark you as someone with cash."

Looking guilty, the man at whom he pointed hurried away.

"From now on," the boy added, "keep your wallet in your front pocket."

That evening the repair shop's owner invited me to take a

shower and eat dinner with his family, then presented a bill for what I'd thought was kindness.

My bittersweet day ended on that sour note, but I couldn't complain. My host had no obligation to do me favors. I'd always avoided treating people badly, but I'd seldom gone out of my way to help them. I hadn't earned the kindness Latin Americans were showing me.

* * *

Since leaving Piura we hadn't had a day off. I'd sent extra feed to Catacocha so my mares and I could rest there for a day. We began by sleeping late and eating leisurely breakfasts. Mine was in a restaurant where I had an interesting conversation with a trucker named Filomeno.

"How did you select your nightly stopping places?" he asked.

"The comandante in Macará did it for me."

"How?"

"From a map."

"Where will you stop between here and La Toma?"

"Nowhere," I replied. "I can go that far in a day. It's only twenty-five miles."

"As the crow flies perhaps," Filomeno exclaimed, "but on the Panamericana it's twice that far. Your friend the comandante must have had an air force map. No wonder Ecuador never won a war."

"The mistake was partly mine," I confessed. "The comandante took the other distances from a map that didn't show La Toma. He guessed at its location, then I calculated the distance to Catacocha with a ruler."

"That explains it," Filomeno declared. "Your estimate ignored the many miles added by the highway's meandering and switchbacks."

Be that as it may, I'd sent the next day's feed to La Toma, and had to get there in a single day no matter how far it was.

When in college and in excellent physical condition, I'd placed second in a marathon by finishing a fifty-mile walking race in a little over eleven hours. Afterward the winner had spent two weeks in a hospital with leg cramps, and I'd been in agony — barely able to walk.

Worse yet, those fifty miles had been on relatively flat terrain while tomorrow's would be in the rugged Andes.

* * *

Long before dawn I set out from Catacocha, hoping against hope Filomeno had been wrong about the distance to La Toma. But exactly as he'd said it would, the highway meandered without regard for the fact that the shortest distance between two points is a straight line.

Ecuador's Panamericana had been built on a budget that didn't allow for bridging canyons, and it couldn't simply drop down one side and climb up the other. It had to maintain a reasonable grade by following the contour of the land.

After walking fast as possible for an hour, I saw Catacocha across a canyon — a stone's throw away. An hour of maximum effort had brought almost no progress. Even if I maintained that pace — which I couldn't — we wouldn't reach La Toma until long after dark.

That afternoon my predicament worsened when we came upon a construction crew surfacing the highway with fresh gravel. I led Hamaca beside the continuous pile of crushed rock in the uphill lane. Behind her — tied to my saddle — Ima soon realized the ground was less rocky in the downhill lane, now congested with two-way traffic.

Repeatedly she veered into the paths of cars, trucks, and

buses—boldly claiming the right of way. When vehicles came head-on she bowed her neck, broke into a *paso llano* gait, and held her ground. When they came from behind, she swished her tail as though ten-ton trucks could be dismissed as easily as flies.

Time and again I shooed her back where she belonged, but she wouldn't stay there. Tied to my empty saddle she put too much strain on its cinch strap, which broke. As the saddle leapt at her—clearly attacking—she bolted and ran, then gathered her courage and whirled to face her pursuer, blocking traffic and angrily swinging her tail.

When the saddle also stopped she let me catch her, then looked at me as if to say, "I showed that thing, didn't I?"

With traffic again moving, I replaced the broken cinch strap with a spare from my duffel bag, mounted Hamaca, then held Ima close—doing my best to keep her out of traffic. A truck came abreast, its driver frantically gesturing. Assuming he was upset I extended both arms palms up, and shrugged. He rolled his window down, but not to scold me.

"I'm going to Quito," he shouted. "I'll take you and your horses free."

"I'll be eternally grateful," I called back, "if you'll just take us to La Toma."

"I'm Manuel," the trucker said. "I'll find a place where we can load your horses and wait there."

When I saw Manuel's truck again, it was backed up to a dirt mound, tailgate open. To get aboard, my mares had to climb the loose pile, step up two feet, and scramble into the cargo area while ducking under a crossbeam.

Manuel held Ima while Hamaca followed me aboard and I tied her behind the cab.

Next Ima—eager to avoid being left behind—frantically

clawed her way into the truck, slamming a forehoof down on my foot.

I said a whole lot more than just ouch.

My foot was too sore to stand on, so I rode in the cab with Manuel, who aggressively squeezed into traffic. With only one lane open and no flagmen directing, we had to alternately stop for downhill traffic, then go uphill until forced to wait for another opening.

The nicknames painted above cabs on oncoming trucks were as entertaining as the old Burma Shave signs I'd read during car trips with my parents. Some boasted of virtues: "Swift and Agile" or "The Lion of the North." Others lamented unrequited love: "You Look But Don't See Me" or "I Sigh When You Glance at Me."

"What's your truck's name?" I asked Manuel.

"I Am Your Salvation," he replied, grinning.

"Perfect. You were definitely mine."

After several miles the long pile of crushed rock ended. With both traffic lanes open, we reached La Toma at sunset.

"Are you sure you don't want me to take you to Quito?" Manuel asked, stopping at an embankment suitable for unloading.

"I've enjoyed your company and am tempted," I told him. "But I prefer to take my time crossing your fascinating country."

* * *

After claiming my feed at La Toma's bus station I rented a corral, then bathed and fed my mares. Next—famished and eating a better-than-average restaurant dinner—I relaxed for the first time all day. But only until an agitated boy burst through the door.

"Señor. Señor. Señor." Wide-eyed with excitement, that was the best he could manage.

Definitely the Señor in question, I asked, "What's wrong?"

"The horses. The horses."

"What about them?"

"Your horses," he said impatiently. "They're loose. Follow me."

Barely able keep up I dashed outside. We tracked Ima and Hamaca across town — not by following hoof prints but by going where people were looking. This took us around a corner to where a policeman had cornered Hamaca and Ima in an alley.

"A boy entered their corral and left the gate open," he said as I took hold of their halters. "You'd better secure it."

Twice I'd foolishly been too cheap to buy a chain and padlock — first after someone in La Tina turned cows in with my mares, then after a thief stole my belt from the gate of that hillside corral at Empalme. This time I didn't hesitate.

Once the gate was securely locked, I returned to the restaurant and found my table cleared.

"Did you by any chance, save my dinner?" I asked the owner.

"Since I should have," he replied, "I'll cook you a fresh one."

* * *

Kneeling in the shed beside Hamaca and Ima's corral I unrolled my sleeping bag, then left the door open so I could keep an eye on them.

Before long the policeman who'd helped me earlier looked inside.

"You should sleep in the empty cell at the police station," he told me. "It's not safe here."

"Thanks," I replied, "but I won't be able to see my horses from there."

"I'll watch over them," he said. "Don't worry. We'll leave your cell door open so you can come and go."

At daybreak I left La Toma with a new concern: altitude sickness. Conventional wisdom said I'd be okay up to ten thousand feet above the elevation to which I was acclimated. That had been sea level until recently. That day however, my mares and I crossed a pass above the safe margin.

We stopped to catch our breath more than usual in the oxygen-poor air, but suffered no ill effects and reached Loja's military fort that afternoon. The comandante read my letter from his counterpart in Macará and welcomed us.

For the rest of that day and all the next Hamaca and Ima rested.

* * *

Up at dawn I began the following day with an outdoor shower in icy seven-thousand-foot air. For days I'd undressed after dark and put my clothes back on before first light, unable to see my aching feet. They were covered with dried blood and huge, puffy blisters.

According to Albright's Theory on Pain, people remember that something hurt but can't recall the actual sensation. This is nature's way of helping us persevere when the going gets tough. And it's effective. I'm not sure I could've set out each morning if I'd been able recollect the previous night's discomfort.

After breakfast a sergeant loaned me an antiquated mechanical typewriter, and I spent hours writing letters and my first article for *The Peruvian Times*. These I mailed at the post office, then took my clothes for laundering and went shopping for hay and grain.

Loja's surprisingly modern feed store offered a reasonably priced grain and molasses mixture. I bought enough for the coming week, intending to send it ahead with cured alfalfa.

"The only alfalfa we sell is fresh," the clerk informed me.

"That will go bad," I said, "before I catch up with it."

"Don't worry. You can buy fresh alfalfa anywhere between here and Quito."

* * *

The Spanish word for endurance is *resistencia*, which I prefer because resisting is better than enduring. So far during my ride — or walk, take your choice — Hamaca and Ima had resisted well. They had a long way to go but had already covered more ground than my geldings.

True, they weren't being ridden. But without preconditioning they'd met every challenge, were in good flesh, and had adjusted to drastic changes in feed, water, altitude, and temperature.

Horses are poorly constituted for travel and don't easily tolerate change. And being prey they don't rest comfortably in unfamiliar places. Nonetheless Hamaca and Ima walked up to me every morning, eager to continue our trip. And at the end of long hard days they settled into new surroundings, ate what was available, and calmly fell asleep.

Would that continue when I started riding them?

20

TOO MUCH ENERGY

My mares were raring to go when we set out for San Lucas. At first I welcomed this evidence that my efforts to get them in condition were succeeding. But that morning they were like hyperactive children. They didn't walk, but danced, pranced, and pirouetted. Twice Ima caught a foreleg over the rope holding her to Hamaca's saddle, then went berserk until I freed it.

Not long after that, Hamaca began plunging. I looked back and saw that rope, now tightly clamped beneath the dock of her tail. Again and again both hind legs lashed out as I struggled to dodge flying hooves and lift Hamaca's tail. She was protesting—not trying to hurt me, but that was of little comfort.

Finally the rope came free and Hamaca stopped lashing out.

* * *

Along the road paralleling a river in Avalanche Canyon, my mares finally settled down. And not a moment too soon.

I'd been warned about that area's toxic plants. Not knowing what they looked like, I needed to make sure Hamaca and Ima didn't eat any vegetation.

My attention focused on yet another threat when watermelon-size boulders bounced across the road ahead and stopped among larger ones that had come downhill previously. After that I seldom looked away from the slope above.

It was almost impossible to predict where these slides would cross the road, and difficult to decide if I should stop, speed up, or turn back. Guessing wrong could have disastrous consequences — especially if my mares froze at a bad time or in the wrong place.

But all's well that ends well.

* * *

Beyond Avalanche Canyon, I saw Serrano women walking along the Panamericana. Most seemed to be amusing themselves with toys that combined the attributes of a yo-yo and a child's top. But they were spinning yarn, as I'd learned years earlier while observing Serranos in Peru from LuBette and Hillary's Jeep.

Speeding along in a distinctive gait, they dropped small rotating wooden spindles that revolved knee-high in midair, twisting wool fibers into yarn and rolling it around a dowel. This required extraordinary dexterity and would've been a fascinating nightclub act, provided George Jones was still looking for ways to make money.

The thought made me chuckle.

Serrano men were equally fascinating. In those days, their sandals had soles cut from tire treads and left what appeared to be vehicle tracks in unlikely places. Nowadays their descendants wear blue jeans and mass produced shirts. But back then they dressed in elaborate traditional outfits that varied from valley to valley.

Near San Lucas they resembled stereotypical witch doctors more than the one in a suit who'd treated Hamaca in Las Playas. Single pigtails hung to their waists. They wore black ponchos with matching knee-length trousers and leather chaps. Machetes in sheaths dangled from their wide leather belts.

Some may have spoken Spanish but if I greeted them, all remained silent, faces expressionless except for the eyes, which betrayed their considerable interest in Hamaca and Ima.

* * *

"You and your horses are welcome to stay the night," San Lucas's leading citizen told me. "But you won't find alfalfa here. You can get some from the American missionary in Saraguro."

I left Hamaca and Ima in his care and took a bus north. When it broke down, I caught a ride with a passing truck. This too was delayed by mechanical problems but reached Saraguro before dark. I set out for the mission on foot, asking directions along the way.

My host in San Lucas had spoken highly of the missionary, who soon showed me why.

"My field barely produces enough alfalfa for my needs," he told me. "I'll give you all I can spare and take you where you can buy more."

He introduced his wife—who seemed cut from similar cloth.

"What are you doing for Thanksgiving tomorrow?" she asked.

"Is tomorrow Thanksgiving?" I was surprised.

"It's easy to lose track of American holidays in the Andes," she said. "There are no reminders from radio, television, family, or friends. Can you get here in time for dinner?"

"Yes. Thank you."

Both medical doctors, she and her husband had forsaken America's comforts and financial rewards to establish a mission and clinic in the Andes. There they were raising a family and tending the physical and spiritual needs of the poor.

As we sat on their porch, waiting for the bus to San Lucas, I enjoyed speaking and hearing English as well as catching up on news from home.

The vehicle that took me back to Hamaca and Ima was custom-made and well-suited for Ecuador's highlands. Its front was a former school bus packed with Serranos. The rear was a truck bed that carried passengers' baggage—everything from firewood and baskets of produce to trussed-up poultry, pigs, and goats.

Feeling like one of the gang I put my alfalfa far from anything that might eat it, then found a seat. My fellow passengers—all Serranos—gave me the Andean silent treatment.

I reached San Lucas just in time for dinner with my host. He was as talkative as my fellow bus passengers had been the opposite. What he said was troubling.

"Your life is at risk, Señor," he began. "Broad daylight robberies are common here. Alone, unarmed, and with two desirable horses, you'll be an irresistible target."

"What precautions would you recommend?" I asked.

"I can't think of anything that will do much good. Traveling as slowly as you are, every bandit for miles will know you're coming. Lady Luck has been with you so far, but sooner or later she'll withdraw her favor."

* * *

After saddling Hamaca and Ima the next morning, I strapped on my Bowie knife for the first time since Piura. Crossing the mountains to Saraguro took us above ten thousand feet. Four hours after leaving San Lucas we reached the mission.

Thanksgiving had almost been just another day. But thanks to the missionary's wife I shared this very American holiday with some delightful countrymen. Because they kept their stallion in the mission's only corral, my mares spent that afternoon tied to a hitching rail beside the road.

As dinner was served, someone knocked on the door.

The missionary answered and a voice said, "One of the Señor's horses dropped something."

I hurried outside where Hamaca had finished her concentrado sooner than expected and removed her feedbag. After picking it up, I smiled, thanked my informant, and returned to the dinner table.

Three mouthfuls later, a second bearer of important information knocked. "One of the horses of the Señor is chewing its rope," another boy told the missionary.

I walked outside to find Ima mouthing her leadline, something she often did. It was wet with saliva but undamaged.

"Thanks for your concern, but she'll be fine," I said politely—no smile this time—and went back to my meal.

Soon another knock and a third bearer of fast-breaking news.

"One of the Señor's horses just stepped on the other's foot," a third boy told the missionary.

From the doorway I saw that all was well and ruffled his hair.

"Sorry for causing these interruptions," I told the lady of the house after returning to the table.

"Don't worry." She smiled. "They're just being sweet. They heard there's a tall gringo in town and are dying to see him."

"Well, if it doesn't bother you," I said, "it's okay with me."

Evidently the last boy brave enough to knock had now seen me, and we ate a tasty and familiar meal: turkey, stuffing, corn, mashed potatoes and gravy. True, the pimento-stuffed olives and cranberry sauce were missing, and there was neither football nor television on which to watch it. But otherwise we enjoyed a classic American Thanksgiving.

"We traditionally have everyone around our table list the blessings for which they're grateful," the missionary told me after dessert. "Would you like to start?"

"On this day," I began, "all my worldly possessions—except Hamaca and Ima Sumac—fit in two duffel bags. But thanks to the kindness of Latin Americans, I'm living the adventure of a lifetime, and courtesy of your wonderful family this has been a Thanksgiving I'll never forget."

I still wasn't comfortable expressing emotion, but was getting better at it.

* * *

Having seen the attention Hamaca and Ima attracted, the missionary chained his stallion to a post so I could put them in with him. There, behind a locked double door and inside high adobe walls topped with barbed wire, they'd be safe. To keep them away from the stallion, I tied them to trees.

The missionary, his wife, and I talked until bedtime. Then they showed me to my room in the mission's hospital, behind their house. I fell asleep soon after they left. Later, the seeds planted by my previous host sprouted, and a premonition of impending evil woke me.

The worst thing I could imagine was someone stealing my

horses. I made my way down a dark corridor to peer through the picture window overlooking the corral. Hamaca, Ima, and the stallion were where they belonged.

Later I was awakened again, this time by what I thought was a commotion in the corral. Another eerie walk brought me back to the picture window. Again I saw no apparent danger.

Starting to leave I was startled by gunshots. Easily visible through the glass I jumped to one side, making myself a less inviting target. Back pressed against the wall I peered through the window at an angle, to avoid exposing my head. A sky-rocket exploded in the night sky.

What an idiot I was. Those weren't gunshots. Someone celebrating something was setting off fireworks.

21

TSCHADES OF TSCHIFFELY

Morning dawned with my mares where I'd left them. I dressed and went outside. As the missionary unlocked and opened the corral's double door I saddled Hamaca, hoping to get an early start. With boys who'd gathered to watch looking on, I tied Hamaca to the tree again and went inside for breakfast.

When I came out, Hamaca was backed up to the still-chained stallion with my saddle rotated beneath her belly. The veterinarian at Sullana's cavalry fort had almost certainly been wrong when he pronounced her pregnant. But now she might be, and if so she couldn't enter the 1967 Tevis Cup Ride, a fundamental reason for my ride.

Having tied her with a knot that's virtually impossible for a horse to untie, I could only guess how she'd gotten loose. Perhaps one of the boys had seen the heart rope that kept her from pulling, and while trying to untangle Hamaca, had accidentally set her free.

One thing was certain. The young busybodies who'd re-peatedly interrupted my hosts' Thanksgiving dinner had sim-ply stood there and watched the stallion breed her.

* * *

On our way to Oña, the Panamericana would cross twelve-thousand-foot Carbonsillo Pass. At a similar altitude during the jeep trip Anne, Vicki, and I made with LuBette and Hillary, I'd suffered an extremely unpleasant attack of alti-tude sickness. I set out that morning dreading and fully ex-pecting a repeat.

The higher we climbed, the more my stomach growled and rumbled. All I could do was hope it was asking for more of what it had received during Thanksgiving dinner. Eventually however, my symptoms expanded to include a headache and flagging energy.

Above the timberline I saw my first Ecuadorian *páramo*. In English these are known as moors or high plains. They're reputed to be the lair of bandits. The one we were crossing was cold, rainy, and covered with hardy grass. Here and there I saw giant rosette plants.

I needn't have worried about altitude sickness or bandits. We made it across without misadventure, and as we dropped down to Oña I felt better. So apparently did Hamaca and Ima. All that remained of their mild symptoms were Ima's huge, jaw-contorting yawns, which had at first worried me but now added a comic touch.

To reach my mares' corral in Oña they had to descend an outdoor stone stairway made with quarried blocks similar to those used to build nearby medieval-looking houses. Horses find it difficult to go down stairs, but Ima was a notable exception. Hamaca however, scraped some hair from a rear pastern.

In the morning both easily went up the same stairs.

That day my frustration with the Panamericana's wandering ways came to a head. I was tired of winding east, turning west, and doubling back south when my goal was to go north. Long tempted to try the mule trail that intersected the highway and eliminated many of its twists and turns, I decided to do just that.

Few things are as easy as I anticipate, but the discrepancy had never been greater.

First my mares and I slid down a slippery channel worn into rock by countless hooves. Then I led them along a ledge nine feet up a sheer wall. Climbing back to the highway we struggled up steps with heights that varied from inches to over two feet.

Back on the Panamericana I estimated how many miles we'd bypassed. My most liberal guess didn't justify the risk taken or the effort expended. But maybe most of that trail's segments weren't as rugged. I tried another and by the time it rejoined the highway, I knew why they weren't called horse trails.

Near Zuzudel however, I saw a downhill shortcut—only slightly steeper than the Panamericana's long curve, but far shorter and free of channels, ledges, and stairs. It looked foolproof and I followed it. All went well for a while.

Then my mares and I slipped off the path in grease-like mud. We slid, legs locked, toward the top of a high cliff. I yanked a foot from the muck. Stamping it as deep as possible—heel first—stopped me. Then Hamaca slammed into me—hammering me closer. Next Ima crashed into Hamaca driving us farther toward a potentially fatal fall.

With cautious baby steps we tiptoed across the slick surface until on solid ground, then made our way back to the Panamericana.

No more shortcuts. Not under any circumstances. No matter how enticing. Period.

* * *

At Hacienda Zuzudel, I approached the main house and asked the owner, a pleasant gentleman named Esteban, if he knew where we might spend the night. As I'd hoped, he showed us to an adobe corral.

"Your horses can stay here if they don't mind sheep," he said.

"They've had quite an assortment of corral mates during our trip," I told him. "It doesn't bother them."

Hamaca and Ima rinsed out their mouths, but wouldn't drink from the trough. I drained, washed, and refilled it. That didn't help. The water had a sulfur smell, similar to burnt gunpowder. To improve its taste, I stirred a cup of their beloved molasses into a bucketful.

Ima sniffed this mixture and walked away. Hamaca took a hopeful sip, then opened her mouth, and let every drop drain on the ground.

"They'll drink when thirsty enough," Esteban assured me after bringing a wheelbarrow-load of cured alfalfa.

I sympathized with my mares after Esteban brought a cup of tea. Even after adding far too much sugar and lemon juice, I couldn't stomach it. My host apologized and offered a glass of milk he'd boiled as a precaution against tuberculosis.

Albright's Book of Useless Facts, page 1: "Boiled milk is far from tasty but infinitely superior to Zuzudel's water."

During a tour of his hacienda, Esteban showed me an adobe structure he said was two centuries old. If that was true, what we Americans would disdainfully call a mud hut had been in service since before our country's Declaration of Independence.

When I checked on my mares before going to bed they were so thirsty they'd stopped eating. I was reminded of Jorge Baca's pithy saying: "Livestock is fattened by water as much as by hay."

* * *

In the morning, eager to find Hamaca and Ima a drink, I set out after several cups of boiled milk and a plate of fried eggs.

We climbed like an airplane after takeoff, steadily gaining altitude until we were inside low-lying clouds. Later we emerged above a fluffy white sea under sunny skies. Around us, peaks protruded—looking like islands with foam lapping their shores.

This majestic scene disappeared as clouds rose to again wrap us in a bone-chilling embrace. Even after drinking little and exercising strenuously, I wasn't thirsty. I was however, concerned about Hamaca and Ima. They'd been twenty hours without water.

The sun had been a formidable enemy in Peru's deserts, but was a welcome friend in the Andes. Every time it appeared I stopped shivering. But when it passed behind clouds, even briefly, I was immediately cold and miserable. No wonder the Incas worshiped it.

That day's spectacular clouds were ever-changing. Some appeared fuzzy and soft. Others looked like frozen explosions. They huddled in valleys or drifted lazily above us, varied from wispy puffs to a single layer stretching from horizon to horizon, and—depending on how much water they carried—were pearly white, any shade of gray, or ominous black.

What I'd thought would be the next valley turned out to be a rugged canyon with a river raging along its floor crashing into spectacular rock formations it had carved.

Raised on one of the world's driest deserts, Hamaca and Ima had never seen water behave like that. Hesitant to get close enough to drink, they did so only after much coaxing.

Hamaca took a long time to drink her fill. Ima worked up the courage to take a sip, then lost her nerve and retreated.

* * *

"Because horses don't talk, read, or watch TV and movies, they don't know anything beyond what they've experienced."

I'd heard those words from O.M."Pat" Smith, the man who sold me my first horse and gave me my initial lessons in horsemanship. They came to mind again when large raindrops hit us with surprising force, leaving my mares puzzled and agitated. True to form, Ima tried to keep them away by swishing her magical tail until a massive cloudburst gave her a dose of humility.

In Alberta, Canada, where I now live, there's a saying: "If you don't like the weather, wait ten minutes." This accurately describes our journey to La Jarata. At times we were bathed in glorious sunshine while storms raged nearby, or vice versa. Wind came and went. Drizzles were abruptly replaced by water falling in sheets — not drops.

During one downpour I stopped Hamaca half-in and half-out of the rain, and sat turning my head back and forth to confirm this was actually happening.

Later, on a páramo for the second time, we spent the night in La Jarata, which turned out to be a collection of huts. One was abandoned and provided shelter for my mares.

At that altitude temperatures nosedive after sunset. Luckily

I'd brought Hamaca and Ima's blankets, which stopped their shivering but didn't improve the taste of La Jarata's water. Neither would drink it, which pretty much guaranteed they wouldn't eat well for a second consecutive night.

In another, larger hut I asked the owner/waiter/cook of a small, dirty restaurant to stop just short of burning my food, clinging to the hope that sufficient heat—applied long enough—kills most germs.

As I ate, the owner asked about my ride and interrupted my answer to tell me, "It's odd that you say *we* when referring to yourself and two horses."

I'd come to regard my mares as partners, not servants, and "we" seemed right to me. But to him, people and animals couldn't be described by the same pronouns.

With his stories of truckers shooting up his establishment fresh in my mind, I hesitated when invited to sleep there. But weary and unwilling to share my mares' tiny hut I said good night, then stepped into his back room and lowered myself fully clothed on his miniature—for me—cot.

No matter how I arranged myself under his small blanket, some body part was cantilevered and cold. I slept fitfully, re-peatedly wakened by arguing truckers. More than once I peered through a gap in the plank wall to make sure no one was armed.

Morning didn't dawn as much as it just showed up. After a short walk through murky gray fog, I found Hamaca and Ima shivering in their hut. They'd eaten their concentrado but less than half the hay, and had frozen dewdrops on their lashes, forelocks, and ear hair.

I honestly believe Ima was offended when I laughed. She turned her back and refused to look at me, but was enough of a lady to refrain from teasing me about the dewdrops in my facial stubble.

Most of that day's trip to Cumbe was above the timberline on land good for nothing but goats. We passed several flocks tended by dark-skinned shepherds whose staffs and flowing garb made me feel I'd wandered into biblical times.

* * *

In Cumbe I felt like an outcast. No one returned my greetings and few answered my questions. Worst of all no one would rent me a corral. I was turned away by private citizens, the so-called political chief, a hacienda owner, and finally the priest.

Beyond town I knocked on the door of a small farmhouse.

"Of course," the man who opened it said in response to my request. "You and your horses are more than welcome."

"Thanks," I sighed. "Your greeting was quite a contrast to my reception in Cumbe."

He shrugged on a coat, then picked up a lantern and led me into the dark night.

"Fate must have brought you here," he said when we reached an adobe corral.

He herded its occupants, two Andean deer, into a small chicken cage. Only about sixteen inches at the shoulder—but fully mature—they easily fit inside. While I lugged pails of water and emptied them into the corral's bathtub, our host dropped an armload of fresh alfalfa into the feed trough.

After a day and a half with little food and only one drink, Hamaca and Ima took a keen interest in both.

"Yes, I'm sure of it," the man said as he gave the deer a handful of leafy alfalfa stalks. "Fate guided you to me."

"Why do you say that?" I asked.

"A traveler on a journey similar to yours stopped here when I was a boy. In those days this was my father's farm, and the man spent a night with us on his way to North America. His horses stayed in this corral, and now it's my turn to be your host."

Was it possible that Hamaca and Ima were in a corral where Mancha and Gato — two of history's most famous horses — had spent a night?

"Do you recall the man's name?" I asked.

"Oh no, señor. It was peculiar and that was long ago. However one of his horses was named Gato."

"Was the other Mancha?"

"Yes, I believe it was. Do you know that man?"

"I know of him. His name was Tschiffely and he's world famous."

"And now you and your horses are recreating his ride."

I was proud of what we'd accomplished, but to mention our petty achievements in the same breath as Tschiffely's was blasphemy.

"Even if we succeed," I said, "Tschiffely, Mancha, and Gato went many times farther than we will."

"He was a man, and you're a boy." He patted my shoulder. "But you'll grow up fast on this journey, and one day you'll be satisfied with what you did."

I enjoyed being compared to my hero, and perhaps what my host had said was true. After our journey ended, maybe I'd be pleased with what we'd accomplished.

The night was still young when my sleep was interrupted... by what? I dozed off, then woke up again and switched on my flashlight. Its beam revealed the biggest rats I'd ever seen, scampering on the floor near my horse gear. I jumped out of bed and hung everything leather high above the floor.

This could be a historical moment I thought, chuckling. *Those may have been descendants of rats that once chewed Tschiffely's saddle.*

* * *

Ima was fit enough to start doing her share of the work, and the next morning I changed our line of march. So far she'd followed directly behind me, carrying the riding saddle I hadn't used since Piura. Burdened by the pack saddle's heavy cargo, Hamaca had been behind her, third in line and tied to a ring on the riding saddle.

After I switched their saddles I moved Ima to third in line because I didn't dare tie Hamaca to the fragile pack saddle, which had already broken twice. Hours later this change in their positions brought unintended consequences.

Surfaced with gravel everywhere else, Ecuador's Panamericana was paved with asphalt where it passed through populated areas. As I led Hamaca and Ima along its shoulder a mile outside Cuenca, it made this change once again.

Not long afterward a fast-moving car closed in from behind us, tires whining on the pavement.

Ima had never heard that sound. With steady, calm Hamaca no longer a buffer behind her, she charged onto the highway. The riding saddle's well-anchored ring held. Ima's leadline brought her up short. And the driver managed to miss her.

Beside the highway I switched my mares' saddles and returned Ima to her usual place between Hamaca and me.

In a residential area where the highway's shoulder was narrow I heard the roaring motor and screaming tires of a truck racing toward us at a speed that would've been impossible on gravel. Ima tried to look back at it, but her leadline was too tight. She infected Hamaca with her terror. They bolted onto the asphalt, and the truck came to a screeching halt.

Like most truckers I'd met in Ecuador, the driver I saw through the windshield was a good sport. He waved, smiled and though time was money for him, patiently waited as I fought to get my mares off the highway.

Now completely unhinged they charged past me on opposite sides, tearing the leadline from my grip. The rope connecting them caught me across the back and flung me to my knees. I leapt to my feet and chased them down the highway shoulder.

A pedestrian — arms spread wide — blocked their path across a front yard long enough for me to grab the dragging leadline.

"Can I do anything more?" he asked, staring at the bloody holes in the knees of my jeans as I led Hamaca and Ima off the lawn.

"Yes," I replied, handing him Ima's leadline. "Hold this horse for a moment please."

The best way to keep my mares under control would be to ride Hamaca. I swung aboard and, when more vehicles came, had no difficulty convincing her I was a worse threat.

Then I washed my throbbing knees and rope-burned hands with water from my canteen, thanked the man profusely, and continued on. Happy to be back in the saddle again, I decided to ride the rest of the way to Los Gatos.

22

COLD WAR SPIRIT

C uenca, Ecuador's third largest city, was founded in the mid-1500s on the ruins of an ancient Inca town in a beautiful forested valley. My destination there was the home of a well-known cavalry detachment, the Cazadores de los Rios, River Hunters. Loja's comandante had promised to arrange for us to rest with them for two days.

When I presented myself at the main gate, the guard said, "No one told me to expect you."

Slowly I worked my way up the chain of command, but met only blank stares from men eager to make me someone else's problem.

When I got to the officer of the day I explained, "I've come all the way from Peru."

Considering the tension between Peru and Ecuador I should've known better. His eyes narrowed with suspicion and he did what any good military man would, referred the matter to a higher authority.

In his office the post commander told me, "You'll have to get permission downtown."

An hour later I walked into District Command's headquarters, quite a sight no doubt — almost seven feet tall, a week's growth of beard, bloody holes in my jeans, Bowie knife hanging from my belt. I was treated with remarkable courtesy and granted permission to spend two days with the Cazadores de los Rios.

After Hamaca and Ima were comfortable and fed, my priority was to get as clean as possible. Hot water was out of the question of course, but at least this shower would be indoors and promised to be less frigid than the one I'd had outdoors at the fort in Loja.

It probably would've been if there'd been glass in the windows.

* * *

The next day I shopped, left my laundry for washing, planned my next itinerary, and sent grain ahead to my nightly stops. Back at the fort I borrowed a typewriter, then wrote letters to people back home and cranked out another article for *The Peruvian Times*.

As I finished, the post commander walked in.

"Will you be kind enough to join us at the officers' luncheon tomorrow," he said as I stood up and resisted the urge to salute. "It isn't often we have the opportunity to talk current events with someone from the States."

"You mustn't expect much from me," I cautioned. "I've been away from home for months."

"Your contributions to our discussion will be welcome," he said. "I look forward to them."

During that afternoon's trip to the post office, I was uneasy.

What could I possibly tell such educated men that they didn't already know?

The highly formal luncheon began amid silverware, linen napkins, and crystal glasses — with me dressed in my Levi's with no holes in the knees and wondering which fork to use first. Seated at the head of a table I was introduced and applauded, to my considerable embarrassment.

Next perspiring draftees rushed here and there serving a splendid meal. One took a liking to me, probably because I was clearly grateful for his efforts. The officers on the other hand, made demands, then barked harsh encouragement.

"Hurry. Fly like a rocket unless you want to wash dishes all night," I heard one tell his server.

After we ate, the *comandante* guided the discussion to its main subject, John F. Kennedy — who three years after his assassination, remained wildly popular from Mexico to Argentina.

The ensuing discussion touched on the Bay of Pigs, the Cuban Missile Crisis, Kennedy's civil rights record, the Peace Corps, and the Alliance for Progress. My few contributions seemed to please the commander.

After he retired to quarters, his subordinates took over.

"Do you think Jacqueline Kennedy will marry Señor Onassis?" one asked me.

"Do you think she should?" another probed, showing his strongest interest yet.

I'd never given that any thought, but it was clearly important to everyone else.

"To us it's unacceptable," one explained, "that the great John Kennedy's widow might lie in another man's bed."

Evidently that possibility offended their machismo a lot more than it did mine.

* * *

In Peru I'd forced myself to be courteous with reporters and photographers. In Ecuador I'd initially been grateful to be free of the time-consuming interviews and photo sessions. But by now I'd learned that without publicity, doors were often opened with suspicion or not at all.

In the absence of reporters chasing me I went to the offices of Cuenca's largest newspaper, *El Diario*. There a well-spoken young man asked questions and took photos. The next day his front page article about my ride concluded:

> *Before his visit to El Diario ended, the young North American asked me to express his gratitude to the many people of Ecuador who in one way or another have helped with his adventure. This country of ours is home to an exceptional people.*

During the following week I met some Ecuadorians who were indeed exceptional, but not in that reporter's flattering sense.

* * *

From Cuenca to Azogues, my ride along a relatively level road was all the more pleasant because I was no longer walking and my mares were relaxed. For the latter blessing I was grateful to the Cazadores de los Rios veterinarian who'd injected both with vitamin B to calm their nerves.

I'd been told I'd find people friendlier as I went north, but the ones I met that night in Azogues were the opposite. I had difficulty finding accommodations and my stay was marred by unpleasant episodes.

Hoping to enjoy a quiet meal I chose an empty restaurant/saloon. The area for drinking was three times the size of the one for dining, which should've been a red flag. By the time my food was served the bar was packed with university students. Staring straight at me, one began a loud anti-American speech protesting what he called Uncle Sam's economic imperialism in Ecuador.

Perhaps Heinz at Casa Grande had been right about our lack of popularity in Latin America. Eager to leave I chewed faster as the student's speech became a list of reasons the U.S. shouldn't be in Vietnam.

"A lot of Johnnies are dying there," he said, now glaring at me, "and they deserve it."

Acting as though I hadn't heard, I left my meal half-eaten but soon felt equally unwelcome outside, where foulmouthed guttersnipes made fun of my height. Their vulgarity troubled me, which made me a hypocrite because my own vocabulary had degenerated disgracefully.

It was a rare day when I didn't launch at least one spirited review of my worst bad words. But in private and not at the top of my voice.

On his ride Aimé Tschiffely had been briefly accompanied by a fellow rider he identified only as Mr. W., and he wrote this about the deterioration of their everyday language:

> *Most horsemen, horsebreakers, and openair men have a special vocabulary of their own. Now a horse did something wrong, again the pack slipped, the trail was rough, or a thousand similar things and happenings demanded suitable remarks at short intervals. I remember soon after we set out together Mr. W. giving me a moral lecture about my strong language, assuring me that if I thus continued I should become so used to this horrible,*

useless and degrading habit, that I should never be able again to mix with decent people.

When upset with myself after a tirade, I often sought consolation in Tschiffely's further comment:

Mr. W had not been long with me before he was very efficient in the use of my private vocabulary, and, thanks to his knowledge of the language, I was able to add a few very original and expressive words to my repertoire.

My next outburst came as I discovered I'd latched but forgotten to lock Hamaca and Ima's gate before going to dinner. It stood wide open and both were gone. I tracked them by asking if people had seen two loose horses and going where they pointed. By the time I caught up, my horses had been captured by two grim policemen who gave me a stern lecture.

A crowd gathered after I returned my mares to their corral and fastened the gate shut with my chain and padlock. These nightly gatherings at my mares' corrals had become my number one pet peeve. After their long hard days Hamaca and Ima needed to relax and eat. But they couldn't do either while surrounded by strangers and had to wait until everyone left — never earlier than 10:00 p.m.

Because of this they didn't finish dinner until about 11:00. Then somewhere between 3:00 and 6:00 a.m., we'd set out for the next town.

I felt an obligation to accommodate spectators and understood their curiosity. But every night they gathered, and unfailingly one would ask to see Hamaca's and Ima's stylish leg action. Hoping they'd leave if I obliged, I'd lead Ima, whose movement was spectacular, back and forth in gait.

If asked why I did this, I would've answered, "To stop people from yelling, waving their arms, and throwing pebbles to make my mares show their interesting way of going."

But if that was the only reason, why did I always choose Ima, who was more likely to impress? The answer of course, is in Marie Ebner von Eschenbach's memorable quote: "We are so vain that we care for the opinion of those we don't care for."

Weary that night in Azogues, I asked people to please leave us in peace. They didn't and in view of the town's anti-American bias I didn't press the matter. Nor did I demonstrate Ima's gait.

Before long two scamps crawled under the locked gate and chased my mares, fascinated by their forelegs' swimming motion.

"Please stop," I said.

Pretending not to hear, they continued.

I vaulted the fence, grabbed each by an arm, slung them over my shoulders, and carried both from the corral as they giggled with enjoyment. Then I set them back on their feet with enough force to take the fun out of it.

* * *

Every night in every town, people asked identical questions in the same words and sequence.

"Where are you going?"

"How far do you travel each day?"

"Where will you spend nights between here and Quito?"

I avoided specific answers in case they were gathering information for a robbery attempt. My stock answers were vague but usually satisfied them. However I never found an effective way to avoid further questions.

"How much did your horses cost?" was the most common.

"I don't remember," I'd respond.

"How much did the big one [Ima] cost?"

"I don't remember."

"How about the little one [Hamaca]?"

"I don't remember."

"More or less?"

"I don't remember. I don't remember."

"How much are you earning for this ride?"

"Nothing."

"Do you want to sell your horses?"

"No."

"Is the big one for sale?"

"No."

"How about the little one?"

"No."

"Will you sell your knife?"

"No."

"Do you have anything for sale?"

"Nothing."

Still the questions continued.

"Are you sure it's possible to go all the way to the United States on horseback?"

"How will you cross the ocean?"

"Why don't you use mules?"

"Why do you feed your horses *this*?"

"Why don't you feed them *that*?"

Their helpful observations came next.

"Did you know that horse is cut on the jaw?"

"Did you know the other is missing some hair on its leg?"

Answering was like trying to fold an octopus into a neat bundle. Every time I thought the job was done, another arm flopped out.

As soon as there were no more questions I was subjected to helpful advice. "The tall horse needs new shoes."

"You shouldn't travel so far every day."

"You should travel farther every day."

"Scraping them with that thing [curry comb] will make them sick."

These endless, pointless conversations were mind-numbing torture. Usually I answered politely, but when feeling less than cordial I'd tell people I was Russian. This simultaneously avoided giving my country a bad name and discredited our Cold War adversary.

* * *

Around midnight in my Azogues hotel, I was awakened by squeals and clicking toenails around the pile of horse tack beside my bed. Rats again. Unable to see in the dark I mustered the courage to feel the floor until my hand touched a boot, then used it to thrash the floor.

Unable to find my other boot and unwilling to expose a bare foot to sharp-toothed rodents, I leaned over and spread my gear until something scurried away. Quickly I jumped out of bed and flicked the light switch, then saw the intruders squeeze under the door of my room.

I plugged that gap with a saddle blanket.

23

STOP THE *AMERICANO*

A t first light with roosters crowing I said farewell to Azogues without regret.

From there the road climbed steadily, then dropped down to the quaint village of Cañar. Where the highway entered town, a teenage boy approached me. Not wanting him and his friends pestering my mares, I considered brushing him off. But he was shy, respectful, and soft-spoken.

"I'm Guillermo, Señor," he told me.

"I'm called Pablito," I said, stopping.

"I know. I read the article in *El Diario* and have been waiting for you."

"How'd you know when I'd arrive?"

"I didn't. This is my third day here. I wanted to be first to offer you a place to stay."

"I accept, with gratitude. Thank you."

Guillermo took charge with maturity and sensitivity beyond his years.

"My house has no place for horses," he explained, starting

down a side street. "I made arrangements for Hamaca and Ima Sumac to stay with my godfather. Follow me."

"You memorized my horses' names," I said, duly impressed.

We were in an above-average residential neighborhood and I was worried about the suitability of the arrangements he'd made for my mares.

Guillermo rang the doorbell on a wall beside a pair of double doors. Someone on the other side swung one open. Inside was a cobblestone-surfaced area, surrounded on three sides by a two-story house with a second-floor balcony. Hamaca and Ima would be safe, dry, and protected there.

"Welcome," the gentleman who'd opened the door said, pumping my hand vigorously. "I'll move my car and bring hay and water."

While I unsaddled, Guillermo's godfather noticed that Hamaca was about to lose a shoe. He sent Guillermo to bring a blacksmith, who re-nailed it for the equivalent of eighteen U.S. cents

* * *

By the time Guillermo and I walked to his house, I had no misgivings about leaving my mares. They were in good hands in a perfect place—except for the rather minor matter of those hard cobblestones.

Surprised when Guillermo introduced me, his mother glared at him when she thought I wasn't looking. Evidently his invitation had been extended without her consent, and she thought I was taking unfair advantage of her son's generous nature. I'd have offered an excuse and left if I could've done that without hurting Guillermo's feelings.

"Welcome," his mother said, recovering quickly. "Dinner's almost ready. Will you join us?"

"Thank you very much," I replied, "but I have another invitation."

Her relief confirmed my suspicion. She'd cooked only enough food for her family.

As I left Guillermo suggested we meet in an hour at the movie theater.

* * *

Standing near the box office when I arrived, Guillermo asked, "You ate at a restaurant, didn't you?"

"You," I countered, "didn't ask your mother if you could invite me, did you?"

He blushed. "I was afraid she'd say no."

Our evening was packed with simple pleasures. The girl selling tickets wouldn't let me pay. The American B-grade feature film was badly scratched after countless trips through projectors that would've been in museums back home. Finally the projectionist managed to sharpen the focus a bit, but he couldn't improve the distorted sound.

This brought protests from the audience.

"Why do they care?" I asked Guillermo. "The subtitles are Spanish."

"Yes, but we learn English by listening to American movies," he explained.

In the States people would've demanded refunds, but in Cañar the film was enjoyed despite its flaws.

Later, not wanting the evening to end, Guillermo and I strolled through town, talking and laughing with several of his friends. They were like young people in Olmos, poor but happy — a combination most Americans consider impossible. Our materialism gives us the world's highest standard of living, but we ignore abundant proof that it also makes us less happy.

Under dim streetlights, Guillermo guided me back to his

home. My mind free of the usual worries about Hamaca and Ima I slept deeply, then woke early and dressed, intending to slip away before Guillermo's mother felt obligated to prepare my breakfast.

I was too late. She was already in the kitchen cooking. Having read the article in *El Diario*, she'd concluded I wasn't an opportunist after all.

* * *

After I finished sweeping up the manure and leftover feed on his patio, Guillermo's godfather came to say goodbye.

"How much do I owe?" I asked.

"Nothing," he replied.

"The least I can do is reimburse you for the hay and grain."

"Forget it. Your money's no good here." Quickly he changed the subject. "By the way, if the *páramo* you crossed yesterday didn't cause you discomfort, you can stop worrying about altitude sickness. That's as high as Ecuador's Panamericana goes."

That day's ride from Cañar to Chunchi promised to be relaxing.

"It's only twenty miles," the agent at Cuenca's bus station had told me when I sent the coming week's concentrado ahead.

I hadn't believed Guillermo's friend who'd said Chunchi was much farther. But he'd planted a nagging doubt.

"How far to Chunchi?" I asked a Serrano standing beside the road outside Cañar. "

Aquícito no más... de la curvita pa' 'lla," he replied with an Andean Indian's high-pitched rhythm. "Just ahead...beyond the curve."

Serranos seem to consider it impolite to give discouraging news. When you ask the distance to a place, they typically select some feature — a bend in the road, upgrade, or gas station for example—and say it's a little beyond that. But they neglect to mention how far away the landmark is.

I asked a *cholo*, half-breed, the same question.

"Farther than a man can ride in a day," he replied.

After I'd gone an estimated twenty miles, everyone but Serranos still said Chunchi was far away.

On a positive note, Hamaca was covering miles effortlessly at high altitude, carrying two hundred and thirty pounds including my saddle. By nightfall we'd come what I estimated was thirty-five miles to a desolate *páramo* near Gun. I pressed on until I saw a house nestled against a hill.

When I asked the owner—a Serrano named Agapito—if he'd rent his corral, he removed a skinny cow, tied her to a post and said, "It's all yours for the night."

What I'd thought was hospitality turned out to be a commercial transaction, and he collected his fee up front.

"Can you also sell me some horse feed?" I asked.

"You and your horses will have to go hungry tonight, Señor," Agapito replied. "I have no food for them or you."

"It won't hurt me to miss a meal," I said, "but I have to find something for my horses."

"For a reasonable price I'll take you to a neighbor who can help."

Again he collected his fee in advance, then lit a kerosene lantern and guided me up the hill on a narrow trail. Barely half my size but accustomed to altitude and familiar with the steep, winding path, he was soon far ahead. I lost sight of him when the moon went behind a dark cloud.

Not sure I could trust Agapito, or find my way back to his house in pitch-darkness on an unfamiliar trail, I climbed faster, stumbling, eyes searching for his lantern's light.

Then with the pride that had kept me from calling out, I

hid my relief when I saw him and another man standing in the doorway of an adobe shack.

"This is Mauricio," Agapito shouted.

He was a few feet away but I barely heard him above the howling wind.

In the living room, which doubled as a general store, Mauricio weighed and sold me rye grass, along with the last of his rice flour. To further capitalize on my arrival, he took me to a room that doubled as a restaurant.

"I'll cook you a special dinner," he offered, "at a comfortable price."

Standing in front of a row of what looked like desks, each with one deep drawer, he opened them one by one so I could inspect his live guinea pigs.

"These were the favorite delicacy of the Incas," he said proudly. "Select one."

During my previous trip to Peru, Carlos Luna had shown me his project to develop larger guinea pigs at Lima's Universidad Agraria La Molina.

"I could never eat a creature that looks like a furry, harmless pet," I told Luna.

"They're like chicken," he assured me, "but much tastier."

"Snakes also are said to have a flavor similar to chicken," I informed him, "and I will never put one of those in my mouth either."

But my ride was after all, an adventure.

"Pick me a good one," I told Mauricio.

He did, then started a fire in a black iron stove and began working in its flickering light.

I didn't watch.

The dinner he set before me looked like what it was, a broiled rodent—all four legs sticking up like a cartoon rendition of Kentucky Fried Rat. True to Mauricio's word guinea pig indeed tasted like chicken, though to me it was less, not more, appetizing.

After paying my bill, I saw Mauricio give Agapito what must have been a referral fee.

Going down the hill, I had difficulty carrying my rye grass and burlap bag of rice flour. But Agapito wanted a tip to help, and I was weary of his never-ending raids on my limited funds.

At Hamaca and Ima's corral, sweaty and puffing, I was rewarded by nickers as they dashed toward me. They ate their hay enthusiastically but barely sampled the rice flour.

A few days earlier I'd sent my seldom-used sleeping bag ahead to lighten the cargo. That night on the hard dirt floor in Agapito's spare room, I shivered beneath loosely woven saddle blankets and woke feeling like the tin man after a light drizzle.

* * *

"You'll fall prey to bandits or be murdered if you continued on," Agapito warned as I left in the morning. "Busloads of people have been waylaid on the road ahead, and men capable of that won't be deterred by a lone man on horseback, no matter how big you are."

One can listen to only so many warnings before their accumulated weight takes effect, and his words filled me with foreboding.

In a brushy valley ideal for an ambush—and expecting one at any moment—I was startled by what I feared were gunshots. Oriental-sounding music echoed hauntingly.

With no birds in sight, I heard calls reminiscent of Geronimo's fierce Apache warriors. Worst of all, I felt the presence of men speaking the harsh Quechua language, but couldn't see them.

Wishing I'd increased my life insurance at the last option, I saw a procession of Serranos coming toward me on the highway. Faces solemn, they wore festive colors and carried a platform bearing a crude statue of Jesus on the cross. Respectfully I stood on the roadside with my suspicious mares and watched them pass.

Finally it dawned on me. Today was a religious holiday, which explained the sounds and activity. Most worshipers, male or female, were intoxicated or well on the way. The icons around the statue on the platform were a curious mixture, some with Catholic origins, others adopted from heathens.

For miles the carnival-like atmosphere continued. On a farm near the highway, a colorfully dressed family was plowing a field. Their oxen wore headbands with flags on sticks fanned out across the tops. Paper currency was pinned to cloths draped across their backs, clearly a plea to their gods for a successful harvest.

I stopped to watch.

"To take pictures, you must pay," one of the women called out, coming toward me.

"I'm only looking." I showed her my empty hands.

"You must pay," she insisted.

"But I'm only looking."

Quickly she removed the oxen's decorations, then ducked down behind them with her family to prevent me from stealing a photograph. If my camera hadn't been in a duffel bag I could've taken far more interesting photos than the posed one she'd tried to sell me.

The more participants drank, the rowdier—or more pathetic—their celebrating.

Eventually men who were so inclined became aggressive.

As I rode Hamaca and led Ima through a hamlet, a man on

a mule reversed course to follow us. This often happened with people on foot and usually meant the person wanted to talk. But this was different. Five men joined him, all riding small scrawny mules, wearing dirty suits, and inebriated. Instead of simply tagging along, they crowded close behind us.

In vain I looked for an army post or police station. Uneasy with riders pushing them, Hamaca and Ima sped up. At the edge of town the group's leader put his mule in a fast trot and came alongside me.

"I'm the Law," he declared, staring at my Bowie knife. "I have to see your passport and inspect your bags."

"Do you have anything to show your authority?" I asked without slowing.

"I'm not making a request," he replied sternly. "I'm giving an order."

"How do I know you have that right?"

"Señor, you must stop immediately."

"As soon as I see proof you're the Law."

We'd reached a stalemate. Obviously he couldn't prove his authority, and I wasn't about to be talked down off Hamaca. Besides, I had a feeling the other five would soon give up and go away. The one beside me, however, was another matter. His determination made me wonder if he might indeed be the Law.

But in nearly eight hundred miles, only border guards had asked to see my papers and even they hadn't inspected my duffel bags. Furthermore I'd slept in police stations without one such request. I was certain I'd regret letting these men go through my belongings.

Incessantly the Law droned on about international law and American imperialism.

When he referred to me as an *Americano*, I pointed out that most South Americans insisted I was a Norteamericano. He ignored my feeble attempt to sidetrack him.

"Stop and dismount," he ordered.

I kept Hamaca a few steps ahead, hoping he'd give up. Abruptly he spurred his mule, and it jumped between my mares. He grabbed Ima's lead rope and started to dismount, intent on searching my bags. By then his companions were surrounding me. I turned Hamaca to face him and untied Ima from my saddle.

"Show me proof of your authority now," I demanded, hoping he'd produce a convincing badge.

He didn't.

"Be careful," I shouted, jumping Hamaca toward him.

He recoiled, still holding the rope. I put slack in it by riding closer, then spun Hamaca and charged in the other direction. Rather than be jerked off his mule, he let go.

"Halt or be shot," he ordered.

I hadn't seen a firearm, but my spine tingled. When I looked back the Law and his men were in hot pursuit, their mules' short legs churning. They looked like chihuahuas in pursuit of greyhounds, but my predicament was hardly laughable.

Never having been galloped under saddle, Hamaca was difficult to control. Worse yet, Ima's packsaddle flopped and swayed, threatening to roll under her belly every time she launched herself and came to ground.

Comfortably ahead I slowed to a sobreandando gait fast enough to maintain our lead and also give the packsaddle a smoother ride. The mules still couldn't keep up, but Hamaca and Ima—unaccustomed to that speed and altitude—would soon tire. And if they didn't, some of our pursuers would detour down a mule trail and close the road ahead while the others blocked our retreat.

We came upon a crew repairing a section of road that had a sheer drop off on one side and a high embankment on the other.

"Stop him," the Law bellowed. "He's an *Americano*."

As I passed each worker I made eye contact, smiled, and greeted him with a cheerful, "*Buenas tardes*."

Pacified they kept working.

We sped past a group of workers clearing a rockslide.

"Stop him. He's an *Americano*."

The grader driver's head whipped around. My smile and wave momentarily disarmed him. Then he stepped on the gas. Sensing a threat as the huge machine drew even, Hamaca sped up. But it continued to inch ahead.

The driver cut his wheels and hit the brake, throwing his vehicle into a slide that would block the road. I aimed for the rapidly closing gap. Somehow we squeezed through before the grader crashed into the embankment. The driver was still attempting to restart it when I went around a curve and passed two teenage boys.

Farther along I looked back and saw them running after us, arms waving.

"Wait please," the older one shouted. "They gave up the chase when the driver couldn't restart his grader."

The packsaddle had slid back toward Ima's rump. I stopped and re-positioned it, then cinched it tight and kept going.

"My name is Rafael," the elder boy said when they caught up. "What happened back there?"

Expecting the Law to reappear at any second, I gave Rafael the *Reader's Digest* version without stopping.

"I live in Chunchi," he said, out of breath. "Would you like to stay with my family tonight?"

"Yes, thank you," I slowed down. "Do you think those men were really law officers?"

Both broke into laughter and I relaxed. Evidently there'd be no wanted posters offering a reward for my capture, dead or alive.

24

THE OUTSIDER

R ather than ride while Rafael and his friend were on foot I dismounted and walked with them. Not long after I stopped looking back over my shoulder to make sure no one was following, my companions started down a mule trail.

"This shortcut is much faster," Rafael said when I didn't follow.

"I already tried several of those," I told him. "They were hard on my horses. I'll stay on the road and meet you in town."

"This is an easy trail," he persisted, "and the highway goes several times as far."

I'd sworn to resist all temptations to try another so-called shortcut. But if the Law suddenly appeared in a commandeered dump truck I'd be safer there, no matter how difficult it was.

In Chunchi Rafael introduced me to a man who offered a corral and feed for Hamaca and Ima.

"When you finish," Rafael offered as I unsaddled and began my nightly routine, "I'll take you to my house."

"Will you please do me a favor?" I asked.

"Of course," he replied. "As long as it's in my power."

"While I care for my mares, please clear your invitation with your parents."

"I'm on my way," he said, turning to go.

I'd finished my chores by the time he returned.

* * *

It was immediately apparent Rafael's mother and father hadn't been home when he'd arrived to ask if I could stay with them. But the story of my run-in with the Law had already reached Chunchi. Both his parents had heard it and instantly warmed to me.

"Your friend the Law," his father greeted, "is a self-appointed vigilante and a well-known bully. Since there are no state sanctioned officers where he lives, he spends most of his time bossing people around. He was long overdue for a comeuppance."

Dinner was already on the stove, and when I saw there wasn't enough for a fourth person, I declined their invitation and ate in a restaurant.

When I returned, Rafael's father asked, "Are you up for some conversation?"

"Always," I replied.

"I'll ask if Rafael wants to join us. He's upstairs."

Moments later he tiptoed down the staircase and quietly told me, "You have to see this. Rafael is in your room, acting out his version of your escape from the Law."

I crept up to the second floor and peeked into the room where I'd sleep that night.

Wonderfully typical of boys his age, Rafael — my Bowie knife in one hand — was galloping around, pretending to be on horseback fending off attackers. Quietly I returned to the landing.

"Rafael," I called from there, "would you care to join your father and me in the living room?"

"Yes, right away," he replied.

Good. I was flattered by his hero worship but didn't want to leave him with the impression that violence was acceptable — except as an unavoidable last resort.

"I think I'll stop wearing my Bowie knife," I told his father as Rafael joined us. "Truth be told, it's probably an invitation to thieves, and someday someone will probably try to take it from me, causing the very problem I'm trying to avoid by wearing it."

Understanding my comment's purpose, Rafael's father subtly helped me stay on that subject long enough for both of us to emphasize our objections to violence in any but dire circumstances.

That night Rafael slept on the living room couch so I could have his bed, where I slept well enough to justify his sacrifice. I woke up with the aches and pains inflicted by Agapito's dirt floor diminished to where I could finally dismiss them from mind.

"I went to the market earlier," Rafael's father told me during breakfast. "An amazingly accurate version of your escape from the Law has reached at least as many people as it would have from our newspaper's front page."

As I rode through Chunchi on my way to Alausi, I was congratulated by strangers who knew almost as much about my escape as I did. Later on the highway, the driver of a dump truck did a double take, then parked on the shoulder and threw his door open.

"I was part of the road crew you passed yesterday," he said, smiling as he jumped out. "After that grader failed to stop you, the Law ordered me to help him continue the chase. I of course, refused. When he and his drunken friends tried to forcibly commandeer my truck, they found out that I have many friends."

All that morning pedestrians showered me with praise as I passed, and people in vehicles stopped long enough to do the same.

"You showed those cretins they can't bother people anytime they get the urge."

"I'm glad you put them in their places."

"Others will stand up to them now that you've done it."

I hadn't stood up. I'd run away, but why parse words? I was a hero and might as well enjoy it.

* * *

In Peru I'd often set out before dawn in order to reach destinations before the worst heat. In Ecuador I began doing the same to avoid torrential late-afternoon rains. So far I hadn't been caught in one and I was ready later that day when my luck ran out. I'd bought an extra large, rubber-coated poncho while my packsaddle was being repaired in Catacaos, Peru.

A few miles short of Alausi, sheets of rain began falling and that garment proved to be an excellent investment. Long and wide it discharged runoff below my boots as I rode, leaving me warm and dry. But Hamaca and Ima were drenched. As we entered town, the deluge worsened.

"It just so happens I have the only one here," Alausi's Chief of Police said after I asked where I might find a covered stall. "It's behind the station and you're welcome to use it."

The stall was in excellent repair, but the floor—raised to keep runoff outside— was surfaced with small stones. This uncomfortable surface would prevent Hamaca and Ima from lying down. Nonetheless they'd be far more comfortable than any of that area's other horses.

"One of my cells is vacant," the Chief offered after my mares were as comfortable as I could make them. "You can sleep there."

"If it's not too much trouble, I—"

"No trouble at all," he interrupted gruffly. "Let's get some dinner."

In a nearby restaurant, the waiter stopped waiting on customers who'd arrived before us and immediately brought our meals. As we ate, the Chief proved to be a skilled conversationalist— intelligent, and well-informed. He even knew about my escape from the Law.

When he requested our check the waiter said, "Compliments of the house as always, *Jefe*."

I tagged along during the Chief's nightly rounds and soon tired of the bowing and scraping that began when he came on the scene. I assumed he disliked it as much as I did, but slowly realized that what I saw as toadying, he saw as respect. One of the most entertaining men I'd ever met, he was also a tin god who used power for his own ends.

Like the stereotypical southern police chiefs in American movies, he went from store to store—occasionally picking up an item he liked and asking its price.

The answer was always the same. "Free of course, for you Jefe."

He saw this coerced generosity as his due and invariably responded with a listless, "*Gracias*."

While I did my shopping, he stood outside unseen until a price had been quoted.

"What? How much?" he'd bark, suddenly appearing. "This gringo is my friend. You can't charge him tourist prices."

Instantly the price plummeted to what local residents paid. Not satisfied, the Chief would beat it down more. I'd never paid such low prices and was grateful he wanted my approval enough to go to all that trouble.

In most South American shops merchandise had a variety of prices. From lowest to highest, they were for: friends and family, local residents, strangers, and foreign tourists. Getting the best possible deal involved a great deal of haggling, an art I was still trying to master.

One couldn't lower outrageous prices harshly because that stung shopkeepers' pride, which was stronger than their greed. They didn't like being bullied any more than I liked having them take advantage of me. It was necessary to talk them down without ruffling any feathers. I had also learned that if initially unsuccessful I should walk away slowly, giving sellers time to reconsider.

With the Chief around, however, all I had to do was wait for him to intervene on my behalf.

* * *

Between Alausi and Guamote we crossed Palmira, which I'd been told was Ecuador's most distinctive *páramo*. There at over eleven thousand feet, I rode into what seemed like a chilly, out-of-place desert. But what looked like sand was fine volcanic cinder — jagged particles that interlocked in ways sand can't.

Howling winds constantly piled and carved these into fantastic, sometimes bizarre shapes. The landscape changed little from one day to the next, but what I saw that afternoon was very different from what I would have seen a few months earlier.

Nothing on Palmira happened half-heartedly, and that afternoon nature displayed a variety of moods. In mere minutes bright, sunny afternoon skies filled with boiling dark clouds that rumbled with ominous thunder. Then bolts of glowing lightning branched out as they raced downward to touch the ground, briefly linking earth to sky.

Next a powerful thunderstorm dropped water in formless masses that might well have been poured from gigantic pails. My mares trudged into Guamote — heads lowered, ears back, and eyes narrowed to slits. The best I could do was pull down my hat brim, and even then it provided little protection from the almost horizontal, windblown rain.

Finding and renting a shed for Hamaca and Ima should've been easy because people had been driven indoors. But few answered when I knocked.

Finally with my mares safe, dry, and fed under a thatched roof, I rented a hotel room — which suggests carpets, drapes, telephone, television, a pool, and maybe a nightclub. But for a dollar these tiny rooms offered dirt floors, pegs instead of closets, small worn-out beds with prickly blankets, and a single bathroom shared by all the guests.

Except for Palmira the geography between towns had settled into a predictable pattern. From a small village near a river in a valley, the highway would climb a mountain, crest a *páramo*, and drop into another valley. There it would cross a similar river, pass a familiar looking village, and head up a mountain almost indistinguishable from the last.

With hay and grain now available everywhere, I could stop almost anywhere. Ideally I would've spent every night in one of those warm valleys. But I usually reached them long before sunset and — if it wasn't raining — gave in to the temptation to try for the next valley.

Too often I ended up on cold mountaintops where the scarcity of flat land forced farmers to build houses on stilts and plant crops on hillsides. The peasants were quite a sight, patiently following their oxen straight up or down steep slopes with no regard for contour plowing, terraces, or erosion control.

* * *

In Cajabamba I settled Hamaca and Ima in the back room of a small hardware store, then strolled plank sidewalks beneath overhanging balconies. The whole town looked like a movie version of America's Wild West, an impression strengthened when a coal-burning engine pulled an ancient train into the railroad station.

Standing among colorfully dressed Indians, I watched it come in belching steam with appropriate sound effects. I might as well have been a character in a Western movie. All I needed was a six shooter, a damsel in distress, and a catchy title—for example: *Gunfight at the Guamote Corral, High-Altitude Noon, From Road Grader to Eternity, The Magnificent Six & Their Subpar Mules, Gone With the Rain,* or *The Lone Gringo.*

George Jones would finance it, and we'd use Andean music for the soundtrack. I had suggested that haunting panpipe music when George asked about Peruvian products to sell in the States. He'd have done well to take that suggestion because Quechua music eventually became quite popular.

But he and I had found it repetitive and mournful, an opinion we shared with Baron Alexander von Humboldt, a legendary German naturalist who in the early 1800s had written:

Ecuador's people are the strangest in the world. They live in poverty on mountains of gold, sleep tranquilly at the foot of volcanoes, and cheer themselves with sad music.

The attire of Serrano men continued to vary. Near Cañar they'd worn black trousers, short sleeve black coats over long sleeve white pullover shirts, and low-crowned, narrow-brimmed felt hats resembling World War I English helmets. Around Cajabamba, most dressed in red pants and ponchos, hats of the Tom Mix cowboy variety, and woolly sheepskin chaps.

Many had slings for hunting. Others carried a flute, held in place rifle-style over one shoulder by a leather strand. Untying one end of this changed a musical instrument into a whip for driving livestock.

The Incas never invented the wheel and almost five centuries after the Spanish conquered them, their Serrano descendants seemed to have a genetic predisposition against its use. They transported even extremely heavy loads on their backs. I had once seen one carrying a perfectly good wheelbarrow that way.

"Is it broken?" I asked.

"No, Señor." He lowered and rolled it a few feet, then put it on his back again and continued on.

The firewood Serranos used for cooking and heating was their most common cargo. Trees around their villages had been cleared and journeys to where more could be found were the women's responsibility. I often saw young girls carrying impressive loads of this fuel and leading toddlers by the hand, already training for their bleak futures.

Serranos lacked my sense of modesty and often took care of personal business in public. Men simply turned their backs. Women fluffed out their full, ankle-length skirts before squatting in a field, and were similarly casual when suckling babies.

At the bottom of Ecuador's ethnic totem pole, these Indians were often exploited. But I never saw them treated nearly as badly as blacks in America. Due to my light skin they assumed I was important and always stepped aside to let me pass. Initially I'd stopped and signaled for them to go first, but I'd discontinued that because it made them uncomfortable.

When speaking to me—which not many did—they addressed me as *jefe* (leader), or *patrón* (boss). If I asked to be called by name, they unfailingly replied, "As you wish, Jefe."

* * *

Near Riobamba the highway ran between fields planted with orderly rows of maguey, then descended into a green valley ringed with craggy snow-capped peaks and at least one inactive volcano. Seeing happy families outside beautiful homes on my way into town, I started thinking about life after my ride.

Would I ever own a house? Would living in it be worth what I'd have to do to pay for it? Where would I work? Would I marry again as Anne had? Would my children and I reunite? My son Scott had been too young to remember me. But my daughter Vicki and I had been extremely close.

She might be interested in a relationship when old enough to be told the man raising her wasn't her natural father.

From porches and yards, residents stared as I rode past. I felt like an outsider—not just from their points of view, but from mine.

25

THE LAST TRUE GENTLEMAN

I'd been more than pleased with Hamaca's recent perform ance. She'd carried me from Cuenca to Riobamba at altitudes three to five thousand feet higher than the highest point on the Tevis Cup trail and seemed to get better by the day. If she continued to improve I just might have an endurance horse on my hands.

She'd earned our coming two-day rest with the Riobamba cavalry and so had I.

In a clean, bug-and-rat-free fort I took full advantage of its cafeteria where I ate tasty healthy meals...the private room where I slept in both mornings...and frequent opportunities for intelligent conversation with officers. I even took hot — yes hot — showers.

Life was good except for my concern that a sentry might shoot me, a notion that took root because one almost did. It happened my first evening there as I returned from the stable after looking in on Hamaca and Ima.

"Halt. Who goes there?" a stern voice demanded.

The sentry's challenge seemed silly. He'd inspected my pass no more than fifteen minutes earlier. My height made me easy to recognize, and I was clearly visible under bright floodlights.

"Halt or be shot." He raised his rifle to his shoulder.

This wasn't the same sentry. Instantly I stopped and raised my hands, trying to look harmless and nonthreatening.

"Show your pass," he demanded.

I did and he relaxed.

The fort's sentries were frequently rotated and it seemed a stranger was on duty every time I checked on my mares. Normally impatient with delays, I never again failed to stop and go through the whole by-the-book routine.

That afternoon the post blacksmith checked Hamaca and Ima's shoes and nailed on eight new ones without charge. Being iron, Ecuador's horseshoes needed frequent replacement, but I'd declined Joe Gavitt's offer to send steel ones. Packages to South America were subject to taxes, and often didn't arrive. Not to mention that so far, iron shoes and their installation had been free.

* * *

During my second day in Riobamba, Sergeant Wilfredo Santiago's eyes lit up whenever he saw me, and I knew why. He was in charge of the post basketball team and having played in high school and college, I was familiar with the way coaches react to my height.

I'd had no interest in that sport before I was hounded into trying it. In junior high I was terrible. After I made the high school team my father tried to motivate me by explaining how proud he'd be to see a headline saying, "Albright Stars as Reno Wins." Finally in my senior year I generated an acceptable substitute: "Albright Hits 30 as Reno Huskies Beat Carson City."

Seven years later in the Riobamba Cavalry mess hall on another continent, Sergeant Santiago sat down beside me and proposed a comeback.

"Our team and another are tied for first place," he said, "and tonight we meet for the second time this year. The other team won the first game by bringing in an outside player. With your help I hope to return the favor."

I hadn't played for years and was hesitant, but he made it impossible to decline. With a sense of foreboding, I agreed to become an Andean ringer.

"I'll put a jeep and driver at your disposal," Santiago said, "so you can finish your chores and errands in time for an early dinner before the game."

This only increased my self-imposed obligation to play well.

"When will we practice?" I asked as we finished our lunches.

"We play to enjoy ourselves," he replied casually, "and practice is work."

"I haven't touched a basketball for years. I desperately need some practice."

"You're taking this too seriously." He winked and patted my back.

* * *

Shortly before the game, the team and I — wearing basketball uniforms under our clothes — went to Riobamba's outdoor court. Inside a high adobe wall, crude bleachers held only a fraction of the people in a standing-room-only crowd.

"Looks like basketball's popular in Riobamba," I whispered to Santiago.

"Not this popular," he said with a shrug. "We've never had such a big crowd. They came to see you."

Oh, great. Just what I needed to calm my nerves.

The team and I stripped off our street clothes in a corner and warmed up. The packed dirt playing surface was rough and the ball did things it wouldn't have on hardwood. On the other hand the court was about half regulation length, something I welcomed at that altitude.

When the game was underway I soon discovered that basketball, like riding a bicycle, is a skill that gets rusty but doesn't go away. With my unfair size advantage, scoring was too easy.

If the Riobamba Cavalry is going to seize sole possession of first place tonight, I told myself, *my teammates will have to do the scoring.*

For the rest of the game I snagged rebounds and passed the ball, but didn't shoot it. After the final buzzer, I celebrated the lopsided win as enthusiastically as anyone on our team.

* * *

In Riobamba no crowds had pestered my mares. Each had a roomy, well-bedded stall where she could lie down, and troopers brought them alfalfa on demand.

Nonetheless they didn't seem to enjoy that stopover nearly as much as I did. Every time I went to the barn they stood, heads protruding over their stall doors, eager to go someplace more interesting.

They were more than ready the morning we set out again. As for me, I left Riobamba's luxuries refreshed and ready for the week-long trek to Quito.

The first day we traveled to Mocha, with Chimborazo — a spectacular twenty thousand plus foot, snow-covered volcano — in view. I was in high spirits and when no one was around to hear sang at the top of my voice.

That afternoon an opportunity to do a good deed made the

day memorable. On a stretch of highway cars, trucks, and buses were swerving to miss something on the road. When closer I realized traffic was skirting a motionless Serrano, prone on the roadway. Determined to prevent a tragedy I tied Hamaca and Ima to a nearby tree.

With no vehicles in sight I hurried to where the man lay — breathing deeply and as far as I could see, unhurt. When rolled onto his back he reeked of urine, alcohol, and nauseatingly bad breath. Instantly I knew why he was receiving no sympathy. He was disgustingly filthy and so drunk he didn't stir as I slid him off the highway.

By the time I'd dragged him out of harm's way and into the shade of a tree, I could almost feel germs crawling up my arms. I backed away resisting the urge to wipe my hands on my pants until I'd thoroughly scrubbed them with lye soap and water from my canteen.

Alcoholism was epidemic among the Andes' native peoples. I'd often seen Serranos who'd overindulged and passed out, sometimes in groups that looked like battlefield casualties. But like everyone else, I'd passed them by.

Later I came upon another traffic hazard, a bloated mule dead on the roadside, presumably after eating toxic plants.

"Look carefully," I ordered a puzzled Ima in my sternest voice. "That could happen to you if you don't do as I tell you."

She didn't understand of course, but being a natural born comedienne she knew looking worried was the correct response.

* * *

The next day after passing a line of stopped cars, trucks, and buses on the Panamericana, I saw the reason for this latest Andean traffic jam. A landslide had closed the highway and the crew clearing it was working with no visible sense of urgency.

People in vehicles could wait or turn back and since the road wouldn't be open anytime soon, most were turning back. But Hamaca, Ima, and I had a third option. We could try to go around the slide, bypassing it on the uphill side. If we succeeded the time saved would be worth the effort, and since I'd have to lead my mares I dismounted.

With every step uphill in soft dirt, we slid backward losing most of our progress. Soon winded we rested, then clawed our way higher with gravity working against us. But we made gradual progress and eventually reached a narrow footpath that led back to the highway beyond the landslide.

Slipping off that path would mean sliding into a jagged jumble of sharp-edged rocks. But the alternative was to spend that night and at least two more days waiting for the road to be cleared. The choice was easy.

Back on the highway we passed a seemingly endless line of stopped vehicles pointed in the opposite direction from those we'd left behind. We had avoided a long wait, but one of Ima's fetlocks was cut and swollen. She wasn't favoring it so we pushed on, and by the time we reached Ambato the swelling was gone.

In early December that fair city was awash in Christmas spirit. Windows in residential districts framed trees hung with handmade ornaments and often lit with candles instead of electric lights. Nativity scenes too were handmade—each distinctive and to me, more appealing than the mass-produced, store-bought variety.

Shops were full of handcrafted one-of-a-kind gifts. The one I most admired was a small, exquisite woodcarving of an old-fashioned high-top shoe with a mouse perched on the toe next to a hole, obviously its handiwork. My finances limited me to admiring it, but on a subsequent trip to Ecuador, I bought a similar carving I've owned for over a half century.

Ambato's Christmas spirit reminded me that even for the adventurous, life's routines can be pleasant and comforting.

In the mood to see a movie, I made a fortunate choice. For more than three hours *Doctor Zhivago* transported me to a world where I identified with Zhivago's passion for writing and fell in love with both Laura and Tonya, the women in his life. Because I was lonely and David Lean's directing was extraordinary, that movie affected me like none I'd ever seen.

In those days—before CDs and reruns on television—I'd never watched a movie more than once. But I would enjoy *Doctor Zhivago* in theaters three more times, and it was my all-time favorite motion picture until I saw another timeless love story, *Out of Africa*, twenty years later.

* * *

Near Latacunga the next day a Ford Bronco stopped on the highway's opposite shoulder. The driver, a man near my age, got out, delighted to see me.

"You must be Verne Albright," he said in English, with perfect pronunciation and no accent.

"I am," I replied, surprised he knew my given name. I'd been Pablito for months.

"I'm Gustavo Moncayo," he told me.

I dismounted to shake his extended hand and asked, "Are you American?"

"We Ecuadorians consider ourselves Americans." He grinned. "But South Americans."

"How did you know my name?"

"I have shortwave radio. I know everything that's happened since you left Chiclayo."

In Lima members of the Asociación had discussed the possibility of setting up a network of so-called hams to follow my progress. But that had been the last I'd heard.

"You're the first ham I've met so far," I told Gustavo.

"The first one you knew was a ham," he corrected. "To me it's unbelievable you rode into the Andes without setting up a network to help in case of emergencies. That would've been my highest priority."

"I doubt there were any radio operators where I've been."

"We're everywhere," he said. "I'll prove it if you stay at my hacienda tonight."

"I'd love to."

"Great. My place is off the highway." He pointed to a nearby farm. "To save your horses a side trip I'll arrange for them to stay there."

Once Hamaca and Ima were settled for the night, Gustavo drove me on a dirt road that soon forced him to switch to four-wheel drive. His brand-new Bronco had every accessory I'd heard of and a few I hadn't.

I pointed to the dashboard's shortwave radio and asked, "Is that how you followed my ride?"

'No," he replied. "I did that on the more powerful equipment at my hacienda. I'll give you a demonstration tonight."

After dinner I was the guest of honor as Gustavo pursued his favorite hobby. His equipment filled two shelves in a small room where we sat while he contacted radio operators in the States. Familiar with American slang he used it freely.

I smiled when he told someone his handle was Gus, after which he passed along a bit of information about my ride and handed me the microphone.

More conversations with strangers about my ride were the last thing I wanted. Sensing this, Gustavo waited until I signed off, then asked, "Would you like to talk with some of your friends and family?"

International phone calls were expensive in those days, and I hadn't spoken with anyone in the States since I'd left.

"I'd love that," I said, "but none of them have shortwave radios."

"No problem. Who would you like to talk to and where does he or she live?"

"My mother. She lives in Reno, Nevada."

"What's her phone number?" he asked, then wrote it down and asked, "Who else?"

"Joe and Pat Gavitt," I paused, then added, "and George Jones. I don't know their phone numbers."

"No problem, my friend. That's why phone companies have information operators."

For hours Gustavo patiently searched the airwaves for hams located near the people to whom I wanted to talk. When he found one—a man near Reno—he said, "I have a young guest who's riding horses from Peru to California. Would you by any chance be willing to put through a phone patch call so he can talk to his mother?"

"Yes, of course," came the reply. "What's her phone number?"

After giving it Gustavo asked, "Is that a long distance call for you?"

"I'll gladly pay the charges," the man replied. "Please be patient. I'm new to this. It'll take a few minutes to connect my radio to my phone and patch the call through."

Being a traveling salesman, my father was, as usual, on the road. I was his illegitimate son and when he'd married the woman who raised me almost single-handedly, she'd become my mom. I hadn't known I also had a natural mother until I was nineteen and needed my birth certificate. I was applying for a passport at the time. It arrived while I was at work, and Anne opened the envelope.

"Your mother's not your mother," she told me when I got home.

"What are you talking about?" I asked.

"She's not your mother," Anne repeated. "The name on your birth certificate isn't hers."

She wasn't my *only* mother, but she was my *real* mother. I loved her and I called her that long ago night to tell her I was grateful for all she'd done for me.

Mom held high hopes for me, but we had very little in common. She didn't share my love of adventure or see how a horseback ride would help me start a career. And my interest in South America and horses hadn't come from her side of the family.

The conversation Gustavo arranged that night—the first mom and I'd had in months—was full of disappointing small talk that couldn't possibly have been any more satisfying for her than for me.

"Have a Merry Christmas and be careful," she said when neither could think of anything else to say.

"I will, mom," I told her. "You too."

"Bye, Vernie."

"Bye, mom."

There was so much more that could've been said that night and in the letters I'd written during my ride. But I never knew how she'd react to my thought and dreams, and the details I'd sent to the Gavitts and George Jones had made their letters pages longer than hers. My best adventures—especially my escape from the Law—would've worried her.

After she and I hung up Gustavo persistently searched for radio operators near the Gavitts and George Jones. Eventually he found some close enough that both calls were free and therefore within my budget.

Both of those conversations exceeded my fondest hopes.

Pat's excitement about riding Hamaca in the Tevis Cup was contagious. Her questions came in a torrent, and she was clearly worried I might not reach Los Gatos in time. Equally enthusiastic, Joe asked for the information he needed to enter Hamaca in that event before its deadline.

Before hanging up, George Jones, true to character, told me, "Keep your eyes peeled for things that might have commercial possibilities in the States."

* * *

The following morning Gustavo opened a copy of the book that had made Charles Darwin famous, *Voyage of the Beagle.* "Read this," he said, pointing to a paragraph that read:

> *A horse is not considered perfectly broken till he can be brought up standing in the midst of his full speed on any particular spot, for instance on a cloak thrown on the ground, or until he will charge a wall, and rearing scrape the surface with his hooves.*

"Those words," Gustavo explained, "describe a demonstration Darwin saw in South America during his HMS *Beagle* voyage. The horses were schooled by a master trainer from Spain. Would you like to see horses trained that same way by a modern-day Spanish master?"

Certain of my answer he'd already arranged a demonstration. After a cross-country jaunt that required four-wheel drive from beginning to end, we were treated to an exhibition of two Spanish high school horses at a neighboring hacienda. The riders were Ecuadorian peasants, also trained by Spanish masters.

The maneuver that most impressed me was the *capriole*, developed for hand-to-hand cavalry engagements. Facing each other, the horses jumped straight up—forelegs drawn in to protect them—then lashed out horizontally with both hind legs before landing exactly where they'd taken off. In actual combat those kicks would've devastated anyone in their paths.

Next, Gustavo drove me to the farm where Hamaca and Ima had spent the night.

After I'd saddled them, he asked, "How far will you go today?"

"Lasso," I replied.

"I'm going there now," he said, getting into his Bronco, "I'll arrange for you and your horses to stay with a friend."

I was halfway to Lasso when Gustavo, now on his way home, stopped and gave me directions to his friend's farm.

"If your greeting there is somewhat unconventional," he cautioned, "it's because there have been some outbreaks of hoof-and-mouth disease in Peru."

Lethal and highly contagious, that incurable ailment affects cloven-hoofed animals. It begins with painful blisters in the mouth and between the hoof segments—followed by lameness, foaming at the mouth, and death by starvation. Back then the discovery of a single affected animal called for immediate destruction of its entire herd, to prevent the virus from spreading.

"My friend is concerned and rightly so," Gustavo explained, "because horses can carry the virus even though it doesn't affect them."

* * *

That evening's host met me at the entrance to his farm, accompanied by employees with buckets of liquid, sponges, and sour expressions.

"This mixture kills hoof-and-mouth virus," he told me crisply.

His men examined Hamaca and Ima's hooves, then thoroughly scrubbed those and their bodies with a vinegary-smelling solution. Next, my saddle, bridle, halters, belt, and boots were submerged in a container of the same liquid.

"Leather products can carry the virus," my host explained. "We'll have to dip your wallet also."

Thinking he was joking I asked, "May I please remove my photos and currency?"

After careful consideration he replied, "Yes, I suppose so."

He was the most thorough Latin American I'd ever met, and his social skills implied that he'd once been a Prussian general, which he hadn't. He was never unkind to me, but obviously considered my ride frivolous and seemed to regret having agreed to host me and my mares.

* * *

Both Hamaca and Ima cringed when I touched them the following morning, a consequence of those disinfectant baths, no doubt. Before setting out I washed both with mild shampoo to remove any residue that might continue to irritate their sensitive hides.

On our way to Machachi that day we crossed a foggy pass near Cotopaxi, the world's highest active volcano. People envy my metabolism because I'm comfortable in short-sleeve shirts when everyone else is wearing at least a jacket. But that day the wind from Cotopaxi's frigid summit cut through my heavy coat and all the way to my bones.

We passed a huge satellite dish and a sign announcing tours at the nearby NASA tracking station, but I was more interested in getting down off that mountain. My attempts to do that were repeatedly interrupted by motorists who stopped or slowed and rolled their windows down to ask what I was doing and why.

Around noon the driver of a silver Mercedes Benz going in the opposite direction pulled off the pavement and parked. When he got out and walked toward me I winced. Answering his questions would delay my descent to warmer temperatures.

I'd never met Luis de Ascásubi but as he came closer I recognized him. He was an expert on Peruvian horses, and his book on that subject had offered the first scientific description of the breed's gaits. Having often heard him praised in Peru and on the verge of meeting him, I dismounted. Sitting on a horse while he was on foot would've been disrespectful.

While visiting Quito years earlier, Manuel Mazzi, a Paso breeder from Peru, had wanted to visit Señor Ascásubi, but Don Luis, who jealously guarded his privacy, wasn't listed in Quito's phone book.

Hoping against hope, Mazzi flagged down a taxi in that city of over a half-million inhabitants and asked, "Do you know Luis de Ascásubi?"

"Ah," the driver had enthused, eyes sparkling, "Don Luis de Ascásubi, the last of the true gentlemen."

Every bit as impressive as his reputation, Don Luis had a neatly trimmed snow-white beard, spoke fluent English with a distinguished accent, and had the unmistakable aura of a very important man.

"I'm keenly interested in long horseback journeys," he told me as we shook hands, "and have been looking forward to your arrival. This morning Gustavo Moncayo informed a mutual friend that you would be between Lasso and Machachi today, and I came looking for you."

After walking around Hamaca and Ima, touching them here and there, he told me, "They're in incredibly good condition. If I hadn't seen them, I wouldn't have believed it."

I was as pleased as I would've been if Aimé Tschiffely himself had said those words. Don Luis knew what he was talking about and having read books he'd written, I knew his approval wasn't given lightly.

26

SURE SHOT AND FRIENDS

"I'll see you again the day after tomorrow at the entrance to Quito," Ascásubi promised before leaving.

I didn't have to wait that long. Less than three hours later I saw his Mercedes again, and this time two men got out. While singing Hamaca and Ima's praises in Quito, Don Luis had become so enthused he'd brought a friend to see them.

"Just look at their weight and general health," he exclaimed. "One would never guess they just came all the way from Peru."

One of the Peruvian breed's most respected authorities was in a state of euphoria over something I was doing. It was more than flattering.

Reading his book, *El Caballo de Paso y Su Equitación*, had been a defining moment for me. By then I'd studied everything I could find about Peruvian horses and even resorted to reading Fernando Ceruti's college thesis. All that material, however, was written for people familiar with the breed—a small group that for centuries had passed on its knowledge by word of mouth.

But after digesting Ascásubi's crystal clear analogies and informative charts, I understood the basics. That had enabled me to learn more, thanks to sometimes day-long conversations with Jose "Pepe" Musante H., a genius who understood the breed as few men ever will.

Not long after Don Luis left for the second time, Gustavo Moncayo passed and pulled over. Bound for Quito on business, he got out and handed me a sack lunch, graciously prepared by his wife, and a map he'd drawn to help me find a friend's hacienda near Machachi.

"Don't worry," he said after I told him what had happened the previous night. "Pedro is more gracious. You'll like him and he'll like you."

At the front gate of Pedro's hacienda, I was stopped by ranch hands with buckets full of the same solution that had irritated Hamaca and Ima's sensitive hides the night before.

"That smells awfully strong," I said, ready to leave if anyone insisted on bathing my mares.

"Don't worry," one responded, holding up a stiff-bristled brush. "This is for their feet only."

With metal picks they cleaned all eight hooves and brushed them with the liquid, working it into every crack and crevice. Next with a much milder solution, they sponged and dipped until Hamaca, Ima, and their gear had been disinfected.

* * *

True to Gustavo's promise Pedro was outstandingly cordial.

"Sorry we had to welcome you that way," he greeted as I rode up to his stable.

"I understand," I said, dismounting, "and am grateful for your hospitality. You have nothing to gain and much to lose by having us here."

"Unfortunately I don't have a stall or corral available," he further apologized, "but your mares can stay in the arena where I test fighting bulls."

After I turned Hamaca and Ima loose, Pedro took me to his house for an early dinner, then drove me to Quito, Ecuador's capital. Its architecture and bustling vitality were all the more appealing set against spectacular views of nearby volcanoes. Anyone from anywhere would've been impressed, and after months away from such sophistication I was enchanted.

My mood changed abruptly when vehicles waiting at a traffic light, ours among them, were engulfed by hundreds of angry young protesters, many carrying signs with slogans that meant nothing to me. When several insolently sat around us on hoods and trunks, Pedro rolled up his vehicle's windows and locked its doors.

Since leaving home I hadn't missed an issue of *Time* magazine and was aware that anti-Vietnam War demonstrations in the States had inspired social protests in Latin America. But I hadn't expected to see one.

"What has them so upset?" I asked Pedro, fervently hoping it wasn't Uncle Sam's economic imperialism.

Agitated he went on at length about his country's problems.

"You're talking awfully loud," I cautioned, "and can probably be heard outside."

"I don't care," he snapped, reaching across me to take a pistol from the glove box. When the demonstrators moved on, Pedro made a U-turn and started back to his hacienda.

"I don't think you fully appreciate the danger," he said, "of making this journey alone on horseback."

"If you mean bandits —"

"No," he interrupted. "I'm referring to the political climate. Serious violence, even revolution, could erupt at any moment.

I keep a submachine gun in my bedroom for protection. You shouldn't go out in public. Norteamericanos aren't safe in Ecuador right now. If I were you I'd sell my horses and go home."

Needless to say, I didn't mention his warning in my next letter to Mom.

* * *

With Pedro's stern warning still on my mind, I took a long time to fall asleep. I'd traveled six hundred miles in his country and felt he'd exaggerated the perils. But the next nation in my path, Colombia, was among the world's most dangerous. According to *Time* magazine, its nineteen-year *La Violencia* had killed more people than the United States lost in World War II.

Colombia's drug lords hadn't yet come on the scene, but already her people had been through hell, starting with a bloody civil war between liberals and conservatives. After that, many of both sides' military units had degenerated into bandit gangs — one led by the infamous Sure Shot, who pretended to have people's best interests at heart while robbing the country blind.

During some years those outlaws' ill-gotten gains had exceeded Colombia's national budget. They'd attacked army posts and wouldn't hesitate to target a lone *Yanqui*. And if I somehow eluded them, I'd be stopped by the Darien Gap in northern Colombia and southern Panama. No one had ever penetrated its dense jungle, not even Tschiffely, Mancha, and Gato.

They'd bypassed it on an ocean-going freighter. I however, had an option not available to them. I could avoid Colombia's bandits, the Darien Gap, and Ecuador's political upheaval by flying from Quito to Panama City. And what the heck...to get to Los Gatos in time for the Tevis Cup, I'd have to transport, not ride or lead, Hamaca and Ima most of the way.

So far I'd ridden—or walked—every inch from Chiclayo, except for a few kilometers near La Toma. Flying to Panama would ruin that almost perfect record, a prospect that made me feel as I had when I'd discovered the first scratch on my first car.

My tossing and turning abruptly stopped when I heard a commotion from Pedro's bullring. Fearing Hamaca and Ima might be in danger I leapt out of bed, pulled on my pants and latex-coated poncho, and hurried out into rainy darkness. In their spacious arena, my mares were huddled near the gate, far from their feed and clearly frightened.

The only sound I heard was rain splattering on my rubberized poncho, and I saw no threat anywhere.

Hamaca and Ima had been raised in fields and were accustomed to looking out across vast panoramas. They clearly didn't like being inside a high wall that hid the sources of unfamiliar noises and smells. As always when in unfamiliar places, they'd selected—by what criteria I don't know—a spot where they felt safe. Evidently I'd put their feed elsewhere.

Occasionally they left their safe haven and rushed over to their hay, grabbed a mouthful, then went back where they wanted to be before chewing. Both greeted me with hungry nickers when I moved what remained of their dinner.

When I returned to the house Pedro was standing at the door in his nightshirt, submachine gun in hand.

"Thank God it's you," he said, visibly relieved. "What on earth were you doing outside in the middle of this miserable night? You do know we have indoor plumbing, right?"

Chuckling I told him, "Sorry I disturbed you. I heard something and wanted to make sure Hamaca and Ima were okay."

"You're a good daddy to your daughters." He smiled and patted my shoulder.

27

WHERE HEMISPHERES MEET

The next day I staged a private horse race—Hamaca and Ima vs. the clock.

They'd rest for at least the next week so I pushed them hard and they responded well. At elevations between eight thousand five hundred and eleven thousand five hundred feet we covered thirty miles in four hours before heavy traffic slowed us to a walk.

As promised, Luis de Ascásubi and Gustavo Moncayo were waiting beside their vehicles on Quito's outskirts.

"Don Luis arranged for your horses to stay at the best horse facility in town," Gustavo greeted me.

"There may be others equally good," Ascásubi corrected with his trademark precision, "but none better."

In his Mercedes he led the way with my mares and me next, followed by Gustavo in his Bronco. Patiently they escorted me along traffic filled streets to an elegant stable at the brick-walled Colegio Militar Eloy Alfaro, Ecuador's West Point and one of

Latin America's outstanding military colleges. Several cavalry officers I'd met in Riobamba had been educated there.

"Don't worry," Don Luis said when he saw my worried expression after getting out of his Mercedes. "They won't charge for your stall. But you'll have to buy your own feed."

While two troopers and I prepared stalls, we were entertained by snippets from a debate between Gustavo and Señor Ascásubi.

"You always criticize my shortwave radios as mere toys," Gustavo began, "but without them we wouldn't have known Verne was in Ecuador."

"It wasn't one of your radios driving along the road the night you first saw him," Don Luis countered. "It was you."

"But I was looking for him," Gustavo said, "because of what I'd heard by radio."

"I too knew where Verne was, because of letters from friends in Lima. And stamps cost far less than those fancy radios."

Back and forth they went, Gustavo bidding for even a small concession, and Ascásubi refusing to give an inch.

"I must apologize," Don Luis told me after Hamaca and Ima were settled. "I have visitors and can't host you in my house. I've arranged for you to stay with a Hungarian friend everyone calls Señor Negro because no one can pronounce his first name."

He drove me to the Negro home, then introduced us and left, clearly in something of a rush. I had arrived at tea time. My new hosts, an energetic husband and wife, seemed delighted to have me as a guest.

"Please forgive us," Señor Negro said motioning for me to sit at the dining room tables' third place setting. "We have full schedules this week and won't be the best of hosts."

"No problem," I assured him. "As busy as I'll be, I won't be a very good guest."

* * *

In the morning I took a bus downtown and spoke with an airline freight agent whose price for flying horses to Panama was well within my budget. Hours later, not having found an equally low price anywhere, I returned.

"When is your next available flight?" I asked.

"In a week," he replied.

"Is there room for my mares?"

"Yes," he said, "but you'll never finish the paperwork that fast. Panama and Ecuador both suffer from Latin America's tendency to wrap everything in paperwork tied with red tape."

"My mares are here in transit," I explained, "and a man at Quito's Ministry of Agriculture told me the paperwork will take less than a week."

"During a normal month perhaps. But you need certificates from Ecuador's Ministry of Agriculture and Panama's Consul, which will take a great deal longer during the Christmas season."

"In that case I'd better leave myself plenty of leeway," I said. "Can you reserve us space on the flight three weeks from now?"

This latest unexpected delay was disheartening but prudent. I wanted plenty of time to get those permits because if I didn't have them on time, I'd forfeit my deposit.

* * *

Friday afternoon after five days of shepherding my mare's health papers I received an exit permit from Ecuador's Ministry of Agriculture. Immediately I rushed it to Panama's Consul.

"What makes you think I'll accept this?" he said, as if I was trying to trick him.

"Why won't you?" I asked.

He answered with a question, "How do I know this signature is genuine?"

"How do you know any signature is genuine?" I made it four questions in a row, then five. "Isn't it enough that the document has all the required seals and stamps?"

"But how do I know the signature is genuine?"

By then the record for consecutive questions in a dialogue was probably within our reach.

"What must I do to verify the signature?" I asked.

"Take it to Ecuador's Department of Exterior Relations," he said as if the answer was obvious, "and have it authenticated."

* * *

"I'm sorry but I can't help you," the man at the Department of Exterior Relations huffed. "The signer is a veterinarian at the Ministry of Agriculture. First the Vice-Minister of Agriculture must authenticate the veterinarian's signature. Then we can authenticate the Vice-Minister's signature."

Faced with the potential for a delay that could cause me to forfeit my deposit, I took a taxi rather than a bus to the Ministry of Agriculture.

"The Vice-Minister of Agriculture doesn't authenticate veterinarians' signatures," a clerk there told me. "His lawyer does that and then the Vice-Minister authenticates the lawyer's signature."

"Which means the lawyer will want a fee for his services," I grumbled, "as well as the Vice-Minister for his. Then the Department of Exterior Relations will charge me to authenticate the Vice-Minister's signature, and I'll have to pay Panama's Consul to authenticate the whole crazy mess."

My little speech didn't bring the sympathy I felt I deserved.

Years before, at an Argentine border station during that jeep trip in the Andes with LuBette, Hilary, Anne, and Vicki, I had seen a wall sign beneath an Argentine flag.

"*Energía y Corrección*," it read. Energy and Accuracy.

A German in line ahead of me and obviously frustrated with Latin American bureaucracy read this aloud and declared, "*Por fin*." At last.

His punishment had come when the immigration officer subjected him to long, rigorous questioning before stamping his passport.

Since then I'd made a hobby of creating comical, to-the-point signs for government offices. The one I came up with for Quito's Ministry of Agriculture was: "Bring us one Problem. Leave with Two."

"Where will I find the Vice-Minister's lawyer?" I asked the clerk.

"Leave your paper here," he said. "He'll authenticate it next time he comes in."

That was a recipe for disaster, especially during the holiday season.

"I'd rather take this directly to him so he can do that now," I said. "Where is he?"

"On Christmas vacation. I'm not sure when he's due back. You'll have to ask his secretary on Monday."

Alone at the Negro home most of that weekend, I couldn't stop worrying about my deposit. One of my three weeks was gone...the elusive paperwork had already taken longer than it was supposed to...and the end was nowhere in sight.

* * *

Bright and early Monday morning I called and spoke with the Minister's secretary.

"I have a power of attorney," she said, "and am authorized to authenticate signatures while the Vice-Minister's lawyer is away."

I walked into her office less than an hour later and she verified the signature while I waited.

Theoretically all that remained was to retrace my steps. But wherever I went, the only person who could help was unavailable. Calling ahead to save time and cab fare was impossible because no one in government offices answered telephones, even when Quito's were working.

More worried by the minute, I redoubled my efforts and two days later delivered all the needed verifications to Panama's Consul, relieved my ordeal was finally over.

But it wasn't.

"Your horses will be quarantined for forty days," the Consul told me for the first time, "if you take them to Panama without prior permission from our Minister of Agriculture."

Cringing I asked, "How do I get that?"

Rather than have my request go by mail, I paid the Consul to send a cable. Ten days and two follow-up cables later, I still had no response. Those cables had cost more than I could afford, but that was the least of my worries.

If my prior permission didn't arrive within the next two days I'd forfeit my deposit, which would be a catastrophic setback.

* * *

While up to my eyes in gobbledygook paperwork, I also made efforts to get Hamaca and Ima's tetanus shots. That potentially fatal malady, also called lockjaw, was a serious threat in hot, humid Panama. In the chilly Andes however, it was rare and none of Quito's veterinarians or stores had the equine vaccine.

"Will the human vaccine work on horses?" I asked a pharmacist in desperation.

"Yes, if you use enough." He wrote out a formula for calculating the dose based on weight and added, "You'll have to give two shots, four to six weeks apart—which will require buying vaccine at several pharmacies. There's not much demand and none of us carries the amount you'll need."

After two other pharmacists verified that human vaccine would do the job nicely, I visited pharmacies buying all their vaccine until I had enough for two injections, the second to be administered in Panama.

When I stopped by the Colegio Militar that evening to feed Hamaca and Ima, I asked the veterinarian if he'd be kind enough to inject the first dose.

"I'm sorry," he apologized, "but if something goes wrong after I administer human vaccine to your horses, a lawyer will find a way to pin the blame on me."

It would've been pointless to assure him I'd never sue anyone for doing me a favor.

"Can I help in some other way?" he offered.

"Is it too early to tell if Hamaca is pregnant?' I asked. "She was bred on November twenty-fifth."

He palpated her and reported, "It's too soon to be absolutely certain, but I'm ninety-nine percent sure she's empty."

The following morning I hired a vet to inject my tetanus vaccine. He did a good job with Ima, but with Hamaca he didn't attach the needle correctly and even though vaccine was leaking, he continued pushing the plunger until the syringe was empty.

"Don't worry," he then said, rubbing the injection site with an alcohol-soaked cotton puff. "I got enough in her."

Not that easy-going, I spent more hours and dollars gathering additional vaccine which another vet managed to put inside Hamaca's neck instead of on it.

* * *

After each of those frantically busy days, I fell asleep exhausted and lonely. Being starved for companionship during the Christmas season was depressing. I wanted to be with people and enjoy the glorious Indian summer that was bathing the city in glorious warmth.

But after seeing those protesters with Pedro and having been warned by Señor Negro to stay out of sight whenever possible, I spent hours alone in his house, waiting for him to return from work. Finally I took two walks in an area he'd guaranteed was safe. Both those walks were unpleasant.

"Hey, giraffe," were the first words I heard in that area and my contribution to its holiday spirit was to be an ideal butt for jokes.

Children relentlessly followed me for blocks, indulging their creativity.

My reaction reminded me of a couplet written by actress Diane Varsi:

"Go away and don't bother me.
Can't you see I'm lonely?"

In the midst of Miss Varsi's flourishing Hollywood career — tired of invasions of her privacy — she had abruptly stopped making movies and left the limelight. At first her flight from fame attracted more of the scrutiny she was trying to avoid. Gossip columnists quoted her little verse as if it proved she wasn't normal.

After all, no sane person would leave fame for obscurity.

But to me those lines made perfect sense, especially in December, 1966.

Some people's company of course, was more than welcome. But Luis de Ascásubi was busy with guests, Señor Negro was seldom home, and Gustavo Moncayo was at his farm.

* * *

When alone at the Negro's house I didn't of course, answer the phone or respond if someone came to their door. One morning however, the knocking went on and on.

"Looks like you're here alone," Gustavo Moncayo said when I opened the door. "I'm in Quito for the day and on my way to visit a friend who procures exotic animals for zoos and pet stores. Would you like to come along?"

"You bet," I responded. "I'd love to."

Our conversation picked up where it had ended a few days earlier and lasted all the way to our destination.

"You've come at an excellent time," Gustavo's friend Julio welcomed us. "I just received some outstanding anacondas. They're in my garage. I'll show them to you."

"I'll wait outside," Gustavo said with no further explanation.

The reason for his decision was soon obvious. Inside the garage I was nearly overcome by a stench my host didn't seem to notice.

"I feel guilty taking so much of your time," I said, eager to finish my tour.

"There's nothing I'd rather be doing," Julio assured me. "Take your time, please."

Rather than hurt his feelings, I strolled from crate to crate, scarcely breathing and asking enough questions to show interest. Thanks to my sense of smell's built-in defense mechanism, the foul odor gradually faded to where I could ignore it.

"These are the biggest snakes I've ever seen," I said, slowing to observe them more carefully, "but they're not as large as I expected."

"They're young," Julio snapped, clearly offended, "but big for their ages."

Damn. I hadn't meant to insult him.

"I've heard they kill monster crocodiles," I explained, softening my remark. "That gave me the impression of something a little larger."

Julio opened a cage and grabbed a snake by its neck — if they can be said to have those — then struggled to lift and set it on a table.

"Return him to his cage," he instructed, still holding its neck. "Don't worry. I won't let him bite."

Almost pure muscle, the snake seemed to make himself heavier as I fought — groaning with effort — to put him back where he belonged. Twice he flexed his body and forced my hands open. I nearly dropped him both times.

"As you can imagine," Julio said after the job was done, "that much weight coiled around a crocodile will quickly exhaust it."

"Point taken," I told him, out of breath but grinning. "Your snakes are every bit as big as they need to be."

He looked pleased.

* * *

I was still waiting for Panama's prior permission the morning Luis de Ascásubi picked me up and drove me to his Hacienda Guachalá, north of Quito. A Mercedes Benz was a rarity and a big deal in those days. I'd long wanted to ride in one but found his less smooth or quiet than expected, partly because the highway was surfaced with cobblestones.

"This is the first time I've seen a highway like this," I told him.

"They're a bit noisy but otherwise excellent," he said, "and due to Ecuador's low cost of labor they're less expensive than asphalt."

Ascásubi's picturesque hacienda offered fighting bulls, horses, gardens, a simple but elegant house, and a man-made lake stocked with bass.

"Those stakes," Don Luis told me, pointing, "mark the equator's path across my land. Someday Guachalá will be a resort where guests wake up in one hemisphere and eat breakfast in the other. Would you like to see a copy of the survey report?"

"That won't be necessary." I smiled. "I believe you."

I wasn't as easily convinced by the claims he made at Guachalá's stable while showing me horses he called Peruvians. They were clearly generations removed from imported stock and showed unmistakable signs of outside blood. Disappointed, I listened to his reasons for considering them superior to their Peruvian cousins.

That was the first time I hadn't agreed with him. For me, his so-called Peruvians lacked the exquisite touches that make pure-bloods unique. They were good, serviceable transportation but had no flair, nothing to fascinate the mind or delight the eye.

On the drive back to Quito Don Luis became as disappointed with me as I'd been with his horses. It was a defining moment in our relationship and afterward he never again showed me the same warmth.

The change began when I said something I thought he knew — that I'd led my mares most of the way to Quito. I hadn't attempted to conceal that, nor did he think I had. But he believed horses were to be ridden — not pampered. And he considered leading my mares dishonest, even though I'd had what I considered an excellent reason.

At first I tried to justify myself, but his mind was made up. Too proud to beg for approval, I stopped trying. I felt hollow inside. Never had anyone withdrawn favor with such devastating effect. Not once did he again show interest in my journey, and I saw him only one more time before leaving Quito.

That blow was softened by the sterling hospitality of Señor and Señora Negro. As soon as their pre-Christmas vacations began, both gave me their full attention. By day they showed me Quito, and several evenings they took me to holiday parties where I felt a delightful sense of participation in a celebration that had been passing me by.

Early one morning—while most of Quito slept—Señor Negro invited me to the country club for a brisk gallop on his polo ponies.

"This may seem a strange way of taking a break from your horseback journey," he said when we were seated in his car, "but I think you'll find it relaxing and enjoyable."

Getting to his stable however, was another matter. He loved testing the limits of his imported Italian sports car as he sped down the winding road from his hilltop home. He steered around the first curve, tires squealing, at a speed that slammed me against the passenger-side door and held me there for too many spine-chilling seconds.

"I should've taken that one faster," he told me, downshifting. "I'll show you. Hold on."

During my escape from the Law I hadn't feared for my life half as much as I did on the next curve. Fortunately he noticed my discomfort and slowed down.

"Sorry," he apologized. "Sometimes I forget that not everyone is a daredevil."

* * *

I would've loved to spend the rest of the holiday season in the Negro home, but they needed their guest room for unexpected out-of-town visitors. Two days before Christmas, Gustavo Moncayo arranged for me to stay at the Colegio Militar for the same bargain price paid by students.

I spent that holiest of weeks in the college's vacant four-patient hospital room, surrounded by dozens of dormitories that were empty and would be for two weeks. Everyone but Giorgio, the maintenance man and my only human contact, was on break. The only time I could leave or reenter the building was when he was there to unlock the door.

Gustavo Moncayo found time to visit me on Christmas Eve. I don't know what he'd heard, but he knew all wasn't well between Don Luis and me.

"Don't worry," he consoled me. "He can be drastic and it's his nature to find fault. But he thinks well of you."

Before driving to his hacienda in Latacunga that night, Gustavo took me to the home of a friend who had a shortwave radio. For over an hour he sat patiently during patch calls to my mom, Joe and Pat Gavitt, and George Jones.

Then I said goodbye with considerable regret. I hadn't felt that close to anyone since Juan Luis Ruesta in Piura. And if Panama's prior permission came before I forfeit my deposit, that evening might well be the last time I'd ever see Gustavo.

* * *

Giorgio didn't work Christmas day or eve, and was kind enough to loan me a key so I wouldn't be locked in. I missed his comforting presence. After forty-eight hours of solitary confinement, I took an early morning walk when there was no one on the sidewalks and no vehicles in the streets. Back in my room I read a used copy of Herman Wouk's *The Winds of War.*

It held my attention. While Quito's families exchanged gifts and sang carols, I set it down only long enough to eat hastily prepared meals or visit the restroom.

Watching Jack Nicholson's movie *The Shining* years later, reminded me of being alone in the sprawling, multistory Colegio Militar after I finished reading that night.

I walked a dark eerie corridor to the showers, imagining danger behind every door and around every corner. Spooked, I considered doubling up on my deodorant and washing my hands and face only. But ultimately I surrendered to mom's carefully instilled rules of hygiene, all the while picturing the shower scene from Alfred Hitchcock's film, *Psycho.*

Afterward I walked back to my room, firmly wedged chair backs under both its doorknobs, and lay in my hospital bed, hearing threats that weren't there and taking too long to fall asleep.

In those days I read a lot of books and went to movies regularly. After that night, however, I steered away from the horror genre.

* * *

Four days into the New Year and one before my flight was scheduled to leave, Panama's Consul summoned me to his office and gave me a certified copy of the cable authorizing Hamaca and Ima to enter his country. My euphoria however, was brief because waiting for that was replaced by waiting for the plane.

"All I know," the airline agent told me firmly, "is that you must be available at all times and will have very little notice before your flight leaves."

Two days later the Colegio Militar's telephone operator called my room with a message. My plane was due and I needed to get ready. At top speed I packed my gear, paid the academy's bill, and rode to the airport.

I'd waited for hours by the time the freight agent arrived with bad news. The plane had been delayed. As discouraged as I'd ever been, I returned to the Colegio Militar...got permission to stay longer...exchanged dollars for *sucres* at a bank — I'd spent my Ecuadorian money in anticipation of leaving...and rushed to the outdoor market to buy horse feed before it closed.

Next day the same thing happened.

On January 9th at noon the agent alerted me a third time. Skeptical this time I phoned the airport control tower.

"Good news," the man there said. "Your aircraft is in Quito and has filed a flight plan."

Well before our scheduled departure, Hamaca, Ima, and I reached the airport, where our pilot, an American, was doing a preflight check on a World War II era Douglas C-47 Skytrain. My mares' shipping crates hadn't arrived so I phoned the freight agent who promised to bring them and a loading ramp.

Not long afterward he delivered the crates and what was more a bridge than a ramp. It had no side rails or legs. As wide as a two-horse trailer, it was too steep after the pilot, co-pilot, and I put it in position. First Hamaca and then Ima refused to climb it.

"Are you waiting to grow claws?" I teased Ima.

As always when I used that tone, she seemed to frown.

Chuckling, the pilot said, "Don't despair. I have an idea."

He hurried toward a hanger, then returned driving a flatbed truck and backed it up near the plane's cargo door. Next we positioned the ramp with its bottom on the ground and its top on the truck's bed. Once Hamaca and Ima had climbed that far, we moved the ramp so it ran from there to the plane. Soon my mares were aboard and in their crates.

Long after scheduled takeoff, the customs agent delivered the health certificates to the airport veterinarian, who cleared Hamaca and Ima. We were ready at last, or so I thought until the pilot walked toward me.

"Mr. Albright," he said calmly, "I wish I'd come to announce our imminent departure. But there's bad news. I've been asked to deliver it because you're almost seven feet tall and about to be in a foul mood. Your flight was postponed until tomorrow."

"Why?" I asked.

"The cargo onboard is incoming, and there are no lift trucks available to unload it."

On my ride back to the academy I sat on Hamaca without once signaling her where to turn or cross a street. Making that trip for the third time, she knew the way by heart. Back at the stable where she and Ima had spent nearly a month, I arranged for them to stay another night, exchanged money, bought horse feed, fed them, and seethed.

Fortunately my room was as I'd left it. No fool, Giorgio had decided not to change the bedding until he'd heard my plane take off.

28

A MEMORABLE FLIGHT

When we reached Mariscal Sucre International Airport at 4:00 the next morning, the incoming cargo had been replaced by merchandise bound for Panama and the United States. After his preflight check the pilot brought the flatbed truck. Under powerful overhead spotlights he helped me load my mares, first into the plane, then into shipping crates.

Having been through that procedure already, they behaved perfectly.

"It's good to see how calmly your horses loaded in the dark," the pilot said as we came down the loading ramp.

Turning to the fuel truck driver he sternly warned, "We're overloaded. If you fill those tanks more than a quarter full we'll be too heavy to take off and you'll have to siphon the excess."

I must have looked concerned because he patted my shoulder and explained, "Quito is about two miles above sea level. The air here is so thin that planes can't get airborne with a capacity load and full tanks. Even with quarter tanks we'll need full throttle and every inch of runway. It'll be rough and noisy in the cargo hold. You'd better ride back there with your horses."

"I'm planning to," I said.

"Good. I don't want a repeat of what happened to that stallion on his way to the Olympic Games. I assume you heard about that?"

"No."

"He went berserk in mid-flight and when his crazed thrashing threatened to bring the plane down, the pilot killed him with the only weapon available, an axe. That's why I carry this when flying livestock." He opened his jacket and showed the pistol in its inside pocket.

* * *

With the sun coming up the pilot taxied his vintage aircraft to the takeoff runway, stopped, and revved up its engines, making the fuselage rattle and vibrate.

"Are you ready, Verne?" I heard the co-pilot shout above the engines' deafening roar.

"Yes," I replied at the top of my voice, turning to face my mare's crates.

Bouncing, swaying, and gradually picking up speed the C-47 labored forward. Near the end of the runway its nose tilted up and we left the ground. Briefly we hung suspended, then the angle of the floor became steeper as we climbed.

At cruising altitude the pilot reduced the flow of gas to the engines. My throat constricted as the engines' loud roar ceased. I thought they had shut off but then became aware of their gentle humming and resumed breathing.

Throughout the dramatic takeoff Hamaca and Ima had behaved like the seasoned travelers they were. By the time the pilot came back to check on them, Ima — eyelids drooping after her preflight tranquilizer shot — was dreamily eating from her hay net.

Hamaca, still remarkably alert, had raised her head high to make sure her traveling companion was still in the next crate.

With Panama to our north, the pilot headed south to top off the tanks in Guayaquil, at sea level. We'd be able to take off from there with full tanks.

The most hazardous moments of any flight, especially those carrying livestock, are takeoffs and landings, and we'd have two of each during our trip that day. To my relief however, the pilot set us down gently in Guayaquil and our second takeoff was much smoother and far less noisy.

When we were again at cruising altitude I wrote a progress report for *Que Pasó*, the newsletter of the American Association of Owners and Breeders of Peruvian Paso Horses. Since I'd replaced my geldings with Hamaca and Ima, my articles had been few and low key. I'd promoted my first failure too enthusiastically and didn't want to repeat that mistake.

When I'd finished writing I leaned my forehead against a window and looked out at the clouds below us. Presumably we were over Colombia, and I indulged my male imagination by pretending we were on a bombing run. Each time Hamaca and Ima relieved themselves, their urine collected in a low spot on the floor where it stayed until the plane banked left.

Then it flowed through the gap under the door and — I sincerely hoped — fell on the heads of Sure Shot and his murderous gang.

* * *

As we descended toward Panama City the cockpit door was open and in the distance I saw Tocumen International

Airport. After this landing and one more sleep, Hamaca, Ima, and I would at last resume our journey.

A Peruvian friend once told me he could distinguish Latin pilots from North American ones by the way they landed. Latins, he said, were more artistic. They floated an aircraft above the runway and set it down so gently that passengers scarcely felt the wheels touch ground. American pilots however, dutifully touched down within the recommended distance.

"Sometimes you can't tell if they landed or were shot down," had been my friend's punch line.

On this flight however, our American pilot brought us to earth quickly and smoothly.

After the C-47 stopped near a hangar, our pilot came back and opened the cargo door. Looking outside we saw two men bent over the plane's forward wheel assembly, hands on knees, watching hot, steaming, red brake fluid gush onto the tarmac.

"Bad luck," one said.

"I'd call it good luck," the pilot told me quietly. "If that brake line had burst sooner we might not have been able to stop before the end of the runway."

"Señor Albright?" a man below yelled through cupped hands.

"Yes," I replied.

"I'm your airline's agent in Panama. Sorry but we don't have a livestock ramp. You'll have to make your own arrangements to unload."

"When a passenger plane arrives," I told him sternly, "the airline has to provide a stairway so people can get off, right?"

"*Si*, Señor, but—"

"Your airline," I interrupted, "has a similar obligation."

"I might be able to borrow a passenger ramp from another airline."

"Horses can't use those," I shot back.

"We don't have a freight ramp." The agent folded his arms across his chest.

I tried a mild threat. "How will your plane continue on to Miami if I can't unload?"

"We'll unload the Panama-bound cargo tomorrow around noon," he called my bluff. "You have until then to make arrangements."

We were stalemated but both had incentive to find a solution. He didn't want his flight delayed, and I didn't want my mares aboard that hot stuffy aircraft all night.

"I've seen horses unloaded with two forklifts," he suggested, "one supporting each end of their crates. I'll give one of the operators a tip if you'll take care of the other."

"I will."

Problem was, the crates were too tall to fit through the door upright. In Quito they'd been brought aboard empty and leaned at an angle to clear the door. But with Hamaca and Ima inside, that was no longer possible.

When the forklifts arrived, several workers and I pushed Ima's crate — with her inside — up to the door, where a man sawed off the tops of its upright corner posts. Then we slid it until one end was cantilevered in mid-air, where a forklift operator supported it — backing up as we continued to push.

When there was room between that forklift and the aircraft, the second driver squeezed in and supported the crate's other end. Talking to Ima all the while. I stepped from the plane to the tip of a fork protruding from beneath her crate.

"I'll ride down with her," I said, hoping that would make the operators extra cautious.

They lowered Ima, trying to coordinate their descents to keep her crate level. But it slanted this way and that, wobbling as she scrambled to keep her balance. The floor beneath her wasn't level until it was on the runway.

We used only the larger lift truck to unload Hamaca, a considerable improvement. By the time my mares were out of their crates and on the runway, night had fallen.

* * *

The next hurdle was the official from Panama's Ministry of Agriculture, who was authorized to quarantine Hamaca and Ima for up to forty days if their paperwork wasn't in order. Fortunately it was. Mine however, wasn't.

"I can't let you in unless you have a ticket for passage out of the country," the man at the immigration desk told me politely.

"My horses are my ticket," I explained.

"Sorry, señor, but you must have a ticket for commercial transportation."

"Why?" I persisted. "If someone enters Panama in his automobile, you don't require him to have a ticket. His car is his transportation, and my horses are mine."

"Almost everyone who comes here can walk, señor," he said as if enjoying our debate. "But we still require a ticket to leave the country. Walking isn't considered satisfactory for international travel and neither is riding horses."

Checkmate. Clearly a better negotiator than I, the official escorted me to the LACSA Airlines ticket counter where I purchased passage to Costa Rica.

With Immigration and the Ministry of Agriculture both satisfied, I moved on to Customs, confident my meager possessions wouldn't be a problem. They weren't, but Hamaca and Ima were.

"You have to leave a deposit," an official told me, "to guarantee you won't sell your mares in Panama without paying taxes."

The substantial deposit would leave me without enough money to cross Panama, but I couldn't say that to a man trained to deny entry to anyone in danger of becoming destitute in his country.

"Is there another option?" I asked.

"One," he replied, then filled out a form. "You can apply tomorrow in Panama City."

"Where do I sign?" I asked, smiling with relief.

"That won't be necessary. I trust you." Handing me the completed application he added, "Give this to an agent at the address on the form."

By then, it was dark and I still had to find a place to spend the night. I'd need local currency, so I stood in line at the airport's money exchange window for at least a half hour. When it was my turn I placed two twenty dollar bills on the counter.

"What do you want me to do with these?" the teller asked.

"Exchange them for Panamanian money please," I replied.

"These *are* Panamanian money." He dismissed me with a backhand wave.

"Most currency and coins circulating here are ours," a nearby, obviously American man informed me. "You'll often receive change made up of both their *balboas* and our dollars. The designs are different, but the sizes, shapes, and values are identical. The coins are interchangeable in vending machines."

* * *

The night was pitch-black when I left the terminal and started toward the hanger where I'd left Hamaca and Ima. Halfway there a porter stopped me.

"You're the one who brought horses, right?" he asked.

"Yes."

"For a small fee you can put them in my corral and sleep in

my tool shed over there." He pointed toward a spot across the runways. "I'm off duty and will show you the way."

"We can't walk across those runways with planes landing and taking off," I said.

"I've been doing it twice a day for years."

"Not with horses."

"The alternative is to go all the way around, which will take at least an hour." He turned to go.

"Wait, please," I said, having decided to do something the easy way for once. "I'll get my horses."

Expecting airport security to suddenly appear and arrest me, I returned, leading my mares, and followed the porter across four busy runways. It was like trying to get to the other side of a four-lane Los Angeles freeway at rush hour. Having done stranger things than that, Hamaca and Ima calmly stopped, started, and waited when I did.

True to the porter's word, no one—other than gawking passengers on incoming planes—paid any attention. But my mom would've been unhappy even though I'd been careful to look both ways as well as up.

Later the porter sold me some of the yucca and wild grass he grew on his farm.

Hamaca and Ima had always eaten whatever I gave them, but not this time.

No problem. They'd stuffed themselves with alfalfa during the flight. Tomorrow in Panama City I'd buy more.

29

THE PORES PORE

At sunup I took the early bus to Panama City, which was bigger, cleaner, and more charming than I'd anticipated. At the Customs Headquarters I handed the form I'd been given to an official and requested an exemption.

I'm sorry," he said, "but we grant very few exceptions on big-ticket items brought into our country. The government has too often been cheated by tourists who bring in everything from children's strollers to cars and sell them without paying taxes."

"I'm hoping that requirement can be waived because of my special circumstances," I told him.

"I can't make an exception for horses," he replied.

"Who can?"

The man he referred me to was no more accommodating. And because Hamaca and Ima's value was difficult to establish, he demanded an outlandish sum.

"May I please speak to your superior?" I asked.

His superior too was adamant.

"How do I get my money back after my horses are out of the country?" I asked.

"You apply for a refund here in this office," he said.

By then I'd be in Costa Rica, more than three hundred miles away. And his use of "apply" distressed me because it implied that Panama might say no or take months to approve my reimbursement.

During the previous night's tossing and turning I'd come up with a last ditch proposal, but I saved it for the superior's superior, who turned out to be a horseman and was more than interested in my ride.

"Could you possibly," I asked, "add a condition to the visa in my passport, requiring me to leave Panama with both mares? That would protect Panama's interests as effectively as a deposit."

"Sounds reasonable to me." He handwrote that condition in my passport beside Panama's visa, then signed and dated it before adding, "Now all you need is a contingency plan, in case one of your horses dies here."

* * *

Under a cloudless sky that afternoon, I couldn't help wondering why so many women were carrying umbrellas. The reason was obvious after I walked a few blocks with the sun's heat beating down on my bare head. Those weren't umbrellas. They were parasols, the female equivalent of the broad-brimmed hats being worn by almost every man in sight.

I hadn't worn mine that day, a mistake I resolved not to repeat.

At the LACSA Airlines office I returned my Costa Rica ticket for a refund. After that I dropped off my laundry, then took a bus to the Guardia Civil post on the city's outskirts and arranged for my mares and me to spend the following night there.

"Would you kindly help me select my next seven nightly stops," I asked the officer in charge, "so I can send alfalfa there for my horses?"

"You won't find alfalfa in Panama," he said, "but you'll find other excellent hay wherever you go. There's no need to ship it ahead."

In a large indoor market I bought a bag of grass hay that had long cylindrical spikes. The vendor called it *heno de fleo*. I'm pretty sure it was timothy, a feed I'd never seen that had an excellent reputation. I left it with the vendor while I did the rest of my shopping, and picked it up on my way out. Pleased to have accomplished so much so quickly I was in high spirits.

Already the sweltering heat and stifling humidity were intolerable. Sidewalks and streets were all but empty, the first sign of something I hadn't anticipated. People there seldom went outdoors between mid-morning and late afternoon.

So far almost nothing I'd seen had been as expected. But at least I didn't have to mentally convert Panama's money to know how much I was spending. And I could automatically appreciate distances, sizes, and weights because everyone used miles, feet, inches, pounds, and ounces, not their metric equivalents.

With people sheltering indoors, the bus to Tocumen was half full, and the roof-covered benches where passengers had waited that morning were mostly empty. With fewer stops than he'd made in the other direction, the driver covered the same distance in about half the time.

At the porter's farm, Hamaca and Ima rushed up to me with flattering nickers. But what they were happy to see was the bag of hay and grain across my shoulders. Having eaten little of the porter's unfamiliar hay, they were hungry. Eagerly they gulped the grain I'd brought, but stopped picking at the *heno de fleo* after eating less than half.

Adjusting to Panama and its drastic changes was going to be as difficult for them as for me. With apologies to Don Luis de Ascásubi, I decided to lead them for a few days while they acclimated to tropical feeds, water, bacteria, climate, and whatever else.

* * *

I'll never forget the sauna-like heat during our twenty-five mile walk to Panama City. We'd been in higher temperatures, but the humidity made this heat the worst I'd ever felt. Even in Peru's brutal desert the Panamericana had been asphalt. But here it was concrete because the harsh conditions would've softened asphalt to where tires left grooves.

In Peru's dry air, evaporation of our perspiration had cooled us a bit. But the air in Panama was saturated with moisture and couldn't absorb more. After taking off my clothes the previous night, I'd hung each piece so air could freely circulate around it.

When I'd dressed that morning my shirt had been every bit as wet as when I'd removed it.

Dripping perspiration, we drank water by the gallon. Sweat streamed into our eyes, accumulated on our skin, soaked my mares' hides and my clothes, and dripped on the ground. And as if more would succeed where less had failed, our pores continued discharging.

In the tropics for less than twenty-four hours, I already had heat rash. Hamaca — plagued by itching even in the cool Andes — never missed a chance to scratch herself against posts, trees, bushes, and me. Already her once flawless coat had bare spots where she'd rubbed the hair off. Ima's skin, thank goodness, was thicker and less sensitive.

Panama, I was learning, was frightfully expensive. When I'd picked up my laundry the previous day, the bill had convinced me to do my own washing from then on.

In the absence of laundromats however, I'd have to do it with a bar of lye soap and a bucket of water. Wasn't it the Greeks who said, "Whomever the gods would destroy, they first make him do his own laundry"?

At day's end we finally found something familiar and comfortable, the hospitality at the Guardia Civil post where we spent the night. But the map on its wall debunked more of my preconceptions about Panama. For example, its famous canal runs north-south — not west-east as I'd thought.

Equally unexpected, our journey along that narrow, horizontal isthmus would take us due west and sometimes south — but seldom north.

There was one more big surprise. The Panama Canal was closer than I'd thought. We'd cross it early tomorrow morning.

* * *

At 3:00 a.m. I led Hamaca and Ima through Panama City's Balboa district, catching occasional glimpses of the Thatcher Ferry Bridge. Spanning the Canal's Pacific approach, it had been new when I'd seen it from the freighter that brought Anne, Vicki, and me back to the States after our jeep trip with LuBette and Hillary.

It looked bigger this time. The mile-long main section was high enough to accommodate all but the world's tallest ships. It was said to carry well over twenty thousand vehicles a day, a dry fact that hadn't prepared me for the heavy traffic. Even at that early hour there were unbroken streams of headlights and taillights.

Competing with that many fast moving vehicles would be perilous, but there was no other way to get to the Canal's other side. Ferry boats had stopped operating, and signs prohibited horses on the bridge's pedestrian walkways.

Thanks to our experiences in Ecuador's traffic, I knew we'd be safer if I rode Hamaca and led Ima. A block from the bridge's east ramp I tightened the cinch on my riding saddle. As I mounted, a Canal Zone Police car stopped beside me. I expected the officer who got out to tell me I couldn't go farther.

"I'll escort you," he shouted from between cupped hands. "We'll talk on the other side."

Back behind his steering wheel he turned on his flashing dome lights and shined his spotlight on me, then waved for us to go first and followed. The other drivers did what drivers do around policemen — slowed to the speed limit and stopped jockeying for position.

At the top of the east ramp we reached the long main span beneath a towering central arch. Artistically lit, the bridge was often photographed at night. Hamaca and Ima couldn't see over its side rails, but from my saddle I could. From that high, looking down at reflections on the Canal's water was spooky.

Even with my mares in a fast sobreandando gait, crossing with vehicles passing, sometimes on both sides, took longer than I liked.

At the end of the main span Hamaca and Ima slowed on their own, then cautiously made their way down the sloping west ramp. We were safely across and on the highway shoulder when our escort passed, parked at a wide spot, and got out of his car.

Profoundly grateful for his assistance I dismounted as he introduced himself.

"I hadn't thought the bridge would be this dangerous at such an early hour," I told him. "I'm lucky you were here."

"It wasn't luck," he said. "I'm a Peruvian horse aficionado. A friend of mine is a ham radio operator who heard you were headed this way. When I saw you and your horses yesterday afternoon outside Panama City, I figured you'd be crossing this morning and made it a point to be here."

"Thank you," I said, genuinely grateful. "You can't imagine how I dreaded this bridge."

"I think I can." He chuckled. "My horse and I have been in some tight spots down here."

We talked a long time. Passing motorists must have thought he'd given me a ticket and I was protesting, especially when our arm gestures grew animated.

Before long he returned to patrolling, and I resumed leading Hamaca and Ima. I'd been with him less than thirty minutes, never saw nor heard from him again, and can't remember his name. But I'll never forget the huge favor he did me.

* * *

That afternoon near Chorrera a car passed and stopped on the highway shoulder.

"My name is Isaacs," a man said, getting out. "I'm a Peruvian horse aficionado as well as a ham radio operator. I heard about you from an Ecuadorian named Gustavo Moncayo. You and your horses are welcome to stay a night or two at my ranchette. It's about a hundred yards from here."

We followed his car a short distance on the highway, then down a driveway past an extremely tempting swimming pool. Beyond that at a barn I unsaddled Hamaca, repeatedly wiping my forehead on my sleeve.

"You and your mares cool can off in my pool if you want,"

Señor Isaacs offered. "It's about four feet deep and quite durable. They won't hurt it."

"Are you sure?" I asked.

"Positive."

"That would be wonderful."

"I want my kids to see this," he said with childlike enthusiasm. "They'll love it. Do you mind waiting while I bring them?"

Later with his wife and children watching, I led Hamaca and Ima into the pool.

They went in willingly and then stood in the cool water, prim, proper, and puzzled.

"Turn them loose if you want," Señor Isaacs encouraged.

After I removed their halters Hamaca stood like a statue while Ima explored until true to her nature, she was bored. At the shallow end she pawed water furiously, throwing it everywhere. Head high and ears back to keep their insides dry, Hamaca retreated to the pool's other end. Ima snorted and lay down in the water.

Holding his sides all the while, the youngest Isaacs boy rolled on the ground laughing.

Later I turned Hamaca and Ima loose in deeply bedded stalls and followed my host up a ladder to his barn's hay loft. From there he dropped generous servings of sweet-smelling cured alfalfa down chutes into their mangers.

As we walked toward his house, he said, "I've arranged a special dinner for you tonight in Panama City. Would you like to shower first?"

* * *

I was freshly scrubbed and dressed in clean clothes when a waiter seated us after handing me a casual jacket and tie so

I'd meet his establishment's dress code. For the next half hour we were joined at a long table by Panamanian gentlemen who exchanged back-slapping *abrazos* with Señor Isaacs before he introduced them to me.

"Everyone here tonight is a Peruvian horse aficionado," Isaacs told me when all the chairs were occupied. "When Gustavo Moncayo told us you were coming, we organized this reception for you."

There is no way my dinner and conversation with those congenial, interesting, full-of-life men could've been more enjoyable.

After dessert, Señor Isaacs looked at his watch and told us, "They're expecting Verne and me at the Canal Zone, and we're late."

* * *

"These folks are all American and share our enthusiasm for Peru's National Horse," Señor Isaacs told me as we approached the group waiting outside the arena.

After I'd been introduced to everyone, we went inside and stood in groups, talking. Being among countrymen who were enthusiastic about Peruvian horses should've been the delightful end to a perfect evening.

But the Canal Zone had been built for Americans by Americans, and our prejudices were alive and well there. Residents rarely left their self-contained world, and few had bothered to become part of Panama's culture or society. All were kind to me, but most acted as if Señor Isaacs wasn't there.

I couldn't tell if they behaved that way because he was Panamanian or had a Jewish-sounding name. But in view of his kindness toward them, it was heartbreaking and explained why many Panamanians saw us as arrogant.

As the night went along, he told two different Americans how much he admired our country, and I wished he hadn't. He was a wonderful person and had no reason to ingratiate himself to anyone.

* * *

The stable's stack of imported American alfalfa brought Hamaca and Ima to mind. Before ravenously attacking Señor Isaacs' alfalfa they'd shown little interest in Panama's hay.

"I'd love to buy a few bales of this," I whispered to Señor Isaacs. "How much does it cost?"

The price was more than I could possibly afford.

"Where do you buy yours?" I asked, hoping he knew a place where alfalfa was cheaper.

"Here," he replied. "As far as I know this is the only place where it's available."

Back at his ranchette we stopped at the American-looking barn.

"I'll give your mares more alfalfa," he said, seeing their empty mangers. "When you're through caring for them, meet me at the car. Take your time. There's no hurry."

Being careful not to dirty his suit he climbed to the loft while I rinsed and filled my mares' water buckets. When I'd finished my nightly routine and stepped outside, Isaacs was putting the second of two alfalfa bales into his car's trunk.

"Damn," he said, grinning sheepishly. "I wanted this to be a surprise. I'm going to Anton in the morning and will leave these for you with the police chief. He's a friend of mine. I'm sure he'll let you and your horses stay at the station, but he won't have anything for them to eat. Two bales should tide you over for a few days while you find an inexpensive local hay they like."

In just a few hours this complete stranger had shown himself to be as aware, attentive, considerate, and responsive as anyone I'd ever had the pleasure of meeting.

"I wish you could read my mind," I told him, "so you'd know how very much I appreciate your unbelievable goodness."

* * *

I had expected Panama's flat, monotonously green panoramas to be dull compared to the Andes. But in the light of the next morning's golden sunrise I saw a spectacular, lush coastal panorama outlined against the cobalt blue Pacific Ocean. It was a view that compared favorably with anything I'd seen in Ecuador's towering mountains.

I was still admiring it when a pickup truck slowed, then stopped behind me. A tall obviously American cowboy climbed out.

"I'm Bob Green," he said. "Remember me?"

"Of course. How are you?"

Back when I was president of the American Association of Owners and Breeders of Peruvian Paso Horses, he and I had exchanged a whirlwind of letters.

"I'm fine, thank you," he said. "Have you had breakfast?"

Before I could answer he pointed to a restaurant near an overpass and told me, "They have a place where you can put your horses while we eat."

Once Hamaca and Ima were in a corral under the overpass, Bob took me inside to a table near a window.

"From here," he said, "you'll be able to keep an eye on your mares."

While waiting for our order we picked up where our correspondence had left off and further debated the virtues of pureblood Peruvians versus the hybrid produced by mating them with Andalusians.

"That outcross produces a more versatile horse," he began.

"Usually," I countered, "but crossing a laterally gaited breed with one that's diagonally gaited results in a jack-of-all-trades but a master of none."

Clearly enjoying our good-natured debate Bob laughed. For the best part of an hour we tried and failed to reach a meeting of the minds.

"I'll pay," he said when the waiter brought the check, "just to prove I can disagree without being disagreeable."

Not long after we'd gone our separate ways a car passed and pulled onto the shoulder ahead, where two more Americans got out. I recognized the Browns, a couple I'd met the previous night at the Canal Zone Stable.

"Boy, are we lucky," he enthused. "We drove here from Panama City on the off chance we might see your mares. They're beautiful. Which has the better gait?"

"Ima Sumac," I replied. "If you'll hold Hamaca, I'll show you."

I haltered Ima back and forth. The Brown's enthusiastic appreciation kept me going until I was out of breath.

"Evidently that *termino* builds up those distinctive chest muscles," Mrs. Brown said, launching a lengthy discussion of the breed's attributes.

They both knew the breed well, and our discussion was stimulating.

Later, looking at her watch, Mrs. Brown told me, "This is fascinating, but we've taken too much of your time. One last question. Where are you staying tonight?"

"At the Police Station in Anton if I'm lucky," I replied.

"Remembering your interest in alfalfa," she said, "we brought you a bale. We'll leave it there for you."

"Thank you very much," I said, touched by their gesture.

I hoped the Chief wouldn't mention Señor Isaacs' two bales because I didn't want the Browns thinking his gift would make theirs less appreciated. More alfalfa would give me additional time to find a more available hay Hamaca and Ima would eat.

Driving back to the Canal Zone after dropping off their gift Mr. Brown saw me too late, made a U-turn, and matched his car's speed to mine.

His wife rolled her window down and said, "We put in a good word for you with the Chief. He's a friend of ours and said you and your horses are welcome to stay the night."

I felt sure the Chief and Señor Isaacs weren't the Browns' only Panamanian friends.

* * *

When I reached the Police Station, the Chief greeted me enthusiastically.

"You're popular in Panama," he said. "I've already received three bales of hay and two requests to let you stay here. You're welcome to do that. The accommodations are humble, but you'll be comfortable and safe."

He pointed to a jail cell.

I would've felt safer if he hadn't added, "I go home before the changing of the guard. Make sure the man on duty tells his replacement not to lock your cell."

By the time the Chief left, I was drowsy and yawning. Determined not to fall asleep I sat on the bed in my cell, wanting to make sure the new guard was told I wasn't a prisoner.

But I fell asleep.

In my dream I woke up with my cell door closed and locked.

"This door should be open," I told the stranger on duty. "I don't belong here."

"That's what they all say." He didn't look up from his newspaper.

"Please. Call the Chief. He'll vouch for me."

"I can't. He's at a conference in Miami."

"Then call the other guard." I try to be polite even in dreams, but in my growing panic I forgot to say please this time.

"He went with the Chief."

Frustration followed frustration as my bizarre dream became a nightmare so believable that my panic persisted even after I really woke up and saw my cell door wide open.

"When I was told you were worried I'd accidentally lock you in," the new guard said, smiling, "I almost did it just to see how you'd react. Now I'll never know."

Maybe not. But thanks to my dream, I did.

30

BELLYING UP TO THE BAR

B efore leaving Anton, I ate a leisurely breakfast and sent my remaining alfalfa by bus to my next destination, in Penonomé. To cushion our transition from the cool Andes to the steamy tropics, I'd scheduled a short day. We covered the twelve miles in three hours.

Leading my mares through town I passed a restaurant with a sign that read: "Grand Opening. American-style Hamburgers."

I'd had to force myself to finish every hamburger I'd ever bought in Latin America. Rather than risk another disappointment I continued on to the home of a man named Valverde, a friend of Señor Isaacs.

"You're welcome to stay the night," Valverde told me. "Unfortunately my wife is in Panama City and I can't offer any meals. But I ate breakfast at a new restaurant, and the food there is excellent."

"Is that the place advertising American-style hamburgers?" I asked.

"Yes. Its owner and cook is a *paisano* of yours."

An American-style hamburger prepared by an American was more than I could resist. I was also curious to know why someone from the States had opened a business in Penonomé of all places.

When we arrived the restaurant was doing a booming business and its cheerful owner, who spoke Spanish as if it were his native tongue, was the center of attention. Periodically the obviously Panamanian men around him burst into laughter.

"That gentleman," I told Valverde, "could improve American-Panamanian relations by teaching social graces in the Canal Zone."

"No insult intended," Valverde said, "but you're right. He's a very unusual American."

"You're my first customer from the States," the owner told me when he came for my order. "I assume you want the specialty of the house?"

"Not if I'll be disappointed," I teased.

"They come with a money back guarantee," he told me.

I could've bought nine for less than a bale of alfalfa cost in the Canal Zone, but my Spartan budget limited me to only one.

Valverde's impeccable manners obliged him to eat his burger with a knife and fork. I ate mine the good old-fashioned America way, with my hands. It was delicious and I chewed small bites slowly to prolong the pleasure.

"Well?" the owner asked, stopping beside me after I'd finished.

"Your version of the sandwich that symbolizes our native land," I began grandiosely, "is as good as any I've ever eaten."

"The world associates the hamburger with America," he said, "but it seems to have originated in Hamburg, Germany. An immigrant from there served them in a restaurant he opened in the States, and the rest is history."

"Really?"

"Who knows? But that would explain how the hamburger got its name, even though it isn't made with ham." Then he announced in Spanish, "*Señores y Señoras*, this is an historic moment. I've just served my first hamburger to my first American customer on the first day of my grand opening, and he gave me the first of what I hope will be many rave reviews."

I had to pay anyhow.

* * *

The next day, still leading my mares, I pressed on to Aguadulce, hoping to spend the night with one of Bob Green's friends. He raised racehorses and since they're fed only the best, I had visions of Hamaca and Ima eating all the alfalfa they wanted without depleting my meager supply.

Unfortunately Bob's friend was out of town and my mares spent the night tied to trees in another man's backyard. I continued my search for a Panamanian fodder they might like. The only one they'd eaten so far had been corn stalks and I wanted something more nourishing.

In Aguadulce's outdoor market a vendor was selling freshly cut *pangola*, reputedly Panama's tastiest, most nutritious hay. I bought his last two bundles, carried them a mile, and proudly set them before Hamaca and Ima. They nibbled half-heartedly and lost interest, forcing me to feed them more of my fast-disappearing alfalfa.

My hotel bed that night had only a bottom sheet and a pillow. Unaware this was standard in all but expensive air-conditioned establishments, I headed for the reception desk but came to my senses in mid-stride.

More bedding? Was I crazy? Even a top sheet would be too much in Panama's heat.

Desperately tired and in bed early, I was awakened by music from powerful speakers outside the hotel. After stuffing my ears with cotton and putting a pillow over my head I could still hear the relentlessly repetitive refrain, sounding as though a phonograph needle was stuck in a groove.

I charged outside determined to stop that racket and was soon joined by another man with the same goal. Aguadulce's buildings however, echoed the music in a way that prevented us from locating its source. That was just as well because every second of searching made us angrier, and we wouldn't have been tactful if we'd found the guilty party.

Unless of course, the culprit had been a pretty woman.

* * *

I'd led my mares since reaching Panama—except when crossing the Thatcher Ferry Bridge. But from Aguadulce to Divisa I was back in the saddle. My eventual goal was to ride Hamaca one day and Ima the next. But I planned to work up to that gradually by riding Hamaca a day and a half and then Ima during the second afternoon.

Hamaca had put in a hard day by the time we reached Divisa and the previous evening she and Ima had finished the last of my alfalfa. This put me under more pressure than ever to find a dinner they'd eat. As soon as they were comfortable in a corral I began my search at Divisa's agricultural school.

"My students grow hay called *pará* in our experimental field outside town," one of the professors told me. "It's nutritious and horses love it. If you'd like to cut some and try it, you can use my bicycle to get there."

After pedaling miles along a dusty road, I reached a lush green field where I cut enough pará to fill the gunnysack I'd brought. Less than a hundred yards into my return trip a

Good Samaritan, picking up people as he went, stopped his pickup beside me.

"My cab and bed are full," he said. "Why don't you throw your bike on the trailer and ride there."

I loaded my bicycle and *pará*, then climbed aboard. We were speeding down the road in a billowing dust cloud when I noticed there was no nut on the bolt holding the trailer to the truck's bumper. Oblivious to my shouts and waving arms the driver kept going until we reached another passenger's destination.

The instant he stopped, I rushed up and knocked on his window.

As he rolled it down I told him, "The nut came off the bolt that holds your trailer."

"Don't worry," he said. "It's been that way for days. The pressure keeps it in place."

"Thanks for the ride." I wasn't in the least reassured. "Give me a second to get my things."

I pedaled back to the school, thanked the professor for the loan of his bicycle, and carried the *pará*, obtained at the risk of life and limb, to my mares' corral. They stopped eating as soon as the edge was off their hunger. I was tempted to make them choose between going hungry and finishing what I'd given them.

But I didn't have the heart after Hamaca's hard day. So, like many a mother of finicky children, I gave up on getting them to eat what was best and settled for getting them to eat what they would, the always reliable corn stalks.

* * *

The following afternoon my mares showed great interest in something we hadn't seen before, sugarcane spilled on the highway by trucks. This alerted me to the availability of an affordable forage I knew they liked. They'd both eaten cane on the plantations where they were raised.

The stalks on the road, however, had been on the way to a refinery and were too mature for horses. I'd have to find someone who sold cane harvested while still young and tender.

In Santiago's outdoor market that afternoon I found what I was looking for and bought enough for the two days we'd be in town.

"If this is for livestock you should supplement it with these pellets," the vendor advised, pointing to a stack of bags.

I bought one.

Hamaca and Ima welcomed that meal with an enthusiasm previously reserved for only alfalfa. To my surprise every stalk and pellet was gone by the morning of our second day in Santiago. At first I thought at least half had been stolen, but the amount of manure in their corral indicated otherwise.

I hurried to the market and bought a duplicate of the previous night's meal. By the time we set out the following morning they'd devoured every last scrap. It looked to me—but was probably wishful thinking—as if those two days of gorging had filled out their hollow flanks. Unfortunately, however, sugarcane wouldn't often be available as we continued north.

My own flanks were becoming leaner as my appetite diminished and my thirst increased. Looking for something nourishing to drink at a roadside kiosk, I discovered *pipas*.

These were coconuts with straws inserted to facilitate drinking their rich milk. After finishing one I broke the husk open, sampled a chunk of its white meat, and shared the rest with my mares. Astonishingly, they liked it. Now all I had to do was find coconut-flavored hay.

At a ranch outside Soná, Hamaca and Ima dined on sugarcane and chicken feed. The best thing about that supplement was that its name described its price. Of course there was also a drawback. To help poultry digest its other ingredients, it usually contained grit—which provokes colic in horses. I made sure the brands I bought didn't have any.

Anticipating a lower temperature, I welcomed that evening's rain. But the additional moisture made the air even more humid and oppressive. Thanks to my hosts, however, I slept comfortably—cooled by a fan and sprawled on two mattresses, end-to-end on the floor.

Beyond the fan's reach the next morning, I was instantly coated with sweat that stung my arms, where microscopic slices had been almost painlessly inflicted by sharp-edged, broad-bladed grass along the highway. Taller than I, it was an ideal environment for ticks and I'd kept Hamaca and Ima out of it except when vehicles forced us off the road.

Beyond La Arena, this grass became so dense we couldn't get off the highway. Several semi-truck-and-trailer rigs—engines roaring and tires whining—passed close enough to slam us with wind gusts. Hamaca and Ima took this in stride, a sharp contrast with that day near Cuenca, Ecuador, when they'd been terrified by traffic not nearly as loud or dangerous.

* * *

That night from a small rural settlement's combination general store and restaurant, I glanced through a doorway. The adjoining saloon had no customers, stools, tables, or chairs—just a bar taller than I was. On its other side the bartender stood on a platform, looking down as I walked toward him on a dirt floor under an extra high ceiling.

"Why," I asked, "is everything here on such a grand scale?"

"Guess," he challenged.

I couldn't. No one in town was as tall as I'd been in the fifth grade, yet the front door could easily have accommodated a truck. When the church bell rang, announcing the end of the work day, a group of men on horseback rode through the oversize door and up to the bar. There they remained in their saddles while the bartender took orders and served drinks.

"What can I get you?" he asked when it was my turn.

"Any soft drink will be fine, thank you," I replied.

With an impish grin he served me a cola with one of those cocktail umbrellas normally reserved for ladies' drinks.

In the States I'd often been complimented for my abstinence, but never in Latin America.

* * *

Soná was days away when we entered an area where indoor plumbing was rare and the only electricity was produced by portable generators. It goes without saying that there were no spraying programs to control parasites. So I redoubled my precautions against piroplasmosis, a sometimes fatal livestock disease that affects equids—horses, donkeys, mules, and zebras.

Piro is transmitted by ticks and mosquitoes. If Hamaca and Ima's blood tests at the U.S. border showed as little as just antibodies, they'd be put down or quarantined for life at my expense. No matter how many ways I tried to protect my mares from this invisible threat, I never felt like I was doing enough.

But I was doing a lot. I immersed all freshly cut hay in water, forcing ticks to float to the surface for air. I never rode in greenery more than inches deep. Twice a day I checked my mares for ticks and wiped their coats with insect repellent.

At night I spread damp shavings or straw on hot coals, producing thick smoke to repel blood-sucking, disease spreading mosquitoes.

* * *

No matter how gently I groomed Hamaca and Ima two mornings later, they pulled away from my rubber curry comb. Examining their mysteriously sensitive hides, I realized how drastically and in how many ways the tropics had affected them. Their distressing loss of weight was but one of many changes.

Their formerly sleek coats were frizzy and dulled by sun, repellents, and insecticides. Their rare, spectacular, true-black colors had faded—Hamaca's to a yellowish hue and Ima's to an anemic red. Insect bites, sweat, and chemicals had left both with rashes and bare spots where they'd rubbed out patches of hair.

"It's better to prevent than lament," Jorge Baca had often cautioned me in Peru.

Yes. If I'd known what was coming I would've toughened my mares' hides with saltwater baths. But now those would be another irritant. To prevent further discomfort, I shipped my saddles and duffel bags ahead. Then I alternately led my mares or rode bareback.

Dreaming of Costa Rica's high country, fewer parasites, alfalfa, and mild temperatures, I also made myself less appetizing to insects by spiking my canteen water with vinegar. Unfortunately adding even small amounts to Hamaca and Ima's grain stopped them from eating it.

North of Soná, between Puerto Vidal and Guabala, the highway changed from a straight concrete line knifing across flat terrain to a crude gravel road winding through foothills.

It was lined with tall grass and surfaced with rocks that varied from the size of a dime to that of a baseball. Often we had no choice but to walk on this so-called gravel and were soon hobbling along on tender feet.

By then my mares were a sorry-looking duo. Their heads were low and for the first time they'd lost interest in their surroundings. Ima's condition deteriorated further after one of her hooves slipped off a rock, leaving her with an ouchy foreleg. But even with all their maladies, there was no short-age of folks interested in buying them.

"Are they for sale?" people called from doorways, passing vehicles, or while running toward us for a closer look.

No wonder Panama's customs had wanted a deposit to guarantee I'd pay taxes if I sold them.

Historically, Central Americans have paid more for Peru-vian horses than Americans do, but I never asked how much anyone would pay. My priorities remained the same as al-ways: to finish what I'd started, publicize Peruvian horses, and enter Hamaca in the Tevis Cup.

I didn't want to leave my mares in Central America even if I could get better prices there. I wanted them in the States, where they'd add their good qualities to our bloodlines.

* * *

Outside Guabala, a man stopped his car and got out. He wasn't however, interested in buying a horse. He'd noticed that we looked like we'd benefit from rest, relaxation, and good food.

"I'm a close friend of the Motta family," he told me. "They have a huge, modern ranch along the highway outside Reme-dios. I'm sure you'll be welcome to stay a few days, and be-lieve me you'll be well-fed and comfortable."

"After three hundred miles in thirteen days," I replied, "that sounds like heaven."

"Just be glad you didn't make this trip a few years back. Before your country financed construction of the highway bridges, you'd have had to swim every river you've crossed." He paused. "I'll see George Motta this evening. Shall I tell him to expect you?"

"Yes, but not tonight."

"Tomorrow then?"

I answered with a Spanish expression that originated with Spain's fatalistic Moors: "God willing."

He gave me directions to the Motta's ranch and went on his way. I hadn't been invited yet, but tomorrow I'd stop by and say hello. If George Motta was surprised, worried about hoof-and-mouth disease, short on space, or less than enthusiastic in any way, I'd continue on. If he welcomed me with open arms I'd thank my lucky stars.

That night in Guabala, ten miles short of the Motta Brothers' ranch, Hamaca's peculiar grazing instinct resurfaced. The first time had been in a newly built adobe corral in Ecuador. Generous amounts of straw are mixed into adobe to bind it, and she'd walked away from perfectly good alfalfa to graze on dry strands protruding from bricks in her corral's walls.

Every time I stopped her, she started again until I tied her where she couldn't reach the wall and fed her there.

At the only accommodation I could find in Guabala, I slept on a porch and tied my mares to posts supporting its roof. Later I was jarred awake by Hamaca who—instead of eating her sugarcane—was chewing sun-bleached grass she'd torn from the thatched roof.

When she resisted all efforts to stop her, I tied her to a tree and fed her there.

* * *

The next morning we traveled on to the Motta brothers' ranch where George received us as cordially as promised. His invitation to stay a couple of days was so enthusiastic it almost seemed I was doing him a favor.

"You can turn your mares loose in there," he said pointing to a lush pasture where three huge Brahman bulls grazed. Seeing my concern he added, "Don't worry. They won't bother your horses."

"I'm more worried about ticks and mosquitoes than your bulls," I explained. "I don't want my mares to get piroplasmosis. It's a disease transmitted—"

"I know all about piro," he interrupted. "But we have a rigorous spraying program for parasites, and some fresh grass will be good for your horses."

The opportunity for Hamaca and Ima to graze to their hearts' content was irresistible, and for the rest of the day I seldom saw either with her nose out of the grass. Late that afternoon three *vaqueros* finished their day's work and turned their cowponies loose to graze.

A gelding headed toward Ima who'd claimed that section of pasture for herself and Hamaca. Seeing this intruder, Ima added a new dimension—bully— to her many-faceted personality. Ears pinned back, she rushed toward him and turned her hindquarter, prepared to kick if he didn't stop.

Emboldened when he retreated, she drove him and his companions farther from her private property. No doubt they'd done more fighting than she—and were probably better at it—but she got away with her bluff and bluster. Tired after a hard day's work the cowponies decided to fill their stomachs elsewhere.

Ima had enjoyed being the boss and next targeted the bulls. In terms of its potential for disaster, this was on a par with Hitler's invasion of Russia. Terrified, I watched her pin her ears and charge the giant toros. When they stood their ground, she stopped and glared. Luckily for her—and me—they blinked first and gave ground.

While Hamaca grazed, Ima continued herding the bulls. Each outweighed her at least three-to-one and had built-in weapons—namely horns—for which she had no defense. When they'd had enough, they became aggravated. It was time to get her out of harm's way.

I caught Ima and Hamaca, then found George Motta and told him, "Ima Sumac was herding your bulls and they didn't like it. Is there a place where she and Hamaca can be alone?"

"I saw her herding them," he said. "Don't worry. She has natural cow sense and won't push too far."

"My mares get along well and can share a stall or a small corral," I pressed, remembering how Ima had refused to yield to even those huge trucks in Ecuador.

George led us to vacant side-by-side stalls.

"After all they've been through, your horses are in great condition," he said after I put them inside. "Panama is hard on livestock. Within a few generations, descendants of imported horses degenerate to where they're no bigger than our native breeds. The only cows that do well are the ones we raise—Cebu, Brahman—an East Indian variety that thrives in hostile environments."

When I finished my nightly routine he said, "There's another precaution you should take. Until well inside Costa Rica, there's a fly that bites out a tiny chunk of flesh and lays an egg in the wound. This hatches into a worm that feeds on its host's flesh and cause serious infections." He handed me a bottle of liquid. "Sponge your mares with this every morning and evening. It repels those flies and kills their larvae."

Great. Just what Hamaca and Ima needed, another harsh chemical on their skins.

* * *

Invigorated by rest, stimulating conversation, and delicious steak dinners, I left the Motta's ranch with considerable regret. With no particular destination in mind, I rode to a farm in a rural area and rented space in its ramshackle barn.

Watching my nightly routine its owner warned, "Before the town of David there's a bridge your mares won't cross." As if concerned I hadn't taken him seriously he added, "Please believe me. They won't walk on that bridge. You need to get there no later than 10:00 a.m. because the detour is long and you shouldn't be on it after the sun sets."

His warning didn't faze me. Hamaca and Ima had been on plenty of bridges, including the one across the Panama Canal at Thatcher's Ferry. They'd even crossed some where we'd had to skirt broken planks or holes where chunks of concrete had dropped out. Through it all, they'd sometimes hesitated but never refused.

Once they were settled I hitchhiked miles to a ranch where I hoped to buy sugar cane.

"That's the only feed I have," the rancher said, pointing to a pile of grass hay.

Hamaca and Ima hadn't yet tried that variety, so I bought some. After sampling it they walked away, obliging me to look for something more appealing—which once again turned out to be the old-reliable, corn stalks.

Reluctant to lie down on the barn's rough concrete floor, Hamaca and Ima spent an uncomfortable night. I slept as well as ever after a liberal bedtime dose of aspirin.

We didn't reach the mysterious bridge the next day, and that evening the only available accommodation was another barn with another concrete floor. We arrived at twilight so I skipped the usual rubdowns and in the absence of traffic, flagged down a man driving an antiquated tractor.

"Pay me by the hour," he proposed, "and I'll take you to farms until we find feed."

Under a fast-darkening sky we traveled the narrow highway with me standing behind him on the tractor's frame. It was a pathetic vehicle that had no lights, couldn't reach anything near highway speed, had a frightening amount of play in the steering, and repeatedly drifted across the centerline.

At the third ranch we visited, I was finally able to buy gritless chicken feed and a grass hay I hadn't seen before. Returning in fading daylight to the barn where I'd left Hamaca and Ima, I made a considerable effort to avoid blocking the tractor's single rear-facing reflector. It was the only warning drivers from behind would see before they were too close to avoid plowing into us.

Though I'd put myself in peril and spent almost two hours finding and bringing this perfectly satisfactory-looking meal, Hamaca and Ima ate only the chicken feed.

Exhausted I gave in to my long-standing temptation to find out if hunger would eventually drive my two spoiled brats to eat.

It did, sort of. They ate the chicken feed and about a third of the hay before sleeping on their feet on a concrete floor for the second consecutive night.

* * *

The next afternoon on my way to David, I saw a bridge's superstructure on the horizon. From that distance it appeared well-built and I saw nothing unusual about it. Was that the span about which my host of two nights ago had warned? If so why had he predicted my mares would refuse to cross it?

Contrary to everything I'd heard or read about horses, Hamaca and Ima were more likely to go where they didn't want to if I led rather than rode them. They might stop to think it over several times, but seemed to trust me and always eventually came along if I went first. In Ecuador they'd even tried to follow me into stores and homes after I'd left them ground tied.

Closer to the bridge I still saw no cause for concern. Nonetheless I dismounted and went ahead, doing my best to time our arrival so there'd be no traffic when we got there.

Stepping from the concrete roadway to the bridge, I froze with one foot on each—unable to force myself to go farther. The bridge's floor was egg crate design steel grates through which I could see all the way to the bottom of the deep canyon. The view produced chills in all the predictable places.

Before Hamaca and Ima saw why I'd stopped, I led them back in the direction from which we'd come, then turned and briskly approached the bridge again. This time I confidently strode onto it and kept going. To my relief they followed, cautiously looking down—but with interest more than distress.

Soon we came to hills where the winding road was surfaced with rocks, some as large as softballs. These rolled beneath my mares' hooves, so I dismounted and led them. Going downhill on such unstable footing jammed my feet against the fronts of my boots with every step. My big toes throbbed with pain by the time we reached the concrete highway near the town of David.

Anton's Police Chief had given me a letter asking David's

mayor to host us. Following the crude map drawn on the envelope, I turned into a driveway, reached a luxurious residence, and knocked on its door.

"I'm the overseer," an elderly man softly said as he came out of a nearby building. "How can I help you?"

I handed him the letter.

After reading it, he said, "The Mayor's on vacation. He'll be distressed to hear he missed you."

Evidently he found it distasteful to turn me away. Twice I started down the driveway and he called me back to explain that the Mayor would've attended me splendidly if only he'd been there. Troubled by his discomfort, I assured him I understood.

"I can offer you a place to stay," he said, "but it's rustic."

After two nights on concrete floors, I was more than satisfied with the small well-kept, bull-free pasture he offered for Hamaca and Ima. And with the spic-and-span shed supporting a water tank he unlocked for me.

"Let me know if I can do anything more," he said as he left.

As I learned when I took my boots off, my big toes hurt because both had blood blisters under the toenail.

Damn. To avoid disappointing a young lady on a high school date, I'd stuffed my size fifteens into a pair of size twelve ice skates, the largest available at the frozen lake in Reno's Idlewild Park. As a result I'd lost both big toenails. After that it became progressively easier to lose them. This would be the fifth time.

I answered a soft knock on the shed's door.

"You'll rest better with this under your sleeping bag," the overseer said, unfolding a chaise lounge.

"Do you know where I can find a horseshoer?" I asked as

he turned to go. "My horses have only four shoes between them, and one is worn through at the toe."

"I'm not sure David has a farrier these days," he replied. "The best I can do is recommend a friend who might know."

* * *

If all went well David would be my last overnight stop in Panama, and the next would be Paso de Canoas, Costa Rica. Before I could cross that border, however, I had much to do.

The caretaker's friend didn't know a horseshoer and referred me to someone who sent me to someone else. While on my way to see him, I stopped at the office of Costa Rica's Consul General and asked about requirements for taking horses into his country.

"You'll need their Peruvian and Ecuadorian health certificates," he informed me, "plus a new one from a veterinarian in David, all three authenticated by me."

At a nearby vet's office I made an appointment to have Hamaca and Ima examined that afternoon, then resumed my search for a farrier. The one I found was probably three times my age.

"I retired years ago and no longer practice my trade," he told me.

"How much will it take to bring you out of retirement?" I asked.

"I have neither nails nor horseshoes," he said. "If you buy some, I'll put them on your horses for my old price minus their cost."

Foregoing an afternoon of badly needed rest I hitchhiked to Concepción where — after considerable searching — I found and bought the first steel horseshoes I'd seen since the States. They'd last far longer than iron shoes, good news because constant re-shoeing was becoming a headache.

In his yard the old farrier labored, perspired, and cursed, but was too frail to remove my mares' remaining shoes. It didn't help that he was using only a machete and a short-handled hammer that was little more than a toy. When I offered to help, he handed his tools to me.

Using his method, I set out to remove the shoes. First I placed his machete blade against the crimped ends of the nails and hit it with his hammer to cut them off. With a rasp and clippers, my shoer at home could've done that and pulled the shoes with tongs in minutes. But with primitive tools and no experience I took an hour.

Trimming my mares' hooves and nailing on new shoes however, would require the old farrier's expertise, and I returned his hammer. I'd have to be patient no matter how long he took to finish the job.

He didn't have hoof clippers, but the previous shoes had worn out quickly and my mares' hooves hadn't grown much. All he had to do was rasp them. Nailing on new shoes however, proved difficult. He bent several nails and looked exhausted by the time he'd put on the first.

Clearly he wasn't capable of finishing the job.

"I might be able to take over," I offered, "if you'll tell me what to do."

Sitting on a nearby chair he patiently gave detailed instructions while I nailed on a shoe. After that, he helped me with another and another, until both mares were shod.

Next I took Hamaca and Ima to the veterinarian's office where he examined them and issued health certificates. After Costa Rica's consul authenticated these, I turned my mares loose in the Mayor's pasture and ate dinner at a restaurant.

In my sleeping bag that evening I wondered how my stay would've been in the Mayor's beautiful, inviting home instead of his tool shed. I decided things had worked out for the best. I was bone-tired and in his house I'd have had social obligations. But in his tool shed I was free to go to bed early and catch up on my sleep.

By the time I woke the next morning the Mayor's helpful caretaker had arranged for a trucker to take Hamaca, Ima, and me to the border. That free ride was a godsend because Costa Rica's Consul hadn't been sure how long Hamaca and Ima's new health certificates were valid.

* * *

Once Panama's border official was satisfied I was leaving with the same horses I'd brought in, he quickly processed the rest of our paperwork. After we crossed the no man's land between that border station and Costa Rica's, I chose the line leading to an agricultural inspector whose name tag read: Raul.

"Your horses' health certificates are signed by a private veterinarian," he told me. "You'll have to return to David and get a new one from a government vet."

"But your consul in David said this would be sufficient." I said.

"All we need is a health certificate from a government vet," Raul insisted.

"So now I'll lose two days while riding my horses eighty miles to and from David because of someone else's mistake?" I complained with what I hoped was the right combination of despair and righteousness.

"Not at all, Señor," he said without a trace of sympathy. "If you take this afternoon's bus, you'll be back in time to cross the border before it closes tonight."

"And my horses?"

"We'll keep them in quarantine until you return."

"If I leave them here, how will the government veterinarian examine them?"

"Show him your certificate from the private vet and he'll issue the one we need. Be sure to have it authenticated by our consul in David."

That made no sense. If the government vet could issue a health certificate based on the one I already had, why couldn't Raul just accept it?

But arguing with him would almost certainly do more harm than good. I was reminded of an incident that began when a small town policeman had demanded to see Aimé Tschiffely's authorization to carry firearms. He didn't have a permit and to get one he would have to backtrack for days.

Suspecting the officer was illiterate, Tschiffely handed over a hotel receipt that bore an impressive signature and several rubber stamped imprints.

That had satisfied the officer.

In Tschiffely's day I might have convinced Raul my invoice for horseshoes and nails was my mares' government health certificate. But time had marched on, and illiteracy was no longer widespread in Latin America.

So why was my mom convinced that education was such a wonderful thing?

I hurried outside, unsaddled my mares, and put them in the quarantine corral. Then I searched for the driver who'd brought me from David. If I could ride back with him I wouldn't have to wait hours for the bus.

He was loading the last of his cargo.

"Do you mind if I ride back to David with you," I asked. "I need to get another health certificate."

"I'll be delighted to have company," he said.

During our drive he tried to make me feel better by describing problems he'd had at Central American borders. But his stories erased all hope that I might someday cross at least one border without wasting more of my fast disappearing time and money.

* * *

"I don't think you should charge another fee," I told the Consul in David, handing him my newly issued government health certificate to authenticate. "The ones I paid yesterday were unnecessary."

"I must be paid for every document I process," he replied, studying me through half-hooded eyes. "According to the bulletins I receive everything I authenticated yesterday is required."

"Not according to the official at the border."

"That's not my fault." The Consul turned toward his private office.

If I didn't apologize fast he'd almost certainly be unavailable to me for days. And for all I knew he was right and Raul was wrong.

"Sorry," I told him. "I shouldn't have questioned you."

"Come back in four hours," he said, taking revenge for my earlier aggressiveness.

Four hours later the Consul collected his fee and handed over my verified certificate.

31

THE WAY TO SAN JOSÉ

My bus reached the Costa Rican border station at Paso de Canoas after dark. I presented my new, freshly authenticated health certificate to the official then on duty, hoping he wouldn't come up with further requirements.

"*Bienvenido*, welcome," he said pleasantly.

Giving him as little time as possible to change his mind, I immediately saddled my mares and started across the parking lot. Every space was full and a line of waiting vehicles with U.S. license plates stretched down the highway. Strange. There hadn't been a single American there that morning.

"Why are so many Americans coming into Panama tonight?" I asked an exhausted-looking man as he hurried toward the border station.

"There's been a revolution," he replied without slowing.

"In Costa Rica?" I called after him.

"No, in Nicaragua," another man answered, stopping to admire Hamaca and Ima. "There was an attempted coup. The rebels took American hostages, and the government closed the borders. No one could get in or out for several days. It's quiet now, but things could heat up at any moment."

"How bad was it?" I asked.

"Damn scary. I'd stay out of there if I were you."

"I had no idea there were so many Americans in Nicaragua," I said.

"What you see here is nothing compared to those who went north." He hurried toward the border station.

Violence in Nicaragua was bad news. Decades earlier, to avoid one of its frequent revolutions, Amie Tschiffely had loaded Mancha and Gato on an oceangoing steamer and by-passed that strife-torn country. I didn't have enough money for that and very much wanted to see what I'd long considered Central America's most fascinating nation.

The night sky was overcast, and without moonlight visibility was poor. Traffic was heavy and drivers were bleary-eyed after many hours on the road. Tonight would be a bad time to travel after dark and I had an alternative. The man in charge of the quarantine corral, knowing what I'd been through that day, had offered to let me sleep in the border station's back room.

"Is it too late to accept your kind offer?" I asked when I found him.

"Not at all." He reached up and patted my shoulder. "Put your mares back in the quarantine corral."

* * *

We started out early and in four invigorating days traveled a hundred fifty miles. In the process we entered a new time zone, which made our progress seem even more dramatic.

This push — our most successful yet — was possible for sev-eral reasons. We'd left the worst of the tropics for a cooler area where we slept well and had more energy. Hamaca and

Ima were eating better and getting over their afflictions. I was riding fulltime and though we were going no faster than before, we felt good enough to spend more hours on the road.

Now that I was riding Ima regularly, the attitude she'd shown the Motta Ranch's cowponies and bulls resurfaced — directed at me. When not inclined to follow orders, which at first was often, she didn't hesitate to challenge me. After several titanic battles she finally submitted, but her attitude soured to where I sometimes wondered if she stuck her tongue out at me when I wasn't looking.

* * *

Passing the first of Costa Rica's banana plantations, I made four observations for *Albright's Book of Useless Facts*.

One: Banana plants are huge, varying from twelve to twenty-five feet high, with leaves up to two feet wide and nine feet long. Two: The fruit itself defies gravity, growing upward from its stems in clusters. Three: These are covered with clear plastic while maturing, to prevent birds from landing and feeding. Four: Bananas are picked while still green and ripen during shipment.

Most plantations I saw in Central America were owned by American companies such as Del Monte, Dole, and Chiquita. Passing thirty-five miles of these the next day, I marveled at the precision required to manage them. Every day — three hundred sixty-five times a year — the needed quantity of fruit had to be at the right stage of ripeness to be harvested and shipped.

When I put myself in the places of workers whose mind-numbing jobs were to hang the plastic sheets or harvest the bunches at top speed, my heart went out to them. This sympathy increased the night I stayed in a shabby hotel at one of their camps and saw how they lived.

At the company store, I bought a gunnysack full of incredibly cheap carrots and carried it to the cattle ranch where I'd left Hamaca and Ima. They were delighted to get more of what they'd eaten by the bushel at Quito's Colegio Militar.

However, I regretted having hogged so many carrots when I realized the company had priced them low so workers could afford nutritious food. My purchase had foiled that plan and condemned hard working men and their families to eat dinners without vegetables. But by the time I realized that, Hamaca and Ima had finished every last one.

I turned my mares loose for a couple of hours in a tick-free pasture where Hamaca seemed to finally realize that grazing was an inefficient way to scrape together a meal. Nickering, she rushed up when I came to return her and Ima to their corral. No fool, she'd seen me put sugar cane in its manger and knew she'd fill her stomach faster there.

Horses don't adjust well to changes of any sort, and the previous four nights mine had eaten sugarcane, corn stalks, carrots, and two tropical grasses — *imperial* and *gigante*. Such abrupt changes of diet can provoke diarrhea, colic, intestinal disorders, irregular hoof growth, inflamed glands, or laminitis. But so far they hadn't.

In fact, Hamaca and Ima had regained some of the weight they'd lost. Their flanks were fuller and their bodies rounder, amazing in view of the distances we were traveling. I'd been told I could buy alfalfa and oats in Costa Rica's high country. If that was true they should soon be back in the condition Luis de Ascásubi had admired.

* * *

After passing a hundred miles of banana plantations we entered a semi-jungle that was less harsh than, and very different from, Panama. Leaving tropical grasslands and scrub forests we entered a tall, dense, broadleaf evergreen forest. Twisted, moss-coated trees with vines dangling from their branches formed a veil along the roadside. Behind it unseen monkeys sounded like the soundtrack of a Tarzan movie.

The highway was often the only evidence of man, and even that would've disappeared if Mother Nature had her way. Vines crawled onto the roadway and branches reached out above it. But passing traffic pruned this fast-growing greenery, keeping the jungle at bay.

When the sun was out we caught glimpses of exotic wildlife — mostly iguanas, sloths, and anteaters. During downpours we saw people huddled under trees. When the sun reappeared, tiny spectacularly colored birds darted from bush to bush as if making sure no damage had been done.

I'd been told the wet season was over and had sent my rain gear ahead, leaving me ill-prepared for these cloudbursts. Following the locals' lead I learned to hold oversize leaves from plants called elephant ears above my head. When these were no longer needed I'd simply throw them away. They were after all, everywhere and biodegradable.

I kept my traveler's checks, passport, and important papers dry by wrapping them in banana leaves. Everything else got soaked by big, hard-hitting, raindrops that stung when they hit bare skin. On hard surfaces they exploded like tiny artillery shells. When they hit standing water, the geysers seemed to have been caused by miniature depth charges.

Yes, we men are inclined to think in military terms.

Windblown rain was the most disagreeable. But electrical storms with bright lightning were particularly unwelcome when they unexpectedly illuminated clearings where I was taking care of personal business at night.

After one early morning deluge, I rode into buzzards gathered in a sunlit clearing. Due to an oversight of nature their feathers weren't water-repellent. They were standing in warm sunlight, too wet to fly, wings spread open to dry quickly. Eager to get airborne and find breakfast, they hopped away from me, wings still extended to avoid interrupting the drying process.

That afternoon I saw tiny tadpole-like creatures swimming in puddles. I don't know what they were or how they came to be in water that had only just collected and would soon dry up.

Perhaps the answer was in a *Los Angeles Times* article I'd saved, intending to quote it in *Albright's Book of Useless Facts*.

> *In what scientists call a biological oddity, the heavy March rains have called to life masses of tiny, dormant shrimp eggs. Many had been deposited long ago on the same clay lake beds where the space shuttles land—usually bone dry but amply flooded in recent months.*

* * *

After starting up into Costa Rica's Talamanca Mountains we paralleled a river with a variety of waterfalls. They were wide or narrow, high or low, and fell in a single cascade or a series of them. Some were airborne all the way down. Others were atomized to mist by protruding rock. All were sensationally beautiful.

One night, determined to reach the town of Buenos Aires, I traveled after dark. In other countries I wouldn't have risked it, but Costa Rica had a well-deserved reputation as a peaceful place. While there I'd never once felt threatened.

Outside Buenos Aires a young, helpful American Peace

Corps volunteer stopped me. He got permission for Hamaca and Ima to stay in a vacant chicken coop, then drove me around in his Jeep while I rounded up crushed corn and sugarcane. Next he left me to share a tool shed with a young English adventurer traveling on a budget as tight as mine.

In the light of a single florescent tube that bleached all color from our enclosure, we sat on the floor talking. Like me he was a "racist" in the purest sense, but didn't condone prejudging or mistreating other ethnicities. Simply stated we both believed the majority of every race has certain inborn qualities that don't mark any as superior or inferior—just different.

Most Americans of goodwill deny the existence of inherent characteristics, usually because racists use those to justify and promote persecution. I freely admit that our country's sometimes deplorable treatment of African Americans, indigenous peoples, Asians, Jewish people, Hispanics, et al was and still is largely based on supposed differences from and inferiority to the white majority.

But that doesn't mean there are no differences or that none are inborn. My perspective is best summed up by one of my favorite jokes:

They say that in Heaven, life is even better than we've been told. This is because English are the policemen, French are the lovers, Germans are the organizers, Italians are the cooks, Japanese manufacture cars, and Americans play basketball.

Hell however, is even more horrible than what Dante described in his *Inferno*, because there Germans are policemen, Swiss are lovers, Italians are organizers, English are cooks, Americans manufacture cars, and Japanese play basketball.

Every race—and everyone in it—has strengths and weaknesses. The same is true of cultures. To me, for example, my companion was typically English, well-spoken, well-informed, thoughtful, interested in a wide variety of subjects, and a sophisticated thinker.

To him I was an untypical American.

"You're the first one I've met," he told me, "who knows how to travel."

"In what sense?" I asked.

"In several," he replied. "The majority of Americans don't travel until they're older. But they could put what they learn while doing that to good use throughout their lives if they did it when younger. Worse yet they sleep in comfortable hotels, eat familiar food, take guided tours, and otherwise isolate themselves from local cultures."

"Your description fits Americans I saw in the Canal Zone," I said, "but not, for example, Peace Corps members. And young Americans usually travel in their own country because they don't have much money."

"But when they're older and go camping, most do it in cocoons—by which I mean motor homes, trailers, or elaborate tents with all the comforts of home, sometimes even television. All I take is a backpack. I drink river or lake water, pick berries, catch fish, and fry them with wild mushrooms and onions. Instead of watching the ten o'clock news, I observe nature and have new experiences."

That night I ignored my desperate need of sleep, so our fascinating conversation could continue into the wee hours.

32

THE MOUNTAIN OF DEATH

R iding to San Isidro del General the next day I saw algarrobo trees different from those in Peru. My mares had loved the Peruvian seedpods so I offered Hamaca a handful of Costa Rica's smaller, darker ones. She nuzzled them, then looked away. After a sniff, Ima the Drama Queen looked at me with an expression that asked: *Are you sure Chinese horses eat those things?*

All day we passed southbound vehicles with U.S. license plates, most no doubt fleeing Nicaragua's revolution. These included numerous large motor homes. Isolated in those cocoons — as my previous night's companion called them — few people waved back and no one stopped to talk.

But their expressions said the situation in Nicaragua wasn't good. Damn. If things didn't stabilize by the time I reached the border, I'd have to hunker down in Costa Rica — perhaps long enough to prevent me from getting to California in time for the Tevis Cup. And maybe, perish the thought, long enough to run out of money.

My discouragement soon infected Hamaca and Ima. All morning they'd been eager to see what was beyond the next hill or curve. But as my spirits dampened they began turning toward every structure and corral. This was their equivalent of being what horsemen call barn sour, a term for horses that persistently try to return to their stalls or corrals rather than go where their riders want.

Problem was, any structure or fenced-in area might be where my mares would eat and sleep. All day they hopefully turned toward each one we passed, with Ima becoming increasingly insistent. By day's end I was as homesick as she and Hamaca were barn sour.

The next day went from bad to worse. On a highway surfaced with crushed rock Ima lost a hind shoe, almost certainly because I'd nailed it badly. I didn't notice her predicament until she began limping on the sharp-edged gravel. By then there was no hope of finding the lost shoe.

That evening I paid a blacksmith in San Isidro to replace it and check the others I'd nailed on in David.

"They should stay put until you get to San José," he told me. Then, as if it were a mere afterthought, he added, "Last night there was a case of Anthrax on a nearby farm. You should immunize your mares if there's any vaccine left at the veterinary supply store."

"There won't be," I said wearily, "not the way things are going these days."

* * *

In a rush to buy anthrax vaccine the next morning, I hurried into San Isidro's central plaza. Halfway across, a street urchin dashed up and stopped as I passed him.

"Señor," he gasped, out of breath. "That man...wants to talk... with you."

"What man?" I asked without slowing.

"The one over there…at the bar…across the plaza," the boy said, scrambling to keep up.

"Maybe later," I told him, eager to be first in line when the veterinary supply store opened.

Even if I hadn't been on a mission, I wouldn't have had any interest in a conversation with someone who was drinking that early. The boy's dejection as he walked away made me suspect he'd been offered a reward to bring me. I couldn't help wondering why.

When I reached the supply store there was no line, and later when the owner unlocked the door I was the only person waiting.

"Please tell me you still have anthrax vaccine," I said, going inside.

"Five vials," he replied. "How many do you need?"

"Enough for two horses. Can you recommend a vet to administer it?"

"Your horses will need a series of easy-to-give intramuscular shots," he said, setting two vials on the counter. "Having a veterinarian administer them is a waste of money. I'll tell you how. It's easy."

"No thank you." As always, I was interested in saving money, but I also wanted to be certain the vaccine was administered correctly. "I shod my own horses a few days back, and one has already lost a shoe. Some jobs are best left to professionals."

"If you insist on using a veterinarian," the owner said, handing me a card from beside his cash register, "this man's office is nearby."

* * *

Determined to save money in the future, I watched carefully

and asked more than my share of questions as the veterinarian gave Ima her shot.

"Would you mind," I asked, "if I inject my other mare while you supervise?"

"I'll be happy to," he said.

He'd inserted the first needle into Ima's neck with the syringe attached.

When I started to do the same with Hamaca he said, "It will be easier if you detach and hold the needle between your thumb and forefinger. Then tap your horse's neck several times with the back of that hand before planting the needle."

I've injected my own horses ever since, using that technique.

After I took Hamaca and Ima back to their corral the same youngster dashed up to me with fresh enthusiasm.

"Señor," he panted, out of breath again. "That man…please go…he came here…to avoid fighting in Vietnam."

He said this without the disapproval I immediately felt. But he'd aroused my curiosity and I followed him into the saloon.

"Is it true the Vietnam war has become unpopular?" the young American on a stool at the bar asked, handing the boy a coin.

"Yes," I replied. "Extremely."

He perked up. "Is there any talk of pardoning draft dodgers?"

"Not that I've heard."

"You don't approve of what I did, do you?"

I didn't answer, but he was right. I didn't yet realize my country had foolishly intervened in a civil war and was employing tactics that violated our most cherished principles.

"I saw you ride into town last night," he continued. "Where are you headed?"

"San José."

"You'll love it there. How long do you intend to stay?"

"Two days," I replied.

He went on to describe the wondrous qualities of San José's women and assured me, "They're delightful."

I started for the door after he slipped back into his melancholy and started drowning his sorrows again.

"I have a prediction," he called out as I left. "A girl will smile at you, and you'll be in San José more than two days."

But women weren't on my itinerary. I had a job to do, and not enough time had passed since my painful divorce.

* * *

In an automobile, the imposing eleven-thousand-foot Cerro de la Muerte—Mountain of Death—can be crossed in less than three hours. But for centuries travelers made that three-to-four-day journey on foot or horseback, and when temperatures plummeted without warning lethal sub-zero weather often killed those who weren't adequately prepared.

Like Aimé Tschiffely thirty years earlier, I'd heard the stories. The one that most stuck in my mind had ended with rescuers finding a virtual forest of travelers frozen solid in standing positions. I didn't ask if any frozen horses had been found. If they had, I didn't want to know.

Even on the Panamericana, the hundred mile crossing of that peak would be a formidable challenge. From San Isidro we'd climb more than nine thousand feet before descending to San José.

On the morning we set out, I packed my horse blankets and warmest clothes at the top of my duffel bag for quick access. I also bought dysentery pills to counteract the debilitating symptoms of what Hispanics call *turistas* because it usually affects foreigners. My symptoms so far had been mild.

Home to abundant flora and fauna, Cerro de la Muerte could also have been called the Mountain of Life. Its flanks are chilled by the world's two largest oceans, and it was foggy that day. Early on we were in a rain forest where the upper branches of huge, moss-covered oak trees formed a canopy, vines hung from branches, and lush underbrush was mixed with flowers and succulents.

I led Hamaca and Ima that first morning. Sicker in the afternoon, I rode when the highway climbed and walked when it headed downhill. At night we camped in a cloud forest of stunted, gnarled trees.

At dawn—weakened by my worsening *turistas*—I forced myself to push on. There was no time to lose. The consequences of being in the high country if temperatures suddenly nosedived would be a whole lot worse than dysentery.

I recognized few of the birds I saw that day, probably because many are found nowhere else on earth. Based on photos I saw later, I probably caught a glimpse of a rare quetzal, a spectacular scarlet-breasted beauty with iridescent green plumage and a long tail.

Much of the third day we were above the timberline in grassland resembling Andean páramos. Several times from the summit's ridge I saw either the Atlantic or Pacific Ocean, but didn't find the promised spot from which both are visible simultaneously. I wasn't all that disappointed. I could've had pretty much the same experience by looking at either, making a half-turn, and looking again.

Many hours later I saw San José in the distance.

Since my arrival, Costa Rica had lived up to its reputation as a land of startling contrasts. In the lowlands I'd perspired while sitting motionless, and on the Mountain of Death I'd shivered during strenuous, ultimately successful efforts to reach the capital in three days instead of four.

* * *

At the Panama/Costa Rica border I had met Marco Vinicio Alvarez. My age, he'd been returning home from a trip. We'd hit it off and he had invited me to stay at his home in San José when I got there.

The American author Mary Catherwood didn't see our first meeting, but she described it perfectly when she wrote: "Two may talk together under the same roof for many years yet never really meet, and two others at first speech are old friends."

After settling Hamaca and Ima in a rather nice commercial stable, I walked to Marco Vinicio's house. His exuberance when he answered the door confirmed he was as glad to see me as I was to see him. But having been previously invited into homes where not everyone welcomed me, I was concerned to find him living with his mother and sister.

Fortunately whatever one Alvarez wanted was automatically important to the others.

"As long as you're in San José, this is your home," his mother told me. "If I see you still in town after you leave us, you'll be in huge trouble."

"Your mother's a jewel," I told Marco Vinicio as she made up the spare bed in his room.

"Your bed is ready," she told me after returning. "You can use my sewing room anytime you need privacy to read, write letters, or just relax."

She was the perfect hostess and served a delicious dinner that night and three meals plus an elaborate afternoon tea the next day. Always available to talk, she never forced a conversation and only once spoke to me without a smile.

"Please don't do that again," she told me the time I didn't

get home at noon and ate in a restaurant rather than oblige her to prepare a late lunch.

The only time I saw her differ with or correct anyone was after I called her son Marco, in the interest of good old Yankee efficiency.

"We always refer to Marco Vinicio," she set me straight, "by both his given names."

No one offered an explanation as to why there was no man in the household, and just in case that subject was painful, I didn't ask.

* * *

The American draft dodger in San Isidro had been right about my spending more than two days in San José, but not because of some smiling girl. I'd arrived late Friday evening and couldn't start processing my horses' health papers for Nicaragua until Monday. That delay however, was pure pleasure.

Intelligent and perceptive, Marco Vinicio was wonderful company.

"I'm already tired of people's remarks about your height," he said during our first afternoon together, "not to mention the endless silly questions about your ride."

He studiously avoided interrogating me and — when not in school or studying— included me in everything he did. One afternoon he even invited me to come along when he visited his girlfriend, Elena.

I declined but he insisted, and while we were there a girl smiled at me.

33

EMILY

Her name was Emily and she appeared on the landing at the top of the stairs while Marco Vinicio, Elena, and I talked in the parlor below. Immediately intrigued, I was disappointed when she reversed course. For what seemed like hours I looked up to see if she'd returned

Finally she did.

All these years later I can't recall how it felt to watch Emily come down those stairs, but I vividly remember her enchanting smile, sparkling eyes, and long shiny hair. I hadn't been that nervous since high school, but wouldn't have traded places with anyone anywhere.

After we were introduced, she sat across from me making polite conversation in Spanish. She was intelligent, upbeat, and confident—qualities I'd always found appealing. At first she seemed to confirm my long-standing impression that Latins are friendlier than people in the States. But then she said something completely unexpected.

"Are you...American?" I asked.

"Yes," she replied in English. "I'm going to the University of Costa Rica under the Rotary Club's Student Exchange Program. Elena and I are friends, which is why I'm here this afternoon."

We talked for over an hour without a single awkward pause. Then at a loss for something to say I complimented Emily on her green eyes, and she amused me with a story.

"I want green eyes just like Emily's," the youngest daughter in the family with which she stayed had said at dinner one night.

"Sorry," her father consoled her, "but you'll have to be satisfied with your beautiful brown ones."

"I want green eyes," the little girl had demanded. "Why can't I have them?"

As Marco Vinicio and I walked back to his house that evening, I was lost in quiet thought.

"You like Emily, don't you?" he asked.

"Is it that obvious?" I braced myself for a teasing.

"If you want, I'll have Elena invite her to have lunch with us tomorrow," he said, ignoring a golden opportunity to give me a hard time.

* * *

The next day Marco Vinicio and I returned to Elena's house where Emily joined the three us. After lunch she mentioned that she liked horses, and I invited her to go for a ride. She accepted and we took a bus to the stable where I'd left Hamaca and Ima.

The manager loaned Emily a riding saddle. After we'd ridden a while I noticed it was uncomfortable for her.

"Mine should fit you better," I told her. "Let's trade."

I was riding Ima — who could be a handful — so I switched my saddle to Hamaca.

"Thank you," Emily said after trying it a while. "This is much better."

"Sorry I took so long to notice you were uncomfortable. My dating skills are a bit rusty."

"Because you've been too busy having adventures?" she teased.

We didn't know each other well enough to require a serious answer, but just in case it mattered, I wanted her to know something.

"No," I replied. "Because I was married for five years."

Those were simple, less open-minded times and she was clearly disappointed. Divorces were rare and seen as evidence of serious character flaws. The atmosphere didn't warm up until we were getting off a bus near the house where she stayed. Then suddenly everything was okay again.

"Would you like to go to a movie," I asked as she turned to go inside.

"Yes, but I'm not sure I can. In the Rotary exchange program we change families every so often, and I move in with a new one tomorrow. Before I can go on a date, I need their permission. Can I let you know Tuesday?"

* * *

Bright and early Monday morning I plunged into getting Hamaca's and Ima's papers for Nicaragua. I assumed that would involve frustrating delays, but the certificates were issued the next day and so was my visa.

Tuesday while Marco Vinicio and Emily attended classes at the university, I toured downtown and liked what I saw. Costa Rica's capital and economic/cultural hub, San José, had cosmopolitan complexity combined with the unhurried atmosphere and friendliness of a small town.

Everyone knew everyone. The economy was basically rural, dominated by bananas and coffee. Business was conducted without urgency. The gaily painted oxcarts many people associate with San José symbolized its casual-but-elegant lifestyle.

Marco Vinicio had proudly informed me that Costa Rica was probably the purest democracy on earth, and perhaps it was. That afternoon the president walked through town without bodyguards, having informal discussions with everyday folks in restaurants or taverns.

Unfortunately, however, visiting female Rotary students were rigorously protected. When I phoned Emily's new residence that afternoon, she reported that she'd been given tentative permission for us to attend a movie. But first her new family wanted to meet me and, by the way, we'd be accompanied by a chaperone.

"Please don't take that personally," she added. "That's how things are here. But the daughter who'll go with us doesn't speak English, so our conversation will be private, sort of."

"Don't worry." I stood up and danced a little jig. "I'm fine with that."

The chaperone had little impact on our date, aside from making it possible. For her trouble she received a free dinner and movie at my expense. She was shy, didn't speak English, and faded into the background. Soon I was paying no attention to her, very little to the movie, and a great deal to Emily.

I wished I'd met her under more auspicious circumstances. Getting to know her would've been delightful. Already I dreaded saying goodbye.

* * *

The day before leaving San José I visited an old friend, Juan Rafael Cabezas, one of the nicest, most interesting men I'd ever met. The day I arrived in San José, I called him from

Marco Vinicio's house and was told he was out of town. The day he was due back I showed up at his door and a houseboy escorted me to the living room.

I was embarrassingly underdressed for the party I'd inadvertently crashed. Don Juan's was the only familiar face in the room and, wishing I could disappear, I watched him move from group to group welcoming guests. Then he hurried toward me, arms outstretched.

"Pablito," he enthused. "I got your message but didn't know where to call and invite you to my party. I'm so glad you came."

I'd met him years earlier when we were in Peru looking for breeding stock to take to our respective countries. Our paths had crossed several times since. Like me — but at seventy years of age — he'd developed a keen interest in Peruvian horses and plunged in with a teenager's energy and a born promoter's skill.

His boisterous, jovial wit had made him such a hit with the Peruvians that no one had paid me the slightest attention when he was around.

That afternoon with his trademark enthusiasm, Don Juan introduced me to several other Peruvian horse aficionados. We talked about my ride until an elegant gentleman joined us.

"You must be Mr. Albright," he said in excellent English.

"I am," I said, puzzled because not even Don Juan knew my surname.

"I'm the Minister of Agriculture," the man continued. "We haven't met, but I signed health certificates for your horses a couple of days ago. I trust our service was satisfactory."

"Highly so," I replied. "I wish all officials were as efficient and gracious as those in your office."

"I can help with that," he offered. "Stop by my office tomorrow afternoon, and I'll write letters recommending you to every minister of agriculture between here and the United States."

"Thank you, but unfortunately I'm leaving at dawn tomorrow."

"Then I'll prepare your letters the instant I get to my office and you can pick them up at 10:00 a.m. Don't worry. They'll save more time than you'll lose by delaying your departure."

"Thank you," I said, knowing how useful letters of introduction can be.

When it was time for dinner—a very formal affair—I tried to leave, but Don Juan wouldn't hear of it. He insisted I sit beside him at his table and seemed genuinely interested in the details of my journey. Soon he put his finger on one of my two greatest concerns.

"By now you must be low on money," he said.

"I'm nearly out of both that and time," I responded. "If I'm going to put Hamaca in the Tevis Cup, I have to reach Los Gatos in two months."

"Will it help if I arrange a free truck ride to Nicaragua?"

"Yes please. Definitely," I replied.

"Are you certain you want to go there right after the revolution?"

"Positive. I've been fascinated by Nicaragua since high school."

"If the shooting starts again," he cautioned, "find a safe place and stay there."

The consensus at our table was that Nicaragua's tensions would flare up again. I hoped to be in Honduras before that happened, and Don Juan's promised truck ride would be a big help.

After his other guests left he told me, "I recently imported more than eighty mares from Hacienda Cayaltí."

"I know. When I was looking for horses for my ride, Pedro Briones told me about that. Did they sell well?"

"Up to a point," he replied. "But I'm afraid I overestimated Central America's market. If you help me sell some, I'll pay a substantial commission."

He handed me a sales list with asking prices that would seem high to Americans.

"How much lower can you go if I sell some without a commission?" I asked.

He took the list back, scratched out the prices, and reduced them significantly.

"When I get to the States," I assured him, "I'll see what I can do."

"Could you stay long enough to see and ride my remaining horses?" he asked.

"I'm sorry, but no. Don't worry. Pedro Briones said you bought their best horses. I'm sure they're outstanding."

"I still have some of the best. Where are your mares stabled? I'll pick you up there at noon tomorrow."

* * *

On Friday February 10th, I went to the Minister of Agriculture's office at 10:00 a.m. His secretary was already typing, and an hour later he handed his letters to me— signed, rubber stamped, and in envelopes with Costa Rica's flag in color above the return address.

"Hope they serve you well," he told me.

"I'm sure they will." Genuinely grateful I thanked him at length. His unsolicited assistance wasn't what I'd come to expect from Latin American officials.

* * *

As promised, Don Juan picked up my mares and me at noon and drove us to the stockyard. There he parked his truck beside a larger one and cheerfully asked where its driver was headed.

I didn't hear the answer.

Turning toward me, Don Juan said, "His destination is a nearby town where you'll have difficulty catching another ride. I'm hoping to find someone who's going all the way to Nicaragua."

Even after every driver there had turned him down, he didn't look discouraged.

"Don't worry," he told me. "We'll find a ride sooner or later."

With undiminished exuberance he solicited each newly arrived driver, his demeanor giving no hint of previous failures. The sky was dark by the time he found someone deadheading north and willing to take a passenger and two horses.

"This gentleman is a commercial hauler," Don Juan began when I returned from the restroom. "He's willing to take you to Las Cañas, which is only a hundred fifty miles north. Do you want to accept or wait until tomorrow?"

"I'll go with him," I said.

"Hope you're not disappointed."

"Not at all," I assured him. "I'm grateful for your help."

"I wish I could have done better."

After the cattle were unloaded, I led my mares aboard and the driver pulled out with me sitting beside him. Tired and in no mood for conversation, he concentrated on guiding his cumbersome vehicle along a winding road, constantly slowing for curves and switchbacks. When he couldn't keep his eyes open any longer he pulled over for a catnap, sitting upright in his seat.

Measured in miles, the trip to Las Cañas was short but we didn't get there until 3:00 a.m. Soon after that a man in another of the same company's trucks offered to take me on to Liberia. The drivers backed their vehicles until they were rear to rear, and I led Hamaca and Ima from one to the other.

During the mostly flat, straight drive to Liberia, a much chattier driver took us seventy-five miles in an hour and a half — a welcome improvement on the previous night's progress. We reached Liberia in time for breakfast, and I paid for his as well as mine.

After we ate I cinched my riding saddle on Ima and headed for La Cruz with Hamaca carrying my duffel bags. Despite having slept little the previous night, I felt fresh. Relaxing in San José had done wonders for me.

The rising sun revealed a distant, clearly active volcano, the first I'd ever seen. In morning's first light the cloud circling its top glowed. When we were closer wispy, grayish smoke stopped coming from its cone. Then abruptly, thick black smoke boiled skyward.

"The first few times Arenal did that," a man along the road told me, "people stood around taking pictures and wondering if it was getting ready to erupt."

But Arenal had obviously played its little trick too often. People were going about their daily routines with scarcely a glance in its direction.

Around noon wind dispersed the tower of smoke, filling the air with what looked like smog — instant Los Angeles with a tiny fraction of the people and vehicles.

Later I looked back for the last time and saw a reddish glow around Arenal's tip.

Irazú was Costa Rica's best know volcano, and a paved road to its twelve thousand foot crater had made it popular with tourists. Two years earlier they'd stopped coming while

Irazú rained ash and cinder on San José and residents wearing cloth masks swept rooftops daily to prevent the accumulating weight from damaging them.

The tourists returned after Irazú began minding her manners.

* * *

The next day I rode from La Cruz, Costa Rica, to La Virgen, Nicaragua. The border crossing was fast and pleasant. Obviously accustomed to livestock entering their country, officials processed our paperwork efficiently and without asking for additional fees.

"There was shooting in Managua," one answered my question about the attempted revolution, "but in most of the country people wouldn't have known anything was happening without news reports."

As I started into Nicaragua its history of bloody revolutions was foremost on my mind. But the area I saw that first day was peaceful and sparsely populated. If it stayed that quiet I'd ride at least as far as Managua, Nicaragua's capital.

34

GOING THE WRONG WAY

Not far down the road, we were attacked—not by revolutionaries but by small flying insects. When swinging my arms didn't drive them away, Hamaca and Ima sped up on their own. I reined them in because the effort of going faster had accelerated their breathing, forcing them to suck in more bugs.

Ima's continuing attempts to rid herself of these pests were hilarious. She reared, lashed out with both hind legs, tried to snort them away from her nostrils, rubbed her nose on her knee, then locked all four legs and stood motionless in silent resignation.

Nothing I tried moved her until a breeze swept our tormentors away.

With huge Lake Nicaragua in view to my right, I was soon basking in the satisfaction of being in a country Tschiffely, Mancha, and Gato had bypassed. That rather small achievement felt better than it should have, but it was the first time we'd done something they hadn't.

Hamaca and Ima spent that night in a barn full of milk cows that were eating something I'd never seen before.

"It's silage," their owner told me. "I make it by mixing chopped wheat and corn—grain, stalks, and all—with molasses and fermenting it in concrete pits. Don't worry it's well tolerated by horses."

I wanted to be sure the warm, sweet smelling mixture wouldn't colic my mares and gave them small amounts, which they ate eagerly. Waiting to see how these samples affected them I turned my attention to a pair of towering volcanoes and the island their lava had formed around them in the lake.

Volcanoes I'd seen in Ecuador could've been snowcapped mountains. These were exotic and as the sun set they abruptly changed color, from dark gray to golden.

"Dinner," my host's wife called from the house.

So far Hamaca and Ima had suffered no ill consequences from eating silage, so I gave them a little more and went inside.

* * *

"How much do you know about Lake Nicaragua?" my host asked as his wife served our meal.

"Only a little," I replied, "most of which happened during and after the California Gold Rush."

"It's over a hundred miles long," he told me, "deep enough for ocean-going ships, and contains hundreds of islands. According to the most widely accepted theory, it was once a Pacific Ocean bay with volcanoes across its mouth. For millions of years those disgorged lava that eventually walled it off from the sea."

"So it's now a saltwater lake?"

"No," he replied. "It's been diluted for centuries by incoming fresh water from over forty rivers and now contains the world's only freshwater sharks, swordfish, and tarpon."

"Over a century ago," his wife added, "cities around Lake Nicaragua grew rich on trade with the orient. English privateers — we call them pirates — repeatedly sacked Granada after sailing up the San Juan River from the Caribbean Sea. To prevent those raids, Spain built a fort overlooking the river. You should go see it."

"You really should," my host said. "It's a little known historical treasure. The same Horatio Nelson who became one of England's greatest naval commanders captured that fort by leading a charge up the slopes later renamed *Lomas de Nelson*."

Before this brief lesson, my knowledge of Nicaragua's history had been limited to its role in the California Gold Rush. Back then thousands of gold-seekers from eastern America had cut three months from the voyage around Cape Horn by following the so-called Vanderbilt Road from the Caribbean Sea, up the San Juan River, across Lake Nicaragua, and north on the Pacific Ocean to San Francisco.

Being an avid sports fan, I also knew that those prospectors — called Forty-Niners because they came to California in 1849 — had inspired the name of San Francisco's football team. And I'd made note of two more pieces of memorabilia in the rough draft of a book I hoped to write.

Albright's Book of Useless Facts, top of page 3: "While planning its canal across Central America, the United States considered a route that more or less followed the old Vanderbilt Road across Nicaragua. But under President Theodore Roosevelt, the canal was built in Panama."

Albright's Book of Useless Facts, bottom of page 3: "Nicaragua's most intriguing historical tidbit involves an

American imperialist, William Walker, who inserted himself into one of Nicaragua's revolutions and led a private army of American volunteers to numerous victories before ruling the country from 1856 to 1857."

After dinner I returned alone to the barn where Hamaca and Ima had suffered no ill effects from eating silage and were hungry. I gave them generous servings and later—over my hosts' objections—slept near their stalls, just in case.

* * *

At the crack of dawn I said goodbye to my ex-schoolteacher friends. Then Hamaca, Ima, and I began our second race against the clock. The one that ended in Quito had been thirty-five miles long. This time I planned to ride fifty, half the length of the Tevis Ride—but in much less challenging terrain.

I rode from La Virgen to Granada as if I had to get there in time to warn of an impending attack by English pirates. Hamaca did her part by carrying me there in seven hours— far from a record but encouraging considering that she'd carried two hundred and thirty pounds. If she continued to improve I just might have an endurance horse on my hands.

Hamaca was listless the next morning. To spare her from carrying my duffel bags I left them at Granada's bus station to be shipped to Managua, and rode Ima the remaining thirty-one miles.

At a stable outside town the manager quoted a price I suspected he'd raised to take advantage of me. Several boarders however, assured me it was the going rate.

As I'd gone farther north, Latin America's cost of living had sharply increased. A stall in Costa Rica had cost a dollar a night, including feed, and a stable boy took care of the horses. In Managua I paid three times that much, bought my own feed, and cared for Hamaca and Ima myself.

Other prices too were a constant reminder that I was running out of money.

*　*　*

Edgy I walked downtown, to where rebels had recently battled government troops. In little more than five years an earthquake would kill five thousand, injure twenty thousand more, and damage Managua so badly that officials would consider rebuilding it elsewhere. And after that, the civil war between U.S.-backed Contras and communist Sandanistas would bring more agony.

But all that was behind the veil that hides the future, and my eyes were on the innovative pyramidal architecture of the International Hotel.

Seeing my interest, a man asked, "Did you know Howard Hughes is in seclusion on the top floor?"

Thanks to *Time* magazine I knew the reclusive billionaire was rumored to be there, but rewarded my informant's intended kindness by exclaiming, "Really? How interesting."

Quoted inflated prices wherever I shopped, I made ample use of my "I'm not a tourist" disclaimer.

Nonetheless I had something in common with tourists in Managua that day. I wanted to see the area around the Gran Hotel, epicenter of the recent revolution. But unable to afford the expensive guided tours, I'd have to see it on my own.

Asking for directions along the way, I finally found the elegant Gran Hotel but saw only well-dressed people going in and out its front door.

Sidling up to a tour group I heard the guide say, "As you can see, they've re-plastered the bullet holes, but the paint doesn't quite match."

He could've said much more. After all, men had fought to the death there only days earlier. But the guide—clearly aware his audience might include government agents—prattled on about the landscaping, the ages of building and such.

Glad I hadn't parted with twenty hard-earned dollars to listen to that, I went to the bus station to claim my duffel bags. Unbelievably a bus driver was unloading them when I walked in. I held out a small tip. He didn't take it.

"In Granada," he said cheerfully, "they told me you don't have much money and are a nice person, for a gringo."

He was enjoying the opportunity to tease me.

* * *

Outside the bus station on the curb, I ignored cab drivers who expectantly slowed their shiny new vehicles to compete for my attention. Finally I saw a dilapidated—and therefore inexpensive—taxi. As it came closer an empty bus stopped in front of me and the door opened.

Its driver was the one who'd brought my duffel bags.

"Where are you going?" he asked.

"To an inexpensive hotel if there is one," I answered.

"There is. I'll drop you off there."

I climbed aboard.

His name was Amos. Engaged in lighthearted conversation we stopped at a traffic signal beside a chauffeur-driven Mercedes Benz. Its haughty-looking back seat passenger looked up at me.

"That man's expression," Amos teased, "says you're his inferior and don't deserve to look at him."

"I wonder what gave him that idea," I played along. "I have a far better chauffeur and a bigger, more expensive vehicle."

That evening in my room I emptied everything from both

duffel bags and divided it into two piles. The first contained supplies I'd soon need. In the other I put items I'd seldom or never used. Hamaca and Ima had carried their useless weight long enough, and Amos had suggested a second-hand store where I could sell them.

No matter how little that transaction brought in, it would come in handy.

* * *

When the embassies of Honduras and El Salvador opened the next morning, I applied for my visas as well as Hamaca and Ima's health certificates. Each time I started by presenting my letter from Costa Rica's Minister of Agriculture. And both times, I was promised everything would be ready *mañana*.

For once *mañana* meant tomorrow. After picking up both sets of documentation, I visited the offices of Nicaragua's excellent national newspaper *La Prensa*. As I gave a reporter named Abraham some basic details, he became more enthusiastic and started interrupting with perceptive questions.

His editor read the rough draft and said, "Get some good photos by ten o'clock and I'll put the story in today's paper."

Quickly Abraham drove me to the stable. After he took several posed photos, I swung aboard Hamaca bareback with only a halter for control. Full of pep after two days rest, she wouldn't go where I wanted, and during the ensuing struggle both hind legs slid out from under her. For an instant she sat doggy style, then bounced up with me still aboard.

Putting his camera back in its case Abraham said, "Let's go."

"Don't you want another picture of me riding?" I asked.

"No. Hurry up."

"Don't wait for me," I said. "I'll clean my mares' stalls and walk back to my hotel."

Walking from the stable to my hotel, I couldn't stop thinking about Emily. I'd enjoyed her company immensely. Leaving San José with no prospect of seeing her again had been painful. For the first time I passed the International Hotel without looking up and wondering if Howard Hughes was really in the suite on its top floor.

After a waitress served my dinner, a haunting Broadway show tune—*Once Upon a Time* sung by Tony Bennett and played on the jukebox—added a soundtrack to my thoughts of Emily. The lyrics didn't fit our situation perfectly, but they didn't miss by far:

> *Once upon a time a girl with moonlight in her eyes*
> *Put her hand in mine and said she loved me so But that*
> *was once upon a time, very long ago*
> *Once upon a time we sat beneath a willow tree Counting*
> *all the stars and waiting for the dawn*
> *But that was once upon a time, now the tree is gone*
> *How the breeze ruffled up her hair*
> *How we always laughed as though tomorrow wasn't*
> *there*
> *We were young and didn't have a care. Where did it go?*
> *Once upon a time the world was sweeter than we knew*
> *Everything was ours, how happy we were then*
> *But somehow once upon a time never comes again...*
> (Composed by Strouse Charles and Adams Lee)

I couldn't get it out of my mind. Twice I interrupted my meal, walked to the jukebox, and played it again. Both times, it filled me with emotion.

Would a telephone call embarrass Emily—or me? What would I say?

The waitress brought a copy of the latest *La Prensa*. Scanning it I came across a photograph of Hamaca sitting like an obedient dog, with me holding her mane to keep from sliding off. Somehow Abraham had resisted the temptation to add a humiliating caption. His written description of what had happened before he snapped that photo made me sound like the master horseman I wasn't.

* * *

Few people were out and about during my Sunday morning walk to the stable, and I had plenty of time to compose and rehearse my offer to go back to San José if Emily wanted me to.

"If I don't come back for a few days," I told the stable boy, just in case, "please feed my horses and clean their stalls. I'll give you a nice tip."

Back downtown — heart pounding and mouth dry — I called.

"I'd like that," Emily responded in her lilting voice. "But I won't have as much time as I'd like. I'm studying for exams."

"I'll call when I get there," I said. "Are you sure you want to do this?"

"Positive."

I packed what I needed in a duffel bag and left everything else in the hotel storage room. At the bus station I bought an economy class ticket on the overnight express. The accountant in me protested the expenditure. But what the heck? I had spoiled myself only four times since leaving California: watching *Doctor Zhivago*, eating an American-style hamburger, my first date with Emily, and listening to Tony Bennett's *Once upon a Time*.

* * *

Advised of my arrival by Emily, Marco Vinicio Alvarez was waiting when I reached San José. He insisted I stay with his family, making this visit reminiscent of my first. Unfortunately the similarities included an unwelcome one. I spent little time with Emily.

Seeing her again had only worsened my loneliness. I would've stayed longer, but she had classes all week and her evenings were full of preparations for an upcoming Rotary convention in Guatemala City.

"Why don't you put your horses in a gallop and meet me there?" she suggested, green eyes twinkling as we said good-bye on her new family's doorstep.

That evening Marco Vinicio accompanied me to the bus station.

"Too bad you weren't able to spend more time with Emily," he sympathized as I waited to board. "Do you think she likes you?"

"At least a little," I replied, then told him what she'd said as we parted.

"This is the name, address, and phone number of the hotel in Guatemala City where she and Elena will stay," he said, handing me a slip of paper.

I tucked it in my shirt pocket, and for the first time Marco Vinicio and I indulged in one of those back-slapping macho hugs Latin American men reserve for male friends.

Awake for most of the return trip to Managua, I formulated a plan that just might get me to Guatemala City in time to see Emily again.

35

IF IT'S MONDAY, THIS MUST BE EL SALVADOR

Long after midnight, the driver made an unscheduled stop to let me out at the stable. There I slept fully clothed on my sleeping bag beside Hamaca and Ima's stalls. After the sun came up, I rode to Managua's largest stockyard — Ganadería Nicaragua, if I remember correctly — determined to find a truck going north with space for two horses.

Ideally I'd find one that could take us all the way to Guatemala City. But the long journey across four nations would probably require stringing together a series of rides.

Only one of the trucks that came that day was headed north, and it wasn't going far enough to do much good.

"It's rare for us to receive so few deliveries," Ganadería Nicaragua's jefe told me before going home. "But a truck from Estelí often delivers cattle at night to The Matadero, a smaller stockyard near here. Why don't you sleep there? If you don't have any luck, come back tomorrow. Our daytime traffic is heavier."

At The Matadero I told the night watchman why I was there.

"I'll wake you if a truck comes," he promised as I unrolled my sleeping bag on the bench outside his office.

With my limited time fast running out I woke every time I heard a vehicle, but none came through the gate. Dog-tired in the morning, I prepared to ride back to Ganadería Nicaragua.

"Don't worry," The Matadero's night watchman told me before I left. "If a northbound truck comes today, my replacement will send it where you are."

Back at Ganadería Nicaragua, a local and two southbound trucks brought cattle and left empty. By noon I'd lost another half day.

Sitting on a fence with the Jefe, I watched a jetliner pass overhead. For all I knew Emily would be on tomorrow's version of that flight. Would she be looking out the window, wondering if I was traveling the highway below? More importantly, would I still be stuck in Managua?

A truck with Guatemalan license plates sped past, its driver clearly in a hurry. The Jefe jumped off the fence, shouting and waving his arms. I leapt down and added my efforts to his. The driver turned a corner.

"Maybe he's circling back," I said, desperate for a ray of hope.

"No," the Jefe said. "He didn't see us and will never know he looked like the answer to your prayers. Come on, I'll share my lunch with you."

At an outdoor table under a lattice sunshade he and two other workers opened lunchboxes containing—not the sandwiches I'd expected, but wide-mouth thermos bottles. The Jefe dished rice from one of his onto two paper plates and covered it with stir fried chicken and vegetables from the other.

"Anyone else want to try this?" he asked setting what remained in the center of the table.

Latin America's workers routinely share food at lunch, and even though I couldn't reciprocate that day, the Jefe and his men were generous with me.

"I'm going to the grocery store," I told them after we'd eaten. "What can I bring you?"

"A beer would go down nicely," the Jefe replied.

Returning with bottles of Corona for the men who'd shared their food with me, I did a double take. The Guatemalan truck that passed earlier was parked at a curb, and its short, lean driver was measuring the air pressure in his tires.

"Please, señor," I said. "Are you going to Guatemala City?"

"Yes," he replied, straightening up.

"When are you leaving?"

"As soon as I finish checking out my truck. Why?"

"I'm looking for a ride and need to get there fast."

"You're in luck." He smiled. "I'll be happy to take you."

"There's a complication. I have two horses."

"I have no objection to transporting livestock," he said. "But I earn my living with this truck and crossing borders with horses could cause delays I can't afford."

Hoping he was a typically romantic Latin, I said, "It's a matter of the heart."

"Why didn't you say so?" His mouth broadened into a grin. "How soon do you have to be there?"

"She arrives tomorrow and will be there three days."

Looking concerned he explained, "Even if we don't stop for meals, have no mechanical problems, and there are no border delays, the trip will take at least thirty-six hours."

"If my horses and I cause any delays you can leave us behind."

"Where are they?" he asked.

"Four blocks from here at Ganadería Nicaragua."

"We'd better get them before those bastards grind them into dog food. My name is Fernando. What's yours?"

"Pablito."

"Whoever gave you that nickname had a twisted sense of humor." He looked up at me. "What's your Christian name?"

"Verne Albright."

"Slower please."

"V...er...ne...All...br...ight."

Working on Albright for the third time, Fernando threw up his hands and declared, "I'll call you Gringo."

As soon as Hamaca and Ima were aboard, Fernando and I began our pursuit of my impossible dream.

Aimé Tschiffely made his ride with no schedule or deadline, but during mine I was spurred on by two unforgiving concerns. My funds were severely limited, and unless I gave up on entering Hamaca in the Tevis Cup so was my time.

At times the pressure had been almost unbearable, and during that mad dash to Guatemala City, it was even greater. Emily would be in Guatemala City only three days. If I didn't see her then I'd probably never see her again.

* * *

Having done the huge favor of sending Fernando, the gods stopped smiling on me. After we stopped for gas on the way out of Managua, his truck wouldn't start. Thanks to his mechanical know-how and impressive supply of replacement parts, he got us going again. But we'd lost two hours and would be lucky to reach the border with Honduras before it closed for the night.

If we made it, Fernando would drive across Honduras to

El Salvador, where we'd sleep until that border opened. Otherwise tomorrow would dawn with us still in Nicaragua and far behind schedule.

I spent hours on the edge of my seat, willing the truck to go faster and the clock slower. At the border we sailed through Nicaragua's exit formalities. Entering Honduras however, was another matter.

"Your horses' health certificates don't meet the requirements," the Ministry of Agriculture official told me. "I'm sorry but you'll have to leave your horses here and get a health certificate in Tegucigalpa."

That side trip would take a long time, and Fernando had made it clear he wouldn't tolerate delays. My chance to see Emily was slipping away.

Leaning on the counter I said, "A health certificate issued without inspecting my horses is simply a way to collect a fee. Can I pay it here?"

"That can be arranged," he whispered, "for forty *Lempiras*."

The back of my neck tingled. He'd accepted the bribe he thought I'd offered. As far as I could tell, he was asking for only about twenty dollars. But the amount wasn't what made bribes wrong, and I'd never offered one—no matter how great the potential benefit.

Fernando put his hand on my shoulder and guided me to where we could talk privately.

"Gringo," he said. "These officials are paid so little that they have to supplement their incomes. Not everyone in Latin American solicits bribes, but everyone pays them. It would be a shame to miss that lady in Guatemala City. I have forty *Lempiras*. You can reimburse me later."

I'm not positive I would've objected, but I'll never know because Fernando's wallet was already out.

Before he could put it away, the man behind the counter said, "One more thing, I'll have to charge a small fee for a custodian who'll ride in your truck to make sure you don't sell your horses without paying the tax."

A master extortionist he'd known Fernando would pay another twenty Lempiras rather than lose the benefit of the first forty.

Our escort—a steel-helmeted, submachine-gun toting soldier—was waiting beside Fernando's truck when we went outside. He kept to himself, spoke only when spoken to, and rode in the cargo area with Hamaca and Ima.

* * *

Between Nicaragua and El Salvador, a hundred miles of the Pan-American Highway passed through Honduras. Fernando drove that stretch in half the time it would've taken in the next morning's heavy traffic.

"This is where we sleep tonight," he said, taking his foot off the accelerator as we approached a half dozen vehicles stopped in the traffic lane ahead.

Over the top of the of the semi-truck-and-trailer in front of us, I saw an unfamiliar flag—El Salvador's no doubt—on a tall pole in the distance.

After Fernando turned off the motor I left the cab, then climbed into its cargo area and untied Hamaca and Ima so they could lie down. Looking apprehensive the custodian climbed on top of the cab, apparently afraid of horses.

Responding to Ima's nickering, I told her, "Sorry. Your hay was confiscated at the border and we won't find any here."

But hay—tied in bundles and stacked on a mule—found us, no more than five minutes later.

"*Heno para la venta*," the man leading the mule called out as he passed the huge semi ahead of us.

"How much?" I asked when he was closer.

He was old, working hard and, as far as I could tell, his price was reasonable.

"Two bundles," I said without haggling.

"This is freshly cut," he told me proudly as I paid.

Freshly pulled from a muddy field would've been more accurate, and the mud clinging to its roots had hardened. Wearing leather gloves I began stripping it away.

"Why don't you just cut the roots off?" Fernando asked, handing me a machete. I sighed. My brain was on strike after two nights of abbreviated sleep.

* * *

Eager to make good time for his reasons as well as mine, Fernando woke me when the driver of the big semi ahead turned on his engine, drove forward a few feet, and stopped.

"The border's open," Fernando said. "I've been thinking. Maybe we had problems entering Honduras because your horses were in my truck. Why don't you ride across this time?"

The big semi blocked our view of the border station. If we couldn't see them, its occupants couldn't see us. Or so I hoped. I held the car behind us in place as Fernando backed up to an embankment where I could unload Hamaca and Ima.

"What are you doing?" the custodian demanded.

"Getting ready," I replied, "to ride across the border."

"Why?"

"I'm not going to sell my horses." I opened my passport and turned a few pages, pointing to entry and exit stamps. "We've crossed six nations so far. If I wanted to sell them, I could've done it a hundred times."

"I'll be watching," he said ominously. "If you don't take them into El Salvador, I'll arrest your friend as an accomplice."

"Go ahead, Gringo," Fernando said dramatically. "I'll be his hostage."

After saddling Hamaca I led her and Ima between Fernando's truck and the semi, which had moved forward twice while I unloaded my mares. Then I alternately rode forward and stopped until we were first in line. Minutes later the crossbar was raised to admit us.

We were in and out of the Honduras' border station before its officials finished searching Fernando's truck. El Salvador's friendly officials simply glanced at my mares' paperwork, stamped my passport, asked a few questions, and wished me good luck.

Looking back, I made sure the custodian saw me ride Hamaca and lead Ima down the highway shoulder into El Salvador. Then not wanting to be seen putting my mares back in Fernando's truck I let Hamaca go as fast as she wanted.

I could no longer see the border stations when Fernando drove past, pointing so I'd know he planned to wait at the next embankment.

His truck was backed up to one with its tailgate open when I next saw it.

"If Emily arrived on schedule," he said, holding Ima while I loaded Hamaca, "she's in Guatemala City and with luck we'll get there the day before she leaves."

Maybe. But there was something I hadn't told him.

In Managua I'd gotten documentation to enter Honduras and El Salvador. But in less than twelve hours I'd need a visa and health certificates for Guatemala, which I hadn't yet had time and opportunity to get.

Would my magic letter be enough to get them while Fernando waited? Would he be willing to wait?

"I'm in a bit of a predicament," I began as he and I ate fresh fruit and bread sticks rather than stop for breakfast.

Taking the news in stride he said, "Your mares can cross borders until the health papers you already have expire. We'll get your visa from the consul near the border."

"Why don't we get my visa in San Salvador," I asked, "instead of waiting until the last minute?"

Raising his eyebrows he said, "Look who's talking."

* * *

As we crossed El Salvador I began seeing something unusual and disturbing, peasants with out-of-date rifles and primitive pistols — or both. Fernando didn't seem to notice them, not even as we passed dozens of armed men working on a vast coffee plantation.

"Seems like everyone in El Salvador carries a firearm," I said. Fernando came to life.

"This whole country is armed to the teeth," he said. "It's like a big CinemaScope cowboy movie, but with an important difference. Here people actually die when they're shot."

"I was often warned to be careful in Nicaragua, but I've already seen far more firearms here than there."

"There's an unbridgeable gap," Fernando said, "between El Salvador's rich and poor. Every day more workers demonstrate for land reform. Last year death squads financed by large land owners murdered hundreds and drove thousands into Honduras."

"And the police...?"

"Are nowhere to be found during massacres because they're also the death squads. This will end in a bloody civil war."

Inside the roadside tavern where we bought lunch to go, clothes and hats were straight out of a Clint Eastwood movie and a sign above the bar warned: "Check your firearms at the door and reclaim them when you leave."

* * *

"This is where we get your visa," Fernando said when we reached the office of the Guatemalan Consul in the last town before the border.

His secretary had bad news.

"Señor Gomez," she said, "is an honorary consul and doesn't issue visas. You need the consul general for that, and—I'm sorry to say—he probably won't be available at this hour."

"Could you please call and check?" Fernando asked.

"Maybe." She picked up her phone and listened for a dial tone. "Sorry the phones are still out of order."

"I have to cross the border tonight before it closes so I can pick up a load in Guatemala City tomorrow morning," Fernando told me. "Maybe you can get a visa in the morning and find another ride."

"I appreciate everything you did for me," I said. "You've been an unbelievably good—"

"I just remembered something," the secretary interrupted. "The Consul General might be available after all. He's a doctor and issues visas at his office. It's open late."

"How badly do you want to see this girl?" Fernando deadpanned.

"You can't imagine," I replied.

"Yes I can. I married the girl of my dreams thirty years ago, and I love her more now than I did then. Let's go get your visa."

The Consul General's office was out of our way, but it was worth the trip. He was there. Pleasant and efficient he quickly stamped a visa in my passport and we set out for the border.

"This will be a difficult crossing," Fernando warned when we were back on the highway. "Guatemala's officials are almost as difficult as Mexico's."

As I unloaded Hamaca and Ima just short of a border that would soon close, Fernando said, "I'll wait a mile inside Guatemala. If you're not there in thirty minutes, I'll have to continue on without you."

I swung aboard Hamaca without taking time to saddle her and started down the road's shoulder, leading Ima. Minutes later Fernando sped past, acting like he'd never seen us before.

This crossing had to go smoothly, which of course, meant it wouldn't.

* * *

As the sun went down I saw Fernando's truck waiting ahead, its cargo area now covered by a rainproof canvas cover. Suspicious, Hamaca was reluctant to go inside but finally did. Ima refused until I tempted her with a handful of oats.

"Why the tarp?" I asked as Fernando shifted gears and merged into traffic. "Are you expecting rain?"

"No," he replied. "Guatemala forbids transporting livestock after dark to prevent cattle-rustling. But with that tarp in place, the police won't see your horses."

"What about the checkpoints?"

"There are seven before we get to Guatemala City, but don't worry. Empty trucks aren't required to stop."

"And if a patrolman stops us?"

"I'll tell him the truth. You aren't paying me and therefore your horses are personal effects — not cargo."

"Will that do any good?"

He shrugged. "It should."

I'll never know why he took that risk, but I think policemen had made his life difficult. He seemed to enjoy putting something over on them and clearly didn't expect to get caught.

I breathed easier when no one came after us as we left the first checkpoint behind. An hour after that we passed another and then five more, all without attracting attention.

Not far from Guatemala City, an erupting volcano lit up the sky like a distant artillery battle, an analogy that once again proves men think in military terms.

But we also think in romantic terms, and that display of nature's fireworks also served as a celebration of my timely, against-all-odds arrival — only one day after Emily's.

Thanks to Fernando I was going to see her again.

36

HELLO, GOODBYE

With me nearby in my sleeping bag, Hamaca and Ima spent the night tied to trees in Fernando's backyard. He woke me before dawn.

"Gringo," he said, "the fairground is nearby. Tell Humberto Morales I sent you. He'll rent you stalls at a special price."

"I'll never forget what you did for me," I told him.

"Especially if you and Emily have the misfortune to marry," he teased. Turning serious, he added. "Make the next two days worth the effort it took to get here. Enjoy every second."

"Would it be possible to meet your wife?"

"Absolutely. In fact, she said she'd like to meet you after I told her how much I enjoyed being your cupid."

Her name was Maria Luisa. Once beautiful, she was still elegant and full of the charm that had held Fernando's interest for thirty years.

* * *

At the fairground Humberto Morales rented me stalls for

Hamaca and Ima. Quickly I made them comfortable then checked into a nearby inexpensive hotel Fernando had recommended.

"Every room," he'd told me, "has a shower, hot water, and a telephone—things you'll need until your lady leaves."

When it was late enough to be sure Emily was awake I called her hotel. She invited me to join her and Elena for breakfast.

The hotel where they were staying was one of Guatemala City's finest. Even dressed in my best Levi's I attracted stares as I crossed the lobby. If I hadn't been Caucasian, I would've been asked to leave before reaching the dining room.

Emily waved when she saw me and I sat next to her, across from Elena. When the waiter took our orders, Emily asked for *huevos pateados*.

Looking puzzled he said, "Can you kindly repeat that, señorita?"

Again she ordered scrambled eggs, using Costa Rican slang, h*uevos pateados*, kicked eggs.

"She means *huevos revueltos*," Elena clarified, blushing.

Giggling uncontrollably the waiter left.

"The expression huevos pateados is used only in Costa Rica," Elena said quietly.

"Why did the waiter find it so funny?" Emily frowned.

"I don't know."

I'm sure Elena knew. And so did I. But with me present it would have been rude to reveal that *huevos* was also slang for testicles. Back then I considered such censorship silly, but when I hear the language used by and around women today, I'm glad I grew up when I did.

* * *

After breakfast Elena considerately excused herself, leaving Emily and me alone in the lobby.

"I had yesterday afternoon free," she told me, "but today I have a tight schedule and am only available from noon to 1:00 and again from 3:30 to 5:30."

"Where shall we meet?" I asked.

* * *

During our noontime stroll through Central America's largest city, Emily stopped to admire an exquisite travel poster on the exterior of a building.

"I'd love to own one of these," she said, "but I haven't been able to find any for sale."

High above the sidewalk, this one was beyond anyone else's reach and in pristine condition.

Taking it was something I wouldn't normally have done, but so was bribing a border official. Embarrassed, I stood on tiptoe and slid my index finger under one edge. The corners were pasted to the wall. Resisting the urge to hurry I slowly worked each corner loose, trying not to damage it.

None too soon I rolled it into a cylinder and carried it myself rather than implicate Emily if a policeman had witnessed my petty larceny.

* * *

For several nights I'd slept no more that four hours. After leaving Emily at her hotel, I went to mine and called reception from my room.

"Can you wake me in two hours?" I said. "Please don't forget. It's important."

It seemed like I'd just fallen asleep when the phone rang.

I answered and said, "Thank you," then hung up and almost went back to sleep.

Still groggy I hurried to the bathroom and combed my hair

in front of the mirror. The image staring back at me with bloodshot eyes looked as weary as I felt. That wasn't how I wanted Emily to see me, but what choice did I have?

I felt better by the time an elevator door slid open in the lobby of Emily's hotel and she stepped out. Lost in conversation we took a municipal bus to one of Guatemala City's beautiful parks. There as close to alone as we'd ever been, we sat on a bench and got to know each other. Everything she said made me want to know more and to tell her more about me.

Later relaxed and comfortable, I saw a beggar approaching prosperous-looking tourists. He looked deserving but was having no luck. On an impulse I called him over and gave him a coin before realizing Emily would almost certainly think I'd done that to impress her.

I hadn't. I'd simply wanted to share my happiness.

On the bus back to Emily's hotel, our driver was the one who'd brought us to the park, and he took the same route he had earlier.

Emily seemed as surprised as I was when we passed beneath a large, impressive wrought-iron tower. Straddling a busy intersection on four curved latticework legs, it resembled the Eiffel tower and seemed out of place.

"Can you believe it?" Emily asked. "There's no doubt we drove under this earlier, but I didn't even notice it."

Nor had I. My attention had been on her.

"It's the Torre del Reformador," the woman across the aisle said pleasantly.

"It's beautiful," Emily whispered, touching my arm as she turned and looked back.

"Are you love birds American?" the woman asked adjusting her gray and black poncho.

"Yes we are," Emily replied, then quietly added, "Americans at least."

"It may interest you to know that tower was built in your country," the woman continued, oblivious to the embarrassment she'd caused.

* * *

Our third catch-as-catch-can get-together — breakfast at Emily's hotel the following morning — was over, and we were in the lobby. As far as I knew this was the last time I'd ever see her.

"It was nice to see you again," I began, "and — "

"We can say goodbye at the airport if you want," Emily interrupted. "I got permission for you to ride on our bus."

We followed her group outside.

"Welcome aboard," the Guatemalan lady chaperone at the bus door greeted as we passed.

Inside we sat behind Elena. Alone in her seat she turned to face us and joined our conversation, inhibiting it.

* * *

At the airport after Emily and Elena checked in for their flight, we stood in the waiting room with their chaperone. When the flight was called, Emily stayed behind.

"Well, goodbye," she said. "Nice seeing you again. Good luck on your ride."

She stood on tiptoe. Thinking she wanted to whisper something, I bent down. She kissed my cheek, bringing cooing from the chaperone. Her gesture had been so innocent that even the official guardian of her virtue could approve.

When we could no longer see Emily the chaperone softly said, "What a jewel. You must love her very much."

"I don't know her well enough yet," I replied, "but I like her a lot."

Wanting to be alone and watch Emily's plane take off, I went outside and circled the terminal. From an embankment I climbed onto a secluded edge of its roof, where I had a clear view of the runway. There I sat, swinging my legs as her plane taxied to its takeoff position. Then it sped down the runway, left the ground, and shrank until it disappeared.

For a while I couldn't summon the energy to move. But stimulated by my long to-do list, I finally climbed down and ambled toward the bus stop—never dreaming the plane I saw landing was Emily's.

As I'd later read in her letter sent in care of Mexico City's American embassy, the pilot had detected mechanical problems and reversed course. We could've spent that whole day together if she'd known where to contact me.

* * *

It was time to return to a less expensive lifestyle. After a last luxurious hot shower at my hotel I checked out and took a bus to the fairground. There Humberto Morales gave me permission to sleep in the stall between Hamaca's and Ima's.

At a nearby store, I bought a small sack of bread rolls and two bananas, then sat on a park bench—lonely and lost in thought.

Later appetite satisfied, I stood intending to buy cheese to supplement my two remaining rolls for dinner. But a sad-eyed dog with protruding ribs was watching. He'd clearly been hungry a long time, so I tossed him my last piece of bread. He gobbled it up and came closer, licking his lips.

With his plaintive eyes following my every move, I bought another roll and fed it slowly to prolong our mutual pleasure. Normally I wouldn't have noticed—let alone spent money on him. But my feelings for Emily had brought out my better side.

In Peru I'd avoided stray dogs because most were aggressive, a generalization my mother would have criticized. She'd taught me to never group people, places, or things before judging them.

Thanks to her I'd grown up with a positive impression of black people. As a teenager my favorite movie actor had been Sidney Poitier, a Bahamian-American. His gentle, decent on-screen persona seemed to reflect the real him—not just the characters he portrayed. My favorite had been Homer Smith in *Lilies of the Field*, the role that won him 1963's Oscar for Best Actor.

As enlightened as my mother was, she had a prejudice. Hers was against Mexicans.

Portrayed in movies, they were bad guys—not heroes. When they were mentioned in newspapers, it was never for doing something good. Those insidious images had influenced millions. In mom's case, she'd come to consider them—and therefore all Hispanics—dangerous.

Hence her fears about my ride.

At the Fairground, Fernando's friend Humberto cheerily invited me to join him in his quarters for dinner. That was when I decided the book I'd write after my ride would portray Latin Americans as I'd come to know them—kind, hardworking, and not inferior to us gringos in anything but opportunity.

* * *

Facing a crucial decision, I slept poorly that night.

To reach California in time to prepare for the Tevis Cup, I'd have to transport—not ride—Hamaca and Ima the rest of the way. But if I did that, what was my real reason? Was it because my once-in-a-lifetime adventure had become an unwelcome chore?

I was down to my last two hundred fifty dollars—not including what I'd set aside for U.S duties, fees, and quarantine. That wouldn't be enough if I rode farther, but would be if I could get enough free rides with truckers. Would doing things the easy way make me feel like a quitter?

Should I borrow enough money to prolong my adventure?

Or should I get on with my life? The way I'd come alive in Emily's company had been an appealing preview of what might happen if I did that. But would it leave me with a sense of defeat?

On the other hand...

My mind was still going back and forth the next morning.

37

"YOUR HORSES WILL BE CONFISCATED"

The next morning I compared Hamaca and Ima in the flesh with a photo I'd taken in Quito. Back then they'd been in good enough condition to impress even Don Luis de Ascásubi. Now they didn't look like the same horses.

In a moment that can only be described as a life-changing epiphany, I saw my future clearly for the first time. Hamaca and Ima had suffered enough. And though I was an adventurer, I wasn't necessarily a wanderer and definitely not a loner. All my life people and places had been here today and gone tomorrow.

I was twenty-six, still hadn't chosen a career, owned nothing but two horses, and wasn't willing to work at a job that bored me. But I had a calling to preserve and promote Hamaca and Ima's magnificent breed and its traditions while protecting it from the Americanization that already threatened to ruin it.

From now on I'd put every drop of my energy into reaching California as soon as possible, helping Pat Gavitt prepare for and compete in the Tevis Cup, and building a business that would allow me to enjoy life while importing and selling Peruvian Horses.

* * *

That afternoon I took a bus to Guatemala City's elegant Spanish colonial Palacio Nacional. At Peru's National Palace soldiers guarding the entrance wore brightly colored uniforms, knee-high boots, plumed helmets, and swords. But after recent terrorist attacks, Guatemalan guards wore practical combat fatigues and carried submachine guns.

Waiting in line I watched as they searched people before allowing them inside. Finally one finished going through a lady's purse and waved me forward. Hoping he hadn't received an all-points bulletin for a tall gringo who'd stolen a poster from a downtown wall in broad daylight, I stopped in front of him.

He swung his arm, gesturing for me to go in. Surprised he hadn't checked the rolled-up sweater in my hand — which could easily have concealed a pistol — I entered the huge lobby and asked directions to the Minister of Agriculture's office. There I handed a clerk my letter from his boss's counterpart in Costa Rica.

Holding that letter — now unfolded — the Minister himself came to the counter and asked, "How can I be of service?"

I told him about my ride and asked, "What do my horses and I need to enter Mexico?"

"Fill this out." He handed me an application. "If your horses are in good health, their papers will be ready tomorrow."

After the government veterinarian examined Hamaca and Ima, I applied for a visa at the Mexican Consulate.

* * **

The next morning I picked up my visa and that afternoon I returned to the Palacio Nacional. There Guatemala's Minister of Agriculture handed me my mares' health certificates along with two letters of recommendation he'd written. The one to the U.S. Secretary of Agriculture wouldn't be of much use, but the one to Mexico's Minister of Agriculture might.

"Where am I most likely find a truck headed for Mexico?" I asked.

"That may be difficult," he replied. "You should check freight rates on our railroad. They're surprisingly low and will be even lower if you show the agent my letter."

At first the railroad's freight agent, who was new at his job, had little interest helping me save money. His attitude changed after he read the Minister's letter. Frowning and clearing his throat, he thumbed through a rate manual that seemed as complicated as the U.S. Tax Code.

"There's no specific rate for horses," he finally said. "That means I can charge you the lowest livestock rate."

By then I'd managed to convince him I was poor — not cheap.

He read more pages, sometimes going back to read a passage again.

"We can also exploit some other technicalities," he said after a while. "For example I can adjust the routing and scheduling so it costs less than a direct trip. But that means layovers and changing trains. Is that okay?"

"Absolutely."

By the time the agent was finished, even I could afford the price.

"Too bad you weren't here two weeks ago," he said. "A local television station offered fifty dollars to the first person at least two meters tall who came into their studio, and the prize went unclaimed."

"Damn. I could've put that fifty dollars to good use."

Handing me a receipt and bill of lading, the agent told me, "Your train leaves tomorrow morning. If you don't have anything better to do, you should tour Antigua. Here's a pamphlet that tells you all about it."

I didn't bother to tell him tours cost more than I could afford.

Sitting on a bench outside I read the intriguing pamphlet.

Before an earthquake leveled it in the late 1700s, Antigua had been Guatemala's capital. At the foot of two volcanoes it was the most important seat of government between Mexico City and Lima, Peru. Most of its destroyed structures had been restored, but some — the huge cathedral among them — remained in ruins, reminders of a long-ago catastrophe.

But how to get there? I stopped a passerby.

"Guatemala City has an excellent, inexpensive public transportation system," he told me proudly, "and one of its buses goes to Antigua."

I took it.

Surprised to see a foreigner arrive on public transportation, a tour bus driver struck up a conversation and invited me to ride with him. His paid passengers — all American tourists — included an elderly hunchback whose knees didn't lock until they were recessed. He walked with two canes and considerable assistance from his wife.

Getting him on and off the bus to tour buildings and ruins required considerable effort from both of them. Each time they took longer and more passengers became impatient. When he was finally back in his seat at one stop, a woman slid into the row behind him and leaned forward.

I cringed, anticipating the worst.

Touching the old man's shoulder the woman said, "I can't tell you how much I admire you for traveling and enjoying your life even though it's so terribly difficult. You're an inspiration."

One by one other passengers — including two who'd earlier shown frustration — chimed in.

So much for the stereotype of insensitive self-centered Americans.

* * *

Up before dawn the next day I rode to Pamplona's train station. We were scheduled to go to Esquintla that day, stay overnight, then continue to Mazatenango. There we'd lay over until the next morning before finishing our three-day trip to Mexico.

I rode with Hamaca and Ima in an otherwise empty boxcar. At the first stop I accepted the engineer's invitation to ride with him. His name was Nestor and we talked nonstop despite the difficulty of making ourselves heard above the engine's roar.

In Esquintla our conversation continued as Nestor drove a World War I vintage switch engine back and forth, uncoupling cars that were staying there and replacing them with others bound for wherever he was going next. After he parked Hamaca and Ima's boxcar on a sidetrack, I turned them loose so they could move around and lie down until our journey resumed the next day.

"Before I leave," Nestor said, "I'll introduce you to Olaf, the stationmaster. He's German, the same as you, and he just might do you a big favor this evening."

Nestor and I had exchanged countless jokes, and I'd remembered two more. We arrived at Olaf's office laughing so hard neither could talk.

"Take good care of this little gringo," Nestor said before leaving. "I want his memories of Guatemala to be good ones."

When Olaf proved to be a man of few words, I excused myself.

At a nearby poultry farm I bought a half-dozen eggs. I'd sold my cooking utensils in Managua, but kept my cans of Sterno fuel. I lit one and boiled the eggs in a tin can near Hamaca and Ima's boxcar. As another train arrived Olaf rushed toward me — waving his arms. I expected him to scold me for lighting a fire.

"Nestor said you're in a hurry to get to Mexico," he began. "How would you like to get there two days ahead of schedule?"

"I'd love it."

"In that case, I'll send you to directly to Tecun Uman with tonight's train. That will get you to Mexico three days ahead of schedule."

* * *

In Tecun Uman the next morning, I rode Hamaca from the tracks to Guatemala's border station, where my exit was processed in under ten minutes. Then back in the saddle, I rode across the International Bridge — a grandiose name for a long, rather simple wooden structure — and reached Mexican soil at 10:00 a.m., three days earlier than expected.

There a customs inspector with a name tag that said Filomeno Mata, ordered me to unpack my duffel bags for inspection. I untied and lowered both from Ima's packsaddle, then spread all my worldly goods on the lawn.

When I walked inside, Filomeno was sitting at the window in the chair from which he hadn't budged since I'd last seen him.

"Ready for your inspection," I said.

"I did that from here," he said. "You can put everything back now."

"Are you sure?"

His expression said my question was ill-advised, and he further delayed me by summoning the official veterinarian from Tapachula, twenty-five miles away. The vet arrived hours later, glanced at my mares, then initialed two boxes on a form, and charged me for services rendered plus travel expenses.

Next Filomeno demanded a deposit to guarantee I'd pay taxes if I sold Hamaca and Ima in Mexico. I didn't know what I'd done to offend him or even if I'd done anything. Perhaps he disliked Americans in general. Either way, I'd had enough.

"I've ridden through eight countries so far," I told him, "without making a single deposit."

"Don't tell me that," he snapped. "I know for a fact that Panama requires one and strictly enforces that requirement."

"They made an exception for me." I opened my passport and pointed to the handwritten notation beside Panama's visa.

"This is Mexico," Filomeno declared without looking. "We don't care what Panama or any other country did."

"May I speak to your superior?" I asked.

"That won't do any good."

"May I speak to him please?"

Filomeno led me to a private office and left me with an elderly gentleman he called Jefe. Exasperated after hours of harassment, I didn't present my case as tactfully as I should have.

"Our job is to enforce the law," Jefe declared when I'd finished, "and that's what we're doing."

"Please, Señor. There must be a way for me to cross Mexico without making a deposit."

That might have worked earlier, but I'd offended him.

"We'll confiscate your horses," he growled, "if you don't make the required deposit."

"How much?"

He gave me an amount in Mexican *pesos*. If I'd told him I didn't have that much, he would've denied me entry on grounds that I might run out of money in his country.

38

NOW WHAT?

L atin Americans place high value on manners. When I was calm and respectful — which I'd been while seeking to avoid Panama's deposit — officials had often accepted reasonable alternatives to their requirements. But after my frustrating day with Filomeno, I'd gotten off on the wrong foot with Jefe.

Fortunately for me, he too had made a mistake by threatening a penalty he couldn't impose. He didn't have the authority to confiscate my horses before they were admitted to Mexico. The worst he could do was deny them entry.

"You'll have to confiscate my horses," I gently called his bluff, "until I can present my letters of introduction to the Minister of Agriculture in Mexico City and ask for an exception."

His manner softened.

"We collect deposits," he explained, "to stop outsiders from bringing merchandise into our country and selling it without paying import taxes."

"I've already had countless opportunities to sell my horses,"

I persisted softly, "but they're not for sale, and I have letters from four Central American Ministers of Agriculture who attest to my honesty."

The Jefe read one, glanced at the others, and with an explosive sigh swiveled his chair and took a volume from the bookshelf behind him. He scanned several pages before stopping to read.

"According to this," he told me, "we can waive the deposit if you transport your horses by train and don't unload them until you reach the United States."

"Perfect," I said. "I'm planning to go by train."

"Your animals will have to board here in Tecun Uman and can't touch Mexican soil again. Where will you cross into California?"

"Mexicali."

He filled in a blank on a form with that destination.

"You can't take your horses off the train anywhere, under any circumstances," he stressed. "If you unload..." pausing he consulted my Guatemalan health certificate, "Hamaca and Ima Sumac anywhere, for any amount of time, they'll immediately be confiscated. And there is no process by which you can appeal for their return. Do you understand?"

"Yes."

Perhaps the Jefe suspected I didn't have enough money to travel the length of Mexico by train, but eager to be rid of me he finished filling out the form, then rubber stamped and signed it.

"Give this to Filomeno," he said, then escorted me to the door and wished me well.

As Filomeno filled out another form, I formulated a plan. I'd go by train as far as Mexico City and get Hamaca and Ima off the train by hook or by crook. Then I'd show the Minister of Agriculture my letters of recommendation and ask his permission to continue my trip by other means.

This simple-sounding plan had three glaring weaknesses:

1. The railroad might insist I purchase passage all the way to Mexicali.

2. When unloaded in Mexico City, Hamaca and Ima might be confiscated.

3. Mexico's Minister of Agriculture might not be inclined to help me.

* * *

That evening I got my first pleasant surprise since Olaf sent me to the border three days faster than I'd paid for. The freight agent didn't bat an eye when I asked to ship Hamaca and Ima to Mexico City — not Mexicali. When I told him about the special rate I'd been charged in Guatemala, he found a loophole under which they could travel as pets, for much less than the livestock rate.

The next morning he accompanied me as I led Hamaca and Ima along the tracks to the express car. The *guardián* in charge appeared in the doorway as I started up its wooden ramp leading Hamaca.

Holding up a hand to stop me, he asked, "Where do you think you're going?"

The freight agent handed him a copy of my bill of lading.

"This car is full of packages that are my responsibility," the guardián huffed after reading it. "I can't allow animals in here."

"You've done it many times," the agent said.

"Those were in crates, and the biggest was a dog. But horses…" he shrugged.

"They're pets," the agent assured him. "We'll separate them from the other cargo."

He and I cleared a path, led Hamaca and Ima to a corner, and penned them in behind side-by-side, five-foot-high crates.

"I'll ride with them so they don't cause problems," I offered, having noticed the guardián's fear of horses.

"Absolutely not," he insisted. "I'm the only person allowed in this car when the train is moving."

Ima—bless her heart—was a wood chewer and picked the perfect time to started reducing the edge of a wooden crate to slivers.

"Oh dear," the guardián moaned. "Stop him from doing that."

On the platform outside, the conductor called the final, "All aboard."

"Can I ride with my horses?" I asked the guardián.

"No," he barked.

I had no choice but to leave and hurried to a seat in the closest passenger car. With any luck the guardián would have a change of heart and I wouldn't be there long.

* * *

In Tapachula I transferred Hamaca and Ima to the express car on another train. This time the ramp was polished steel — suitable for hand trucks, but too slick for metal shoes. Fortunately the last blacksmith who'd shod them had used large-headed nails that protruded and gripped the ramp. These helped Hamaca cautiously make her way down.

The guardián nervously held her while I went back for Ima, who slipped, then scrambled frantically, but managed to stay on her feet until safely on the ground. On a similar ramp—with gravity working against us—the uphill portion of the transfer was more challenging.

Standing in the car's doorway I kept constant pressure on the lead rope to steady Hamaca, but she repeatedly lost traction and slid backward. To her credit, she kept trying and finally reached the top.

Ima made it in one mad dash.

Technically this transfer had violated the prohibition against unloading Hamaca and Ima. But no one except the guardián had paid any attention. I could've led them anywhere and only he would've cared. Evidently he knew they couldn't leave the train.

To my dismay he transferred with us.

* * *

Every time the Mexican Express slowed to a stop between Tapachula and Veracruz, the conductor hurried through the passenger cards shouting, "If you leave the train and don't re-board before it departs you'll be left behind."

As soon as waiting passengers and freight were aboard, we continued on.

The first stops weren't long enough for me to check on Hamaca and Ima. When one was, I dashed to the express car where I watered, fed, and cleaned up after them before sprinting back to my seat.

Later during a longer stop, I begged the guardián to please let me ride with my horses. But I had to plead my case while rushing around the platform looking for a water spigot, holding Hamaca and Ima's buckets while they drank, and stuffing their hay nets. This ruled out eye-contact and face-to-face sincerity. But I doubt either would've changed that stubborn man's mind.

I spent that afternoon trying to make myself less uncomfortable on my tiny, increasingly uncomfortable seat. But there wasn't enough room, and why would there be? People my size were so rare in that part of the world that a Guatemalan television station had offered a significant reward and failed to find even one.

To make matters worse I was one of three passengers in a seat designed for two. Unlike me, the other two were accustomed to crowded conditions and had no difficulty sleeping.

"Ladies and gentlemen," the conductor announced when the train stopped again. "This car will be attached to a train bound for Chilpancingo. If your destination is Mexico City, you must transfer to the train ahead, which leaves in a half hour."

I helped Hamaca and Ima down and up two more slippery ramps, then claimed a seat in a passenger car. No matter how I squirmed, the bones in my skinny behind pinched my skin against its widely spaced slats. Happily no one sat next to me and I was able to curl up on my side and find a position almost as comfortable as a bed of nails.

Around midnight the train stopped in Oaxaca. Still half-asleep I sprinted to the express car and checked on Hamaca and Ima. Back in my seat and asleep before the train left the station, I didn't wake again until 6:00 a.m.

I felt fortunate to have slept so well until I realized why.

The engine had been turned off and the train was still in Oaxaca. None of my fellow passengers knew why we'd been delayed or for how long. Hoping to find out, I stepped onto the platform. It was empty, and I didn't want to go farther from a train that might depart at any moment.

After a while—alert for signs the engine was building up steam—I went inside the station.

"Can you please tell me," I asked a porter, "why the train to Mexico City was delayed?"

"There was an accident, señor," he replied. "The tracks are blocked."

"Any idea how long it will take to clear them?"

"None. You should stay near the train. It might leave at any moment."

When I checked on Hamaca and Ima, both were finishing the last hay I'd given them. They looked contented, and why not? For them, train travel was effortless and comfortable. Out of the sun and cooled by the guardián's fan, they ate and slept whenever they wanted. And no blood-hungry insects or curious people pestered them.

* * *

Around noon a group of my fellow travelers headed to town for a meal and sightseeing. I was tempted to join them but didn't dare risk having Hamaca and Ima continue to Mexico City without me.

Sitting on the ground shaded by the hot car where I'd ridden, I opened a secondhand paperback novel that had cost pennies in Guatemala City. I'd intended to read it while Hamaca and Ima were in U.S. quarantine.

In need of exercise after several chapters I walked briskly around the train until tired enough—I hoped—to sleep that night.

Soon after I went back to reading, the grossly misnamed Mexican Express pulled out after a thirteen-and-a-half hour delay. One of the three days given to me by kindly Olaf in Guatemala had been taken back. But I was still ahead and complaining would've been ungrateful.

39

THE GREAT ESCAPE

Due to Southern Mexico's long history of violent bandit gangs, there was a conspicuous military and police presence there. The government had provided Tschiffely with an armed escort when he'd passed through. Over thirty years later a new generation of outlaws was active.

Every time our train stopped, the soldiers it carried for protection took a keen interest as I rushed to the express car. Finally one stopped me.

"Your documents please," he said politely, then questioned me so long I had to return to my seat without looking in on Hamaca and Ima.

By then armed policemen were frisking the car's passengers and brusquely going through their dilapidated suitcases, gunnysacks, and cardboard boxes.

"Where's your luggage?" an officer asked after patting me down.

"In the express car with my horses," I replied.

He looked at me suspiciously, then followed his partner to the next car.

"Are the police always this rude?" I asked the man sitting beside me.

"They're famous for abusing their power," he replied.

"The soldiers don't seem that way."

"They aren't. Without them we couldn't travel safely."

The soldiers were well-mannered and from poor families. They called passengers sir or ma'am. When there was no place to sit they stood — unlike the arrogant police sergeant who'd displaced a boy from the seat across the aisle.

The man in the window seat next to me threw his trash into the desert, but spit on the floor — probably because hot, gritty incoming air would've blown spittle back on him. Uncomfortable breathing the overcrowded car's stuffy air, I walked to the door at the end of the aisle, opened it, and stepped onto the open platform outside.

There it was noisier but smelled better.

* * *

In Veracruz we changed trains again. This time the car carrying Hamaca and Ima stopped across from the one to which they had to transfer, and a portable bridge was secured between them. Then workers with hand trucks transferred crates and packages in both directions. Last but not least I led Hamaca and then Ima across.

Mercifully the guardián who'd been watching over my mares stayed on the other train. His friendly counterpart succumbed to my pleas and let me ride with my mares. If there was indeed a rule against that, he didn't care. This raised the welcome possibility that he might not know I'd been forbidden to take my horses off the train.

Standing between Hamaca and Ima I braced them during our jerky departure, then stopped Ima from gnawing on crates. After that the guardián and I sat talking in the open doorway for hours—legs hanging out, hands grabbing at leaves on trees that flashed past while hot dirty winds tore at us.

Near Mexico City we passed extensive ruins at San Juan Teotihuacán, an abandoned city built around impressive pyramids. It is believed to have been the sixth largest city in the world during its heyday. I could almost see families enjoying themselves outside its single story apartment buildings.

A half hour later we rolled through Mexico City's poorly lit outskirts. Farther along the bright lights and busy streets of North America's largest metropolis stretched in every direction like sparkling jewels.

* * *

At the railway station soldiers and police were everywhere, making this a bad place to illegally unload Hamaca and Ima. I gathered my courage, and the guardián didn't object when I led Hamaca down yet another slippery ramp.

Then a uniformed freight agent rushed up and showed me his badge.

"I'm Cipriano Maldonado," he introduced himself.

He held Hamaca while I unloaded Ima.

"If you want," he offered, "your horses can spend the night in a vacant boxcar near here."

I could scarcely believe my good luck.

Cipriano put my sleeping bag, remaining hay, and duffel bags on a cart. Pushing it, he cleared a path as I led Hamaca and Ima away from the crowd and bright lights.

"Your horses can sleep in there." He pointed to a boxcar on a spur track beside an abandoned warehouse.

Following him I led Hamaca and Ima up a ramp and across a loading platform, then borrowed his flashlight to illuminate the boxcar's interior. There were no hazards.

As I slid the door shut, Cipriano took out a padlock and told me, "Use this. I'll come back in the morning and open it for you."

"I'd rather not lock their door," I said.

"You should. There are many thieves here." His key ring jingled as he removed one. "Put this and the padlock on the ledge above the door if you leave before I get here tomorrow. You can sleep in the warehouse."

Lighting the way with his flashlight Cipriano guided me inside, then rolled a freight cart near the door and showed me how to operate its deadbolt.

"Good night," he said, "and welcome to Mexico City."

He didn't seem to expect a tip and I couldn't afford one, but I made sure he knew how much I appreciated his helpfulness.

Even after my eyes adjusted to the dark interior I could barely see. Guided by my sense of touch, I found the flashlight in my duffel bag. In its feeble light I unrolled my sleeping bag on the freight cart and lay on top, fully dressed so I'd be ready to go at first light.

* * *

I woke feeling as though I'd just fallen asleep.

While in the future my impending escape had been a terrifying prospect, especially after I'd read an article that ranked Mexico as the world's fifth worst place to be imprisoned. But I was surprisingly calm considering that I was about to risk losing Hamaca and Ima and might soon be in a Mexican jail.

I opened the warehouse door.

The men troweling a concrete pad in the distance were in a

hurry to finish before it set up. Only one looked at me when I stepped outside. I stretched to show I was in no hurry, then opened the padlock and slid the boxcar door as far as it would go.

When Hamaca was saddled and my bags were on Ima's packsaddle I led them outside and put the padlock and key where Cipriano had requested.

I could've yelled, "I hope nobody confiscates my illegally disembarked horses," and the concrete finishers would probably have continued working.

But a curious policeman or soldier could ruin everything.

After riding off the platform and following a spur track, I saw an arrow-shaped sign pointing toward Mexico City's stockyard. That would be the perfect place to leave Hamaca and Ima while I visited the Minister of Agriculture. Among pens full of cattle, they'd be like needles in a haystack.

And if my meeting with the Minister went well, the stockyard would also be a good place to find a truck heading north.

* * *

As the guard at the gate proudly informed me, Mexico City's stockyard was the world's second largest, behind only Chicago's. Hoping Hamaca and Ima would be allowed to stay in one of its many empty corrals, I asked directions to the office.

There I told the assistant manager about my ride and asked, "May I please stay here with my horses for a few days?"

"Only the *mayordomo del campo* can give you permission to do that," he replied. "You'll probably find him in the slaughterhouse or at the unloading ramp."

I didn't. He had left the grounds on errands and didn't return until it was too late for me to go to the Minister's office.

To my considerable relief, he was as kind as he'd been hard to find and showed me to one of the seemingly endless corrals with concrete feeders along one side.

"Your horses can stay free," he said, "and you can sleep in their feed trough if you want."

He was surprised when I accepted his invitation to sleep in my mares' corral, having no doubt suspected I was exaggerating when I'd said I was almost out of money.

* * *

In the morning before leaving for my all-important visit with the Minister of Agriculture, I took a shower in the slaughterhouse's worker clean-up facility. Its smell — produced by incinerated waste, mostly intestines and stomachs — was so foul I feared I'd acquire a worse scent than the one I washed away.

Because fabric readily absorbs odors, I didn't take my clean clothes and wore my dirty ones back to the corral. There, beyond reach of the slaughterhouse's awful smell, I changed.

That done I walked to a nearby boulevard and caught the first in a series of buses that eventually took me to the Ministry of Agriculture.

"You can't just walk in and see the Minister," his receptionist told me. "You need an appointment, which I warn you will be difficult to get."

Her indignation wasn't surprising. My clothes were clean but shabby, and I'd asked for one of Mexico's most important officials.

"Please show him these," I said, handing her my letters of recommendation.

She looked at the return addresses on the envelopes and had a clerk deliver them.

To my astonishment and everyone else's, the Minister sent his personal secretary to escort me to his desk, where he stood up with great dignity and shook my hand.

"How can I be of service?" he asked.

Briefly and honestly I told my story.

"You're a fugitive from the law," he said. "I could have you arrested. But you wouldn't have come here if you weren't honest, right? Besides I've heard about your ride. Have a seat in the waiting room. This won't take long."

Later, his personal secretary brought a manila envelope and showed me the signed, rubber stamped certificates and notarized letter inside.

"If anyone bothers you, show these," she said, returning her handiwork to its envelope. "Good luck."

* * *

With livestock trucks constantly coming and going from the stockyard, I'd hoped to find a ride all the way to Mexicali. But no one was going that far. Most trucks going north already had return cargo, and I could offer only a token payment. One after another drivers scoffed and shook their heads.

"I wouldn't take two horses to Mexicali for ten times that much," one told me.

The next morning on the mayordomo's advice, I visited the headquarters of the Asociación de Charros — perhaps Mexico's most powerful horse-related organization. Its busy receptionist took no interest in my problem except to tell me what I already feared.

"It will be impossible to find such transportation without paying a lot more than you're offering."

I'd made a long trip for nothing and returned to the bus

stop where a man with a steaming metal cart periodically shouted, *"Perros calientes,"* a literal translation of hot dogs that brings to mind canines — not sandwiches. His were inexpensive, but at the slaughterhouse I'd seen what went into them.

Back at the stockyard's unloading area I resumed my search for transportation. As before, the mayordomo did his best to help when he had time, but today's luck was no better than yesterday's.

Finally, discouraged, he told me, "I can get you a ride to the border, but you'll have to go without your horses. I'll help sell them if you want."

40

HOME STRETCH

Desperately needing to pick up my spirits after a much needed nap, I went to the stockyard's office and studied a newspaper's movie section. To my surprise — and delight — *Doctor Zhivago* was showing at an inexpensive theater. Seeing it again would be the perfect antidote for my sagging morale.

"That theater is clear across Mexico City," the receptionist told me. "To get there by bus will take two hours and require numerous transfers. You'll be lucky to get there on time."

I set out at once. Nowhere on my journey from Peru had I been as worried about getting lost. I transferred from bus to bus to streetcar, to bus — checking with each driver to be sure I was going the right way. Even after a wrong transfer forced me to backtrack, I arrived in time for the last showing and enjoyed David Lean's masterpiece more than enough to justify the effort.

Getting my bearings on Mexico City's confusing, seldom parallel streets was difficult. When I returned to the stockyard that night I was extra cautious — especially when transferring. And for good reason. It was almost midnight and buses would soon stop running. One wrong transfer and I'd be stranded without a place to sleep.

* * *

I awoke with renewed enthusiasm and a new strategy. Rather than attempt to go most or all the way to the border with my first ride, I'd settle for the first available truck going in my direction — on the theory that assistance might be easier to get in smaller amounts.

For two days this approach produced the same result as the one it had replaced. Then early Saturday morning, two drivers traveling together delivered cattle.

"We're returning to Guadalajara with partial loads," one told me, "and each of us has room for one horse."

Thanks to the mayordomo's intervention, they offered an extremely reasonable price. But I was down to eighty dollars. They wanted thirty dollars per horse, and Guadalajara was more than two thousand kilometers from Mexicali.

"I can't pay more than five dollars each," I said, embarrassed to haggle over an already spectacular price. "I know a ride to Guadalajara is worth much more, but I don't have it."

The drivers looked at one another and the taller one said, "Make it twenty-five for both."

"I can pay twenty," I said, "but not a penny more."

"Done," he replied. "Bring your horses to the loading ramp."

When we got there, both trucks were backed up to ramps with their rear gates open. Except for a few feet at the rear, each was full of fresh cowhides. The pleasant smell of tanned leather was off in the future, and their ripe scent was attracting flies.

As a boy I'd competed in trail horse classes and learned how difficult it can be to get a horse anywhere near a cowhide. But I was determined not to let Hamaca and Ima veto an incredible price. My resolve didn't get tested. Both loaded easily, taking little notice of the hides.

Being separated, however, upset them. For the first time since Piura neither could see the other, and both needed reassurance they were still together. They continued calling back and forth after the trucks were underway. The neighs and whinnies grew more frequent every time we stopped for fuel or food and kept me awake all night.

After their joyous reunion at daybreak in Guadalajara's central market, I was exhausted for obvious reasons, and nauseated because I could no longer afford to be as careful as I should when buying food.

Less than ten minutes after unloading my mares, I was negotiating with a tomato truck driver who was headed north with room to spare.

"In two days," he told me, "I'm going to Culiacán. I'll take you and your horses for ten dollars, but I'm offering such a low price because I need the money now, in advance."

His price was indeed excellent, and Culiacán was seven hundred kilometers closer to the border. Furthermore I could use the rest to get over what seemed like another bout with dysentery. But should I trust a stranger?

I wanted to and did.

By then I was feverish and powerful intestinal cramps periodically reminded me of the reason Mexicans call dysentery Montezuma's revenge. Fitfully I slept the rest of that day and all night, outside a stall shared by Hamaca and Ima.

Feeling better in the morning I borrowed a bicycle and toured a picturesque Guadalajara neighborhood featuring plazas and parks that had walkways covered with cobble-stones or colorful tile. I saw fountains, statues, and beautifully manicured gardens where shrubs were trimmed to resemble animals and flowers were planted so they spelled out words.

After running out of energy I watched two movies for a few cents each. Neither was as interesting as its venue. Inside and out, both theaters were impressively ornate compared to our rather plain movie houses in the States.

* * *

The trucker met my mares and me at the appointed time in the central market. By the following afternoon he'd driven us to Culiacán. Feeling much better by that time I rented a corral for Hamaca and Ima. Then at the outdoor market, I bought the smallest bale of alfalfa I'd ever seen. The vendor weighed it and charged by the kilo.

Later I opened my bale with the man who'd rented me the corral looking on. Like me, he was disgusted when I peeled off two flakes of moldy hay.

"One of our fine, upstanding merchants," he informed me, "pours water in his bales to make them heavier so he can charge more. Every day his leftover bales get the same treatment, which is why yours is rotten."

If I'd simply put that bale in Hamaca and Ima's corral and removed the string, they might well have eaten or breathed in toxic mold spores. Angry I returned to the market — determined to get my money back. But the dishonest merchant was gone. All I could do was break open a bale offered by another vendor before paying him.

* * *

The following day, a Wednesday, I was fortunate enough

to catch a ten-dollar truck ride from Culiacán to Ciudad Obregón. On Friday ten more dollars took us to Hermosillo, four hundred miles from the border at Mexicali. By then I'd spent all I could spare for transportation.

From Mexicali, if Hamaca and Ima's blood tests came back negative, Joe Gavitt would take us to our final destination—his and Pat's aptly named Pleasant Hill Farm near Los Gatos, California.

But he could hardly be expected to leave his job...pull a horse trailer half the length of California and four hundred miles into Mexico, bring us to Mexicali, wait at least a week for Hamaca and Ima to be released from U.S. quarantine... then drive six hundred miles home.

I was still looking for a free ride when a local rancher offered the next best thing, a job.

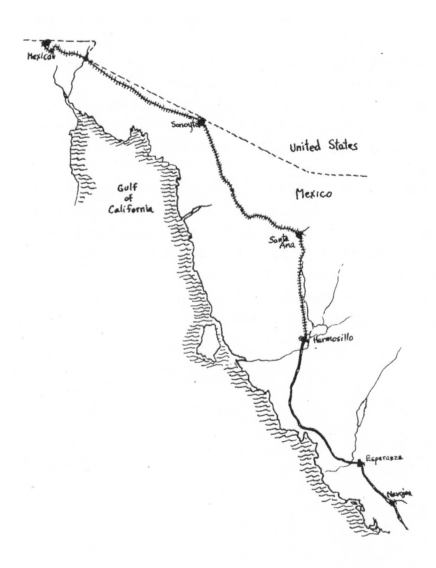

41

FINISH LINE

That job was as a *picador*, but I wasn't destined to enter a bullring in front of cheering thousands. There are two kinds of *picadores*: courageous mounted lancers who defy death to joust with brave bulls in front of cheering thousands, and dirty, tired men who endure foul odors to care for frightened cattle on railroad trains. I was one of the latter.

The rancher who hired me was shipping a herd north by train to Mexicali, and my wages were free passage for me and my mares. As I unloaded them from his truck at the train yard, a little popinjay of a man strutted from the Sonora State Government office and zeroed in on me—arms away from his body in an obvious attempt to look big and imposing.

He wore a Livestock Deputy's uniform and clearly saw me as a potential source of income.

"Be careful," the rancher whispered in English. "This idiot has small man's complex and will enjoy lording it over someone your size."

"Where are you going with those horses?" the deputy demanded.

"Mexicali," I replied.

"We'll see about that. Come with me." He led the way into his office, gestured for me to stand in front of his desk, then sat in the swivel chair behind it.

"Are you aware," he demanded, his tone making it clear I should be, "that you need a permit from the State of Sonora to transport horses by train?"

I was tempted to say I was fresh out of money but would gladly bribe him with a few inches of my height, but good sense prevailed.

"Not until now," I replied.

"Show me your horses' papers."

"These are from the federal government," he growled, returning them. Where's your permit from the State of Sonora?"

"Do I need one?"

"Absolutely and the office that issues them is closed for the weekend. You won't be able to travel on today's train."

I ignored what may have been an invitation to offer a bribe and took a deep breath, drew myself to my full height and said, "But I have a job on that train."

"A job." His eyes opened wide with anticipation. "You're a foreigner. Do you have a work permit?"

Me and my big mouth.

If ever there was a time to unveil the documents I'd been given by the Minister of Agriculture, this was it. I started with the smallest, intending to present the others one-by-one for greater effect. The Deputy started to return it, then did an unintentionally comical double take and passed it to his clerk.

Suddenly my would-be tormentor's utterances were limited to "yes, sir, no, sir, and if you like, sir."

With no further mention of permits he told me, "You're free to go. With that paper no one can stop you."

"Unless you commit a crime," his clerk clarified.

* * *

Well after dark, the rancher brought my fellow picador to the train yard.

"Carlos has taken thousands of my cattle to Mexicali over the years," the rancher said after introducing us. "Do as he says and you'll be fine."

"We'll be up most of the night loading steers," Carlos told me between yawns, "and should rest while we have the chance. I usually sleep in the caboose with the brakeman. Do you mind sleeping over there?"

He pointed to a broken-down truck. Before curling up on its front seat, I prepared for my coming trip.

First I fenced in Hamaca and Ima with stout horizontal poles at one end of a boxcar. The steers Carlos and I would later drive into that car were only generations removed from wild ancestors. I wanted a barrier between their long, sharp horns and my mares.

Next I hung my duffel bags from the ceiling, where they'd stay clean, dry, and untrampled.

Then I put opposite ends of a plank between corresponding slats on each of the car's side walls and slid it against the end wall, making a ledge. On the way to Mexicali that was where I'd sit by day and sleep at night.

Looking down, I imagined thirty-two steers below — each with sharp horns and hooves that supported hundreds of pounds. Sleeping on my little ledge would be difficult, and not only because it was narrow.

In the end wall above my makeshift bed was a crawl hole

that would be the only way into or out of that boxcar when we were underway. I opened its door and saw a metal ladder that went up to the roof and down to the coupling between cars. Even with the train stopped, I found it extremely difficult to slide through that opening onto the ladder.

It would be dangerous when the train was moving.

* * *

Just before dawn I helped Carlos drive the cattle along chutes and into boxcars. Then we made sure every steer in each car was on its feet. If any were down when the train started moving, they could suffocate or be trampled. And as they struggled to get up, their horns would threaten the soft underbellies above them.

When the train stopped, Carlos and I walked along opposite sides — keeping cranky, tired steers on their feet. When the train was underway, we walked the tops of moving boxcars, opening access hole to see if all the cattle inside were standing. If one wasn't we crawled in, lowered ourselves to the floor, and used prod poles to clear enough space for it to get up.

The rest of the time we rode on the roof talking, laughing, and eating delicious, juicy oranges while the desert seemed to flow past. When the sky suddenly darkened and a desert downpour caught us outside, we slid through the access hole above my makeshift bed.

Sitting there giggling boyishly, we wiped our faces on our sleeves. When I looked down I saw something troubling.

Hamaca and Ima were still eating the alfalfa I'd given them earlier. The hungry steers on the other side of the barricade I'd built were putting considerable pressure on it.

I had unwittingly set the stage for a dangerous conflict.

"Next time we stop," I told Carlos, "I'll get rid of that hay."

"If I were you I'd do it now," he said.

* * *

After dark the chilly desert air became bitterly cold and Carlos retired to the caboose. I untied my sleeping bag from the boxcar's roof, unrolled it on the scaffold and crawled inside. Repeatedly the car's swaying and jerking roused me from a half-sleep. Finally I wrapped a length of rope twice around me and the plank, then tied it firmly — making a crude safety belt.

Nonetheless I slept little and badly.

At dawn my career as a picador ended. I said goodbye to Carlos in the hamlet of Pascualitos, a few miles from Mexicali's quarantine station. Then, as I'd done so often during my ride, I saddled Hamaca, loaded my baggage on Ima, and mounted up. We soon reached our — or more accurately my — final goal, Mexicali.

This abrupt end to my adventure was jolting. I was sorry the often lonely and arduous trip was over. Already the unpleasant memories were fading, and all I could remember was beautiful country, wonderful people, and fascinating experiences.

The stretch from Mexico City had tested my persistence more than my mares' endurance. But it had been an interesting challenge, and its apparent defeats had been overcome. We even set what might be an unofficial world record by traveling fifteen hundred miles on only sixty-some dollars — not bad for a man, a pair of horses, and two hundred pounds of baggage.

As I dismounted at the quarantine facility my curiosity got the best of me. I opened one of my duffel bags and took out the sealed envelope given to me by Jorge Baca's elderly neighbor the day I left Chiclayo.

Inside the outer envelope were three smaller ones. Feeling like a presenter at the Academy Awards, I opened the first and found a postcard with an image of Saint Christopher, the patron saint of travelers. All in all he'd looked after me nicely, so I resisted the temptation to suggest a few small improvements in his service.

In the second envelope was a sheet of paper bearing the old man's prediction of my arrival date, *Noviembre de 1967*, written in his shaky scrawl. He'd been wrong, but it wasn't his fault I'd changed my plans after he'd made his guess.

The surprise gift in the last envelope was a color lithograph of the palomino Peruvian stallion, Mantequilla, looking as stunning as he had in life. Hamaca and Ima had represented their breed less spectacularly — but in an equally important way. They too would be remembered. I'd make sure of that.

At the reception desk in the quarantine station, a secretary told me, "The requirements for bringing horses into the United States have become more complicated. If you hire a customs agent, it'll save you time and money in the long run."

I'd already set aside enough to cover that expense.

Letters of recommendation wouldn't help at this border. In the United States — theoretically at least — rules were the same for everyone no matter who they were or knew. Crossing its border would depend on meeting requirements, period, and a professional agent could do that better than I.

"Can you recommend an agent?" I asked the secretary.

"I'm not allowed to do that," she replied.

I selected a name from the list under the glass countertop.

"Good choice," the secretary said, then dialed his number and handed me her phone's receiver.

The agent quickly proved his worth.

"Since your horses are registered purebreds," he told me, "I can get you exempted from import duties. That alone will save you more than my fee."

So far our conversation had been in Spanish, and we'd each assumed the other was Latino. Then he asked my name.

"Verne Albright," I told him.

"Are you American?" he asked in perfect English.

Months earlier he'd have known I was a gringo halfway through my first sentence.

"Yes," I replied.

"Me, too. Your Spanish is so good I figured you were Peruvian or maybe Mexican."

"Thank you, but my Spanish isn't nearly as good as yours."

"I was raised in Latin America and grew up bilingual."

* * *

That night I called Joe and Pat Gavitt from a pay phone and told them Hamaca and Ima would be released from quarantine in a week, if their blood tests were negative.

"Our plans have changed," Joe informed me. "A new Peruvian Paso breeder named John DeLozier wants to talk with you and will pick you up in Mexicali. He'll trailer Hamaca and Ima Sumac to his ranch in Cantil, and I'll meet you there."

Shortly before leaving on my ride I'd sold John and his wife, Angie, two horses. It didn't seem likely he was driving several hundred miles just to tell me how pleased they were.

42

BACK TO COSTA RICA

With little to do while Hamaca and Ima were in quarantine, I thought back to conversations I'd had with the owner of the Ecuadorian hacienda where Aimé Tschiffely had stayed forty-one years before me.

As predicted, I was already beginning to appreciate what Hamaca, Ima, and I had done, even though we'd fallen far short of what Tschiffely, Mancha, and Gato accomplished. All things considered we'd done well, and our merits weren't diminished simply because three of history's greatest travelers had done more.

Several times I wondered if I'd see Emily again. We'd said goodbye three times, thinking each was our last. But twice Lady Luck had brought us back together, and I had answered the letter she'd sent in care of the America Embassy. Was her response waiting at the Gavitt's ranch in Los Gatos?

The afternoon before Hamaca and Ima were scheduled to be released, Judy, the quarantine station receptionist, introduced me to a cattle importer who took an immediate interest in my ride.

"I have a proposition for you," he said as I started to go. "Would you like to discuss it over dinner at The Steakhouse?"

If I remember correctly his name was Bob. I'll call him that here.

"I manage the Cattle Call Horse Show and Rodeo," Bob told me as I savored an outstanding cut of meat he'd recommended. "If we invite you and your horses to take a lap of the arena during our show this Friday, will you accept? A camera crew from ABC's *Wide World of Sports* will be there and might be interested in an interview. And you can stay at my house until then."

I was sleeping in a park and eating french fries at McDonald's. His invitation would've been irresistible even without the prospect of national television publicity.

When the waiter brought the check, Bob handed him almost as much as I'd spent to travel from Mexico City to Mexicali.

That evening from Bob's house, I phoned John DeLozier and asked him to pick me up there two days later than planned. John was pleased with the possible publicity for our breed, and our conversation ended with no hint of why he wanted to talk.

* * *

The Cattle Call Show began with thunderous applause as the grand entry — a steady stream of horses and riders — filled the arena. During the National Anthem two Quarter Horses circled on the rail in opposite directions at a dead run, their riders holding rippling American flags and masterfully priming spectators for the coming show.

As the last horse and rider left, Hamaca, Ima, and I entered. The announcer introduced us with great enthusiasm. Problem was, we weren't all that interesting compared to the spectacle the crowd had just witnessed. I simply circled the large, otherwise empty arena — riding a small, sun-bleached black mare and leading another.

A short journey compared to the one we'd completed eight days earlier, it was too long for the audience. My mares — taught to dispense with their normally elegant carriages and flashy leg action — attracted little attention. My battered hat, faded shirt, and worn-out jeans were dull compared to colorfully dressed cowboys and Indians.

We were less than halfway around when announcer finished the script I'd written.

He tried to ad-lib but didn't know what to say. His rich, booming voice went silent. No one — me least of all — had thought to provide some stirring music.

Bored, the audience settled back, waiting for this unavoidable delay to give way to high-spirited cowboys and bucking broncos. As we left, the announcer repeated my name and mispronounced Hamaca and Ima's. His request for a round of applause brought scattered clapping.

By then *Wide World of Sports* cameras had long since stopped filming. What little videotape they'd shot would no doubt wind up on a cutting room floor.

I had a lot to learn if I was going to promote Peruvian horses.

* * *

"I'm completely satisfied with one mare you sold me," John DeLozier told me a few miles after I'd loaded Hamaca and Ima in his horse trailer, "but the other turned out to be sterile."

He handed me a vet certificate.

After reading it I said, "I know a man who's selling outstanding Peruvian horses from hard-to-get bloodlines. I can help you get excellent prices. Will that compensate you?"

The next day at John's Thunderbird Ranch, he and I finalized arrangements for our trip to Costa Rica. He wanted to go soon, before Central American buyers skimmed off the cream of Juan Rafael Cabezas' horses.

Two days after Joe Gavitt trailered Hamaca, Ima, and me to his Pleasant Hill Farm near Los Gatos, John and I were in Alajuela, Costa Rica. Don Juan Rafael Cabezas had prepared an impressive showing of the best mares he had for sale. If I'd had his flair, my exhibition with Hamaca and Ima at the Cattle Call Show would've achieved its purpose.

As John watched one mare after another circle an arena surrounded by flowering bougainvillea, Don Juan took me aside.

"I'll add your commission to my horses' prices," he told me. "How much do you want?"

"Nothing has changed," I replied. "I won't charge anything, but I'll appreciate it if you give Mr. DeLozier the best prices you possibly can."

The two mares John selected were the best he'd been shown. Nonetheless he and I thought Don Juan was asking too much.

As negotiations dragged on, I repeatedly tried to see Emily. But the family she was then living with was stricter than its predecessors. I saw her only once—without permission— while she was at school and surrounded by friends.

To make a long story short, John returned to Thunderbird Ranch after buying both the mares. Don Juan and I arranged to have them shipped. And I flew back to Los Gatos.

* * *

My return flight from Costa Rica landed in California's beautiful Santa Clara Valley. Only decades earlier that area had been covered by vast orchards. Remnants of those still blossomed every spring among the homes and businesses of San Jose.

Beneath that sprawling city, the roots of hundreds of thousands of felled fruit and nut trees were still infested with termites. Numbering in the billions they'd become a threat to San Jose's wooden structures — but had also provided Joe Gavitt with a good job as lead inspector for Rose Exterminator Company.

Two years earlier Joe had gotten me a job there. After a year of repairing termite and water damage, I'd gone on my ride. Thanks to Joe, my job was waiting and I was due to report on Monday. My old room at his and Pat's house in the Santa Cruz Mountains behind nearby Los Gatos was also waiting.

It was good to be home. I was eager to restart the life that had been boring when I'd left but looked promising now that I knew what I wanted to do with it.

EPILOGUE

Part One: Emily

After John DeLozier and I returned from Costa Rica, I stayed a while with the Gavitts. At the time, Pat had six hens — one, coincidentally, named Emily. Whichever laid the fewest eggs that month was destined for the cooking pot.

Every morning I checked the cages, hoping there'd be an egg in the one occupied by Emily (the hen). There usually was and her final total was the highest of all.

Emily (the woman) and I exchanged more letters. She signed her first: "Thinking of you, Emily." After that they were never again as promising.

A couple of years later she attended UCLA. I drove down from San Jose and we went to dinner. Then I took her to Santa Barbara to visit friends she had there. On the way back to UCLA she fell asleep with her head on my lap.

The theme song for that night could've been Stephen Sondheim's poignant ballad about two people who could never quite get together, *Send in the Clowns*.

Not long after that Emily and I got married, but not to each other.

Part Two: The Tevis Cup

By the time my Peru-to-California journey ended in 1967, The Tevis Cup Ride was almost certainly the best-known, most grueling endurance race on the planet. Annually it began on the shore of Lake Tahoe and ended twenty-four hours later under July's bright riding moon at the fairground in Auburn, California.

All told, its rugged Western States Trail climbed over fifteen thousand feet and descended almost twenty-three thousand. Temperatures varied from below freezing on Cougar Rock to 114 degrees in California's century-old gold camps.

Near Emigrant Gap the climbs were so steep pioneers had been forced to lower covered wagons with ropes. On nights when clouds blocked the moonlight, contestants forded the American River at a crossing marked with floating light sticks.

Winners had finished in as little as eleven hours and thirty-eight minutes riding time, but any riders to do so in less than twenty-four hours received one of the ride's coveted belt buckles.

Pat Gavitt was looking forward to testing herself against that ride's many challenges, and I was hoping she had enough time to get Hamaca ready.

"Hamaca tries hard to please," Pat told me early on, "but after all she's been through, I fear she's not ready for another challenge."

To find out, Pat rode Hamaca up and down California's rugged Santa Cruz Mountains with Julie Suhr and her Peruvian mare, Marinera. I'd bought Marinera in Peru, then sold her to Julie and the two had finished the Tevis Cup in very respectable time.

Later — on an Arabian — Julie won three Haggin Cups, awarded to the best conditioned horse among the Tevis Cup's first ten finishers. This tied her for the record, but Marinera is still her all-time favorite endurance horse. Twice the gallant little mare carried her across the finish line, 22nd of 92 entries the first time and 24th of 125 the second.

In retrospect Julie once wrote: "I'd give anything to have had the knowledge I have at this time. I could have done much, much better!"

A month after first riding Hamaca, Pat told me, "She can't begin to keep up with Marinera. Even if we wait until next year, it will probably take her almost twenty hours to finish."

Back then, few Americans had heard of Peruvian horses and most would judge the entire breed by the first individuals they saw. Our goal had been to finish in the top third. But Pat knew horses. Shaking my lowered head I deferred to her. A cherished dream was dead, along with what I feared was my last chance to show the breed's virtues to a national audience.

Part Three: John Delozier

John DeLozier was the most loyal friend I ever had, and I believe I was the same to him. We couldn't have been more different in appearance and manner, but our souls were almost identical. We had the same taste in people as well as horses and seldom disagreed on anything.

Starting with the fertile mare I sold them and the two John bought from Juan Rafael Cabezas, he and his wife Angie methodically built their Thunderbird Ranch into one of the leading Peruvian horse ranches in the United States.

By the mid-1970s they had four outstanding breeding animals.

The first had been La Nata, the Cayaltí mare John bought in Costa Rica. Next he'd acquired Cleopatra and Duquesa from the Hacienda Pucalá, where I'd bought Ima Sumac. And finally Alfredo Elias — Peru's all-time best breeder in my opinion — had sold him Gacela.

With such mares to be bred John wanted the best sire he could possibly get. I helped him buy the incomparable Piloto, the stallion José Antonio Onrubia had shown me the day he and I first met.

Gacela never gave the DeLoziers a live foal, but their other mares' offspring won an impressive number of championships.

* * *

I never saw John plod to a decision. They seemed to pop into his head from nowhere as if divinely inspired.

His ability to assess situations and make decisions quickly had kept him ahead of competitors back when he'd been in Alaska's towing and wrecking business. He was proud of his success there, and never missed an opportunity to tell the story of a three thousand dollar check he'd tried to cash one afternoon.

"I'm sorry, Mr. DeLozier," the teller had said after consulting a large rectangular ledger. "There aren't sufficient funds to cover this."

Bad news. The man who'd written that check was leaving Alaska the next day.

"How much is there?" John asked.

"You know I can't tell you that," she replied.

"Why not?" Leaning closer John quietly said. "He'll never know. He's moving to California tomorrow."

She looked around to be sure they were alone and whispered, "A little over twenty-five hundred dollars."

"Okay," he pounced. "I'll deposit five hundred dollars so I can cash his check."

He pulled five crisp new bills from his wallet.

Startled she said, "You can't make a deposit to someone else's account."

"May I speak to the manager please?"

The manager told John, "I can't let you make a deposit to another person's account."

"Why not?"

"It's against the rules."

"Can you show me that in writing?"

John's continuing discussion with that dignified gentleman ended with the manager thumbing through his bank's thick policy manual without finding the rule he wanted—after which John had made his deposit and cashed his check.

He and I were still friends when John passed away years after he'd moved to Texas and I'd gone to Canada.

Part Four: More About Luis De Ascásubi

During one of my subsequent adventures I managed to disappoint Don Luis de Ascásubi again. At the time I was taking twenty-two of José Antonio Onrubia's Peruvians to sell in the States. And for a long, complicated reason they were in Manizales, Colombia, where they were a special attraction at that city's popular Exposición Equina.

When the man in charge asked how I'd recommend generating publicity, I suggested he invite Ascásubi as guest of honor.

While Don Luis was in Manizales I agreed to translate his book *El Caballo de Paso y Su Equitación* into English without changing a word. I began while we were still in Colombia, and briefly we were drawn close again.

Parts of his book discussed the breed's deficiencies. All purebred domestic animals — horses included — have genetic issues that should be acknowledged and managed by breeders. I was very much in favor of pointing out the ones in our breed. But Ascásubi's book did that again and again — sometimes verbatim.

"My book contains repetition because it's a collection of essays, written over many years," he explained, "and I want it left that way for emphasis."

We couldn't resolve this disagreement and our project came to a halt.

Later in my similarly named *The Peruvian Paso and His Classic Equitation*, I quoted passages I'd translated from Ascásubi's book — with credit to him. He considered this a violation of our agreement and from then until he passed away, our contacts were limited to chance encounters in Peru. I greatly regret that and wish I could've continued to learn from him.

He was one of the most interesting, intelligent, and articulate people I've ever known. Though I disagreed with some of his opinions about Peruvian Pasos, I believe the breed would've benefitted from his continued influence — especially his opposition to training and showing at too high a speed, a major problem for years before judges got it under control.

Part Five: More About the Great Aimé Tschiffely

Considering the geographical obstacles he was forced to deal with before the construction of the Pan American Highway, Tschiffely's ride was infinitely more difficult and impressive than mine. Psychologically however, mine might have been more stressful.

With no deadline, he was often able to relax and enjoy himself. I almost never was. Too, he wasn't constantly disheartened by motor vehicles speeding past — mocking his slow pace — or by overhead jetliners that would soon land in cities he wouldn't reach for months.

Tschiffely rode at least five times as far as I, and his journey lasted four times as long. His reward, too, was similarly greater. For a decade after he rode Mancha and Gato into our nation's capital, his was a household name from coast to coast.

He was listed with his era's most prominent persons in *Who's Who* and met many of America's high and mighty, including President Calvin Coolidge. Feature articles about him appeared in newspapers and magazines — including *National Geographic*, which rarely features individuals.

But his best reward, and the one that makes me most envious, was that for years he earned a good living from sales of his popular books.

Part Six: More About Me

Following my journey I earned a living working with Joe Gavitt at Rose Exterminator, then graduated to better jobs as a carpenter. After work and on weekends I devoted my spare time to promoting Peruvian horses. Tired of waiting for publicity to magically materialize, I began writing what eventually became several hundred articles published in magazines big and small.

Those initial efforts cost mostly time, but it was soon obvious that promoting this new breed would require more money than I had left over after paying my monthly bills. To raise funds I did something difficult. I sold Hamaca and Ima.

My ultimate goal during our journey had been to start a business. But during our intense trip I'd come to know my mares' quirks, preferences, fears, and opinions. I chose their new owners based on the homes I thought they'd provide. No one could have treated Ima better than Joe and Pat Gavitt did, and Hamaca was spoiled for the rest of her long life by Betty Bowe.

Confident that Peruvian horses would sell themselves, I used part of the proceeds to put them in front of as many people as possible. The difficulty of entering an unknown breed in California's big parades was inevitably rewarded by invitations to return next year. And when our exhibitions at horse shows were over, spectators flocked to the barn area, full of questions.

Next I borrowed the letters I'd written the Gavitts during my ride and used the contents as a foundation for a book which, later expanded and republished, became a best-seller.

A few years after my ride, *Western Horseman* magazine generously dubbed me "Mr. Peruvian Paso," a tribute to my enthusiasm more than my knowledge.

For years the breed grew steadily, but too slowly for George Jones, who lost interest.

Throughout the 1980s — thanks to the efforts of many aficionados — the Peruvian Paso was an up-and-coming breed with a seemingly unlimited future. By then a stallion had sold for a hundred thousand dollars, and I'd announced some two hundred shows and training clinics as well as numerous exhibitions — one in front of a hundred thousand spectators in Pasadena's Rose Bowl.

In 1985 the U.S. National Championship Show was held in the San Francisco Cow Palace where it attracted over four hundred entries and six thousand spectators. By the end of the decade there were thousands of purebreds in North America, and the breed had spread to Ecuador, Argentina, Central America, Germany, England, and Australia.

During those exciting years I traveled to Peru sixty-four more times for purposes as varied as importing horses, bringing trainers and tack, and researching articles about everything from the breed's characteristics and training to its bloodlines and foundation breeders. Twice I was an advisor during the filming of documentaries that were widely televised.

In 1996 however, the Reagan Income Tax Reform eliminated deductions for losses on so-called "hobby farms." That severely impacted the U.S. horse industry in general and the Peruvian Paso in particular. In its homeland, however, the breed prospered to the point where Peru's National Championship Show now regularly attracts in excess of seven hundred horses.

I don't for an instant believe this splendid breed owed its astonishing early success to me or my efforts. It sold itself on its own considerable merits and was brought to the world's attention by many fans in Peru, the United States, and elsewhere.

Notable among those were: Vivienne Lundquist of Meadow Springs Ranch, the Texas Ladies Aside drill team, and the Southern California Peruvian Paso Horse Club parade group, whose appearances in the Pasadena Tournament of Roses New Year's Parades were televised to millions.

I will admit to being proud of the small role I played in keeping the breed alive during the late 1960s and early '70s, when I helped sell enough horses to keep a few of Peru's breeders from scaling back the numbers of horses they produced after the Agrarian Reform.

Though tax reform marginalized the breed in the United States, I never once wished I'd done something else with my life. Even if I could relive it a hundred times, I couldn't possibly make it more enjoyable, interesting, or fulfilling.

* * *

As I look back, my greatest regret is losing touch with special people I met during my journey. I had intended to get back in touch with them when my ride ended, and over the years I tried—with differing results.

José Antonio Onrubia and I formed a close friendship that lasted for the rest of his life, but lost all meaning when he was stricken with Alzheimer's.

For years I saw Juan Luis Ruesta—who'd sold Huascarán, Lucero, and Inca in Piura—every time I went to Peru. We're still in touch and I think, would be close friends if we didn't live so far apart.

Sadly, I never again had the pleasure of seeing Hugo Bustamante, who'd thrilled that capacity crowd in Lima's Plaza de Acho after he, his trainer, and I rode across Lima together. But in 2014 I read that he'd passed away the previous year.

I finally got around to writing Gustavo Moncayo, who'd arranged those memorable ham radio calls from Ecuador to my mom, the Gavitts, and George Jones. His answer subtly told me he'd been puzzled by my long silence, and in view of all he'd done for me it was understandable when I didn't hear from him again.

I never did find an address or telephone number for Señor Isaacs—the Jewish gentleman whose kindness in Panama had included those two welcome bales of alfalfa.

Soon after I finally wrote Marco Vinicio Alvarez—who'd introduced me to Emily in Costa Rica—I received a newsy reply that showed he'd lost none of his wonderful enthusiasm. He didn't answer my next letter, but if we meet again I'm sure we'll enjoy each other as much we did in 1967.

My daughter Vicki—about whom I so often thought during

my ride — welcomed me back into her life four decades ago. She's more like me than anyone else I've ever known and within months told me we were "two peas in a pod."

A year after we got back together, she provided me with an extremely poignant moment. Without ever asking why I hadn't been there to raise her, she said, from the bottom of her heart, "I'm grateful we weren't together during my teen years. We're both stubborn, and I don't think we'd be such good friends if we'd been under one roof."

Part Seven: The Peruvian Paso as a Pleasure Horse

T he following article — published several times and written by Verne Albright — may be republished anywhere by anyone who credits this book, *Horseback Across Three Americas*, as its source and Verne Albright as its author.

> *Doctors had told Sharon Reynolds her riding days were over. A lifetime in the saddle had caused discs in her lower back to deteriorate, and getting on a horse had gone from exhilarating to painful to downright dangerous. Sharon risked paralysis if she didn't stop her favorite activity.*
>
> *"It was the worse news of my life," she remembers, "and yet I had to admit the doctors were right. Every time I rode, it wouldn't be thirty seconds before I'd start feeling those painful twinges. And they were getting worse."*
>
> *In an unexpected turn of events, Sharon had the opportunity to ride a horse imported from South America.*
>
> *"It was unbelievable," she exclaimed. "The ride was so smooth it felt as though the horse was floating. There*

was no pain or discomfort—just the marvelous sensation of riding again."

What made the difference? Sharon had ridden a Peruvian
Paso, which offers the smoothest ride of any horse on earth.

One of the breed's foremost experts, Luis de Ascásubi,
once said, "There are many kinds of ambling horse, but
only the Peruvian is a true artist."

To those not familiar with the paso gait, it may appear a bit peculiar. Most people are accustomed to seeing
horses trot, with the diagonal legs leaving and returning
to ground together. The trot also has an aerial phase—
after which two legs hit the ground with jarring impact.

By contrast, the Peruvian Paso's gait is lateral and
each leg is raised and lowered individually. The horse
always has at least two feet on the ground, similar to a
baby crawling. Peruvian horses perform this gait with
spectacular style. The front knees are lifted high and the
forelegs arc toward the outside as the horse strides forward, a movement similar to the arm motion of a swim-
mer doing the Australian crawl.

Reading about this breed is no substitute for seeing it.
Interested parties will find a directory of owners who
welcome visitors at the website of NAPHA, the North
American Peruvian Horse Association.

Part Eight: The Peruvian Paso As a Show Horse

The following article—written by Verne Albright and
originally published on the website of the Peruvian Paso
Longevity Project—may be republished anywhere by anyone
who credits this book, *Horseback Across Three Americas*, as
its source and Verne Albright as its author.

The Peruvian Paso's creators chose goals with no regard for the difficulty of achieving them. They wanted a naturally gaited, non-trotting breed—a traveler's horse for long journeys back when no highways crossed Peru's brutal, unforgiving deserts. They demanded a precise gait that produces four equally spaced beats and stays smooth and efficient at a range of speeds. And they insisted their breed inherit its characteristics genetically.

When automobiles replaced equines, horses remained popular due to horse shows and pleasure riding. At that critical moment one of the Peruvian Association's founders urged breeders to concentrate on "a work horse suitable for showing—not a show horse suitable for working."

To assure that trainers didn't enhance horses' performance by artificial means, another founder insisted that show rules require horses to be trained without artificial appliances and to be shown unshod.

The breed's architects painstakingly combined virtues most horsemen consider mutually exclusive:

• Long, efficient strides with proud carriage.

• Smoothness with strength and eye-catching leg action.

• Boundless energy with manageability and fluid movement.

Their ultimate triumph was blending these characteristics without resorting to devices or training methods that make horses do what they don't do naturally. This breed has been patiently improved for centuries by men who weren't pressured by commercial considerations and sometimes worked toward goals that wouldn't be reached in their lifetimes.

They gave horses to one another rather than sell them and considered it impolite to charge stud fees. When a friend admired one of their mares, they often "made him a gift of her womb," in other words let him breed her to a stallion of his choice and keep the foal.

The achievement of these extraordinary breeders is living functional art, a unique breed that calls attention and is so rare they're outnumbered by many endangered species. There are for example, fewer Peruvian horses in the entire world than bald eagles in Alaska.

Riding a Peruvian horse is effortless. You experience a powerful, utterly smooth floating sensation, as if on a magic carpet. The power and energy make you feel like a Spanish conquistador riding toward Inca Kings, your horse so magnificent it seems heaven-sent.

Don't just imagine yourself astride one of these stunning animals. Call a breeder today and arrange a test ride.

ACKNOWLEDGMENTS

N one of my books would've been good enough to publish without the help of my hardworking, , sharp-eyed, creative test readers. In this case they were: Michelle Baer, Ruth Bloom, Kay Galbraith, Tina Clavelle Meyer, Sylvia Reusser, Lucille Rider, and Jan Swagerty.

Special thanks also to my brothers, Deane and Harold, for their suggestions and encouragement; my brother Ralph, who assisted in countless important ways; my stepdaughter Krista Weber, who so willingly helped me set scenes and define characters; my Peruvian friend Robbie Watson, my Reno High School classmates Jim Colgan and Kay Galbraith, and my newly discovered uncles Bryan and Gordon Shrake, all of whom—with nothing to gain—tirelessly promote my books; Russell Róbe who taught me a great deal about storytelling and contributed to this book's predecessor, *The Long Way to Los Gatos*; my publisher Harley Patrick of Hellgate

Press, whose assistance and support were phenomenal; Mimi Busk Downey, a friend for over a half-century, who has helped me edit my manuscripts since I became an author; and finally my wife Laurie, who repeatedly came through when I needed the benefit of her artistry with words.

This book was written at a time when America's white supremacists were loudly and energetically demonizing Hispanics with the objective of keeping them out of our country. I sincerely hope reading about my experiences in Latin America will show my countrymen and the world how wonderful most Hispanic people really are.

NOTE: Back when I made this journey a half-century ago, Peru was a primitive member of the third-world, and the descriptions in this text reflect that. Since then however, Peruvian industriousness has transformed that country into a prosperous nation with its first-ever middle class and an exceedingly bright future.

ABOUT THE AUTHOR

"**M**y earliest memory," six-foot-nine-inch Verne Albright remembers, "is of an English class where the teacher assigned a one-page story. The other students' reaction was summed up by a boy who exclaimed, 'How will I ever write a whole page!' I, however, wrote twenty and in the process discovered my life's first passion."

At twenty-one Verne traveled to Peru and was enchanted by the country and its people. During that first visit he, his wife, and their year-old daughter traveled by jeep in the Andes Mountains of four nations. Over the next half-century he returned to Peru sixty-four times and imported over two hundred of its Paso horses--including a pair he took overland to California, a nine-month trek of more then five thousand miles in eleven nations. Riding much of the way he came face-to-face

with killer deserts, witch doctors, bandits, avalanches, poisonous reptiles, vampire bats, and a violent revolution.

"Finding a true calling is a miracle experienced by few,"
he once said, "and Peru provided me with two. I promoted
its Paso horses worldwide for over fifty years and more recently began writing historical fiction set in its fascinating
past and rich culture."

Verne is a master story teller and his novels are so well
written that they've already begun appearing on Best-Seller
Lists. And why not? He has lived adventures at least as exciting as the ones he writes about.